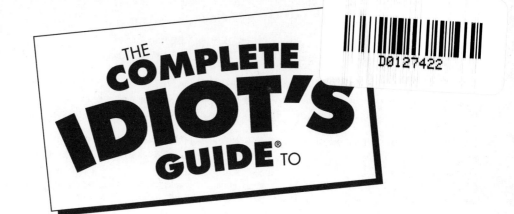

THE COMPLETE IDIOT'S GUIDE® TO

Commercial Real Estate Investing

Third Edition

by Stuart Leland Rider

ALPHA

A member of Penguin Group (USA) Inc.

ALPHA BOOKS

Published by the Penguin Group

Penguin Group (USA) Inc., 375 Hudson Street, New York, New York 10014, U.S.A.

Penguin Group (Canada), 10 Alcorn Avenue, Toronto, Ontario, Canada M4V 3B2 (a division of Pearson Penguin Canada Inc.)

Penguin Books Ltd, 80 Strand, London WC2R 0RL, England

Penguin Ireland, 25 St Stephen's Green, Dublin 2, Ireland (a division of Penguin Books Ltd)

Penguin Group (Australia), 250 Camberwell Road, Camberwell, Victoria 3124, Australia (a division of Pearson Australia Group Pty Ltd)

Penguin Books India Pvt Ltd, 11 Community Centre, Panchsheel Park, New Delhi—110 017, India

Penguin Group (NZ), cnr Airborne and Rosedale Roads, Albany, Auckland 1310, New Zealand (a division of Pearson New Zealand Ltd)

Penguin Books (South Africa) (Pty) Ltd, 24 Sturdee Avenue, Rosebank, Johannesburg 2196, South Africa

Penguin Books Ltd, Registered Offices: 80 Strand, London WC2R 0RL, England

International Standard Book Number: 1-59257-468-8
Library of Congress Catalog Card Number: 2005935927

08 07 06   8 7 6 5 4 3 2 1

Interpretation of the printing code: The rightmost number of the first series of numbers is the year of the book's printing; the rightmost number of the second series of numbers is the number of the book's printing. For example, a printing code of 06-1 shows that the first printing occurred in 2006.

Printed in the United States of America

Note: This publication contains the opinions and ideas of its author. It is intended to provide helpful and informative material on the subject matter covered. It is sold with the understanding that the author and publisher are not engaged in rendering professional services in the book. If the reader requires personal assistance or advice, a competent professional should be consulted.

The author and publisher specifically disclaim any responsibility for any liability, loss, or risk, personal or otherwise, which is incurred as a consequence, directly or indirectly, of the use and application of any of the contents of this book.

Most Alpha books are available at special quantity discounts for bulk purchases for sales promotions, premiums, fund-raising, or educational use. Special books, or book excerpts, can also be created to fit specific needs.

For details, write: Special Markets, Alpha Books, 375 Hudson Street, New York, NY 10014.

Publisher: *Marie Butler-Knight*
Editorial Director/Acquiring Editor: *Mike Sanders*
Senior Managing Editor: *Jennifer Bowles*
Development Editor: *Michael Thomas*
Senior Production Editor: *Billy Fields*
Copy Editor: *Amy Borrelli*
Cartoonist: *Jody Schaeffer*
Cover Designer: *Bill Thomas*
Book Designer: *Trina Wurst*
Indexer: *Brad Herriman*
Layout: *Brian Massey, Trina Wurst*
Proofreading: *Mary Hunt*

No one's career is due solely to the individual's effort. Along the way, people can become successful when granted a special opportunity by someone who is in a position to do so. The smart ones realize that they are in the right place at the right time and act on it. There is no way to pay someone back for providing such a pivotal opportunity; you can only pass it on.

I have been trying for years to do so. In the process, I have been instrumental in the real estate careers of three people who are, today, very wealthy and accomplished investor/developers. I'd like to dedicate this book to the two men who each gave me an invaluable opportunity at a crucial time in my career. They are David Schoales, past president of Texon, Inc., in South Hadley, Massachusetts, and Mr. Charles Branagh, past president of Branagh Construction, Inc., of Oakland, California. Without the confidence of Dave and Charlie and their personal investment in my abilities, I would not have had the career I have today. I hope this book will pass along some of that opportunity to you, the reader.

Contents at a Glance

Contents

Appendixes

Foreword

So you think you want to invest in real estate. Think again … and again. Then think some more. Do some homework. Lots of it. Investing in real estate isn't as effortless as calling up your stock broker or clicking online to move your money around.

What you're thinking about doing is lending your money—and, eventually, your expertise—to the tangible progress of the material world, not to mere ticks on a chart and potential gains that show up only on paper or a computer screen.

Come to think of it, if more people investing in the stock market had thought more like real estate investors, no speculative bubble would have formed on Wall Street, and it wouldn't have burst, and maybe we'd all still be partying like it was 1999.

Forget Wall Street for the moment. Think Main Street. Think New Apartment Complex Circle. Think Office Building Boulevard. Think Retail Road. Think Warehouse Way.

Think Real Estate Development Drive—not a short path to quick riches, but a winding road to long-term wealth, with lots of turnoffs and switchbacks, some blind hills, and the occasional runaway truck lane.

Think dirt on the ground, bricks and mortar, new homes, grand warehouses, and shiny office buildings. Think little retail niches and big boxes—the utilitarian kind of buildings that are the way stations for our basic needs as well as our mad material desires: retail stores, without which the economy, as we know it, wouldn't exist.

Daunting, yes? It's not rocket science, as author-developer Stuart Leland Rider points out—but it's not "easy," either. It takes guts and know-how.

You have to bring the guts; no book can provide that. But *The Complete Idiot's Guide to Commercial Real Estate Investing, Third Edition*, can introduce you to what you need to know: the nuts and bolts of what it takes to find partners, land a deal, build a building, fill it with tenants, keep them happy, hold a property for years, and sell it for profit or exchange it for tax purposes.

Investing in real estate is not for everyone. And investing in real estate Rider's way—hands on, mind engaged, and money on the line—is not for the weak. There's a reason that entrepreneurs are universally admired.

New passive investors, say, those who've recently put money in a real estate investment trust, aren't Rider's main audience, but even they should have the information in the following pages, to understand the forces and the types of strong, entrepreneurial personalities at work in the real estate and development business.

New silent partners, those who've put their money on the line but eschew involvement in the day-to-day management of a development project, need this kind of scoop even more. Sometimes such stakeholders have to break their silence. When times are good they want to sing. When times are bad they want to cry. Either way, they need to know what they're singing, or crying, about.

For those seeking a more hands-on investment, those ready to jump right in, form an LLC, and put their money to work, this book is more than a primer for all aspects of real estate investment. It is a basic introduction, but it's laced with something Rider has and you probably don't: expertise—and if you don't know what "LLC" stands for, you most definitely should read on to learn about limited liability companies and other mechanics of real estate finance, investment, and business structure.

You've got guts, or you wouldn't have read this far—and if you don't, you need to know that, too, and this book will help you decide. The best kind of knowledge is experience, which no book can provide. So, better get started. You've made an important investment already. Better start reading it.

Richard Mize
Real Estate Editor, *The Daily Oklahoman*

Introduction

Investing your money and time in real estate is not reinventing the wheel, nor does it take incredible insight or great intelligence. Like anything else in this world, it just takes a little hard work, some common sense, and an ability to stay focused and see it through.

Real estate has several advantages that other commodities do not have. It is a finite commodity. It is location-exclusive, as each parcel is immovable, and it comes complete with tax shelter designed to enhance your return on investment. This cannot be said for stocks, bonds, debt instruments, or any other form of investment that I am aware of.

In this book, you will learn …

- What investment property is, and where to find it.

- How to evaluate and select a solid investment property.

- How to improve on what you have purchased.

- Finally, how to sell your property for a good profit and start over.

Absolutely nothing you will learn in this book is a secret, and there is no inside information offered here. Everything you need to know you can find out. What you cannot do yourself, you can hire to be done at a reasonable price.

This book is designed to organize your approach, and to stimulate you into creating your own system for your own style of investing. Every single day of your life you are surrounded by someone else's real estate investments; if they can do it, why not you? You are, after all, as smart as the next guy, aren't you? Just reading this book will put you light-years ahead of the people who do not read it.

The beauty of real estate is that there is something for everyone. The variety is endless, and you will, most likely, add to that variety. One advantage of starting out fresh is that you come to it with few preconceived notions. Do what makes the most sense to you. Chances are that your first hunch will be correct.

Talk to as many people as you can find willing to talk, but keep your own counsel. Keep your game plan to yourself and stay flexible. Work hard at it and prosper.

What You Will Learn in This Book

The Complete Idiot's Guide to Commercial Real Estate Investing, Third Edition, is divided into seven sections.

Part 1, "Why Invest in Real Estate?," introduces you to the world of real property investments to make you aware of the fact that it is literally everywhere. You live in it, work in it, and are buried in it. (Cemeteries are real estate developments, and plots are sold at a profit.) It also points out the problems with the overheated stock market and the lack of investment logic that took it to unsustainable heights. Understand what's at work in today's market. You will learn why real estate can create a steady, reliable, and profitable income stream for you.

Part 2, "Types of Real Estate: The Good and the Not-So-Good," delves into the endless variety of real estate products and investment ploys, examining their relative advantages and their limitations. There is a deal out there with your name on it—you simply need to look. Take your time and do what feels comfortable to you. It has to make sense to you or you will not be able to work with it.

Part 3, "Stepping Up to Your First Deal," examines the methodology of dissecting a potential investment property to see if it will fit your needs. The chapter on purchasing agreements will guide you through the drafting and execution of an offer to purchase. This document will give you time to do your homework and cut the risks down to a manageable few. It will give you the confidence to proceed, or the ammunition to back off and try another property.

Part 4, "Ownership and Financing," will give you a choice whether to go it alone or bring in partners. It discusses the positive and negative effects associated with both approaches. It discusses the alternate forms of ownership, the value of cash, and the importance of hands-on management. It shows you how to structure the deal and where to look for equity money and financing. This section will give you a place to start your financial planning.

Part 5, "Documentation," deals with the proliferation of paper that defines any estate investment. Whatever you buy, whatever you lease, and whatever you sell, all of it involves paperwork. This section will introduce you to all of the required documentation. It will end the confusion and intimidation by attorneys. You can, and will, understand the documents and the financial analysis involved in real estate transactions. In fact, you will learn that you can create most of it yourself. At the very least, you will be able to save a fortune on legal bills because you understand what's needed, and can direct others in a time- and money-saving approach to documentation.

Part 6, "Managing Your Investment," looks into the realm of ownership and management. When you buy a piece of real estate, you are purchasing an opportunity to create an entrepreneurial profit. You can buy an income stream with the building, but you can also increase it and make a handsome profit in the process, while enjoying cash flow and tax shelter. This section guides you through the systematic improvement of any deal and provides you with tools and a guide for that effort.

Part 7, "How to Sell and Reinvest—or Not!" brings you to the endgame or exit strategy in any investment. You have four choices in any deal: you can keep it as is, you can keep it and refinance it using the proceeds to acquire more property, you can sell it, or you can roll it over into another deal. Learn how and why each avenue can work for you. In the end, it is your long-range plan that will guide you.

In Appendix B, you'll find a prototype purchase agreement that will give you a template from which you can draft your first purchase agreement. The second sample document, the commercial lease, gives you the main body and general provisions—parts one and two of a three-part lease. It is a working commercial lease that is in use today with my projects. It will give you something to start with. You and your attorney may use it to create the perfect lease for your investment property. The third part of the lease, the exhibits, is omitted due to length of this manuscript, but it is available on the CD-ROM mentioned below.

Also available from the author for $35.00 plus postage and handling is a CD-ROM containing usable versions of the following documents and spreadsheets. The current version, revised in 2005, contains the following (all files are Microsoft Word and/or Microsoft Excel):

Documents	
Commercial Lease—Main Body	Business section of a three-part lease (Part 1 of 3)
Commercial Lease—General Provisions	The boilerplate provisions (Part 2 of 3)
Commercial Lease—Exhibits	Exhibits (Part 3 of 3)
Agreement of Purchase and Sale and Joint Escrow Instructions	For purchase or land or income property
Note	General purpose
Deed of Trust	For use with a note
Development Services Agreement	Fee agreement between owner and developer
Exclusive Leasing Agreement	For commercial property

Documents

Exclusive Right To sell	For commercial property
Notary Page	For use with any documents requiring a notary
Independent Contractor Employment Agreement	For salespeople or consultants
Property Management Agreement	For commercial property
General Power of Attorney	General purpose
General Contractor Agreement	For construction
Subcontractor Agreement	For construction
LLC Operating Agreement	For forming an LLC
LLC Articles of Organization	For recording with the state

Spreadsheets

Appreciation Calculator	General purpose
Construction cost breakdown	General purpose
Critical Path Schedule	General scheduling
Five-Year Cash Flow Projection	Income property
Land Speculation Analysis	Quick analysis for land purchase
One-page Pro Formas	Income and expense and cost breakdown
Personal Financial Analysis	Your financial statement
Investment Schedule	A target game plan
ROI Analysis on Single-Family Home	Analysis for your home
Tenant Information Spreadsheet	Full information management document

Disclaimer

All sample documents included on the CD-ROM are intended to be used only as a guide to suggested topics for inclusion in commercial real estate transactions, and no representation is made as to their sufficiency or legality in your state, or their appropriateness for your proposed project. All legal documents should be reviewed by your attorney prior to use.

To obtain a copy of the CD-ROM, log on to the website www.riderland.com, or contact the author at slrider@riderland.com.

Extras

In addition to all these goodies, *The Complete Idiot's Guide to Commercial Real Estate Investing, Third Edition*, has sprinkled through each chapter small snippets of information in boxed sidebars. These sidebars provide you with additional tips, definitions of key terms, and warnings of potential dangers.

The signposts are up ahead—you are entering the sidebar zone:

 Buzzwords _____

Here's where you will find definitions of key terms introduced in the chapter. The definitions also appear in the glossary along with a number of other helpful terms.

 The Straight Skinny _____

These sidebars are designed to be a "heads up" for you along the way, adding to, and amplifying, important points to give you extra illumination.

 Better Believe It! _____

These sidebars contain warnings and caution flags. They are intended to make you aware of issues that may be pivotal to your deal.

Acknowledgments

Special thanks to Nancy Lewis, my development editor on the original edition. She had the unenviable task of shepherding a new author through the process of creating something intelligible, and making it reach out to you.

Heartfelt thanks to my wife, and best friend, Christine, the English teacher who kept my grammar within acceptable limits.

Special Thanks to the Technical Reviewer

The Complete Idiot's Guide to Real Estate Investing, Third Edition, was reviewed by an expert who double-checked the accuracy of what you'll learn here, to help us ensure that this book gives you everything you need to know about real estate investing. Special thanks are extended to Doug Jones.

Trademarks

All terms mentioned in this book that are known to be or are suspected of being trademarks or service marks have been appropriately capitalized. Alpha Books and Penguin Group (USA) Inc. cannot attest to the accuracy of this information. Use of a term in this book should not be regarded as affecting the validity of any trademark or service mark.

Part 1

Why Invest in Real Estate?

I have always felt that anyone who wants to can make a living. If you work hard and get a decent education, you can make a very good living. If you want more than just a good living, you must take risks. Investing in real estate is the act of taking a series of calculated risks. This part of the book looks at real estate and what it can offer you versus what the conventional stock, bond, and debt markets now offer. Stock and bond profits today seem to hinge on the "bigger fool" theory rather than serious investment analysis, and current investors are paring the price for investing in stocks that had no real value behind the prices. Real estate offers annual income, depreciation to shelter some of that income, and long-term capital gain. It's hard to beat.

Chapter 1

The Compelling Facts About Real Estate

In This Chapter

- Why real estate has the edge over stocks, bonds, and other debt instruments
- Where to start
- A little background on real estate
- Defining commercial real estate

With all the investment choices available today, why should you consider placing your money in real estate investments instead of the stock market or any other investment vehicle? The fundamental difference lies in the characteristics of the stock market and the basic nature of real estate investment. In this chapter, we'll examine the stock market and see why real estate investing is such an attractive alternative.

What Happened to the Stock Market?

The traditional investment for most Americans not actively involved in the investment industry falls into two major categories: stocks and notes. Stocks are shares of ownership in companies, and notes are debt instruments issued by a borrower. They differ in fundamental ways. Stocks can pay a dividend, and the per-share value of the stock may go up or down in price. Notes pay only interest, based upon the purchase price of the note; the interest rate may vary from investor to investor. Other investment choices are futures, hedges, currency trading, and a plethora of derivatives of the above. The modern investor has so many choices that it becomes confusing unless a deliberate study is made to sort it all out.

Buzzwords

A **mutual fund** is a company formed to hold stock in other companies, providing a mix of stocks and mutual funds that theoretically give an individual a choice between high-, medium-, and low-risk investments. A **REIT** is a Real Estate Investment Trust, a mutual fund whose assets are real estate properties or real estate–backed, debt-based securities (mortgages). It is usually publicly owned.

Most people have neither the time nor the inclination to sort out this menu of investment choices. They prefer to leave the work to the self-proclaimed experts. For the individual with no desire or time to analyze all these choices, this multiplicity of investment vehicles has given birth to yet another class of investment called the *mutual fund*.

There are funds that trade only certain stocks, such as high-tech companies, single industries, foreign companies, foreign currencies, certificates of deposit, or treasury bills; the list is endless. Suffice it to say, there is something for everyone. Someday there will be a fund that holds shares in other mutual funds. With the resulting management overhead and brokerage fees, the net result is that dividends get pretty thin by the time they reach the investor.

Miraculously, there is even a type of security (a certificate of ownership issued against an equity) or mutual fund, if you will, called a *REIT*. This type of fund was first formed in the 1970s for the purpose of allowing the public to invest in real estate. Its shares provide the investing public with an undivided interest in a variety of large, commercial real estate projects.

Other than buying a home, American investors have always looked to the stock market as their primary way of achieving a piece of the American dream. Their only other hope was to start a business of their own. For those who work for wages, the only viable venue for equity investment has been the stock market.

Why Is the Small Investor Switching to Real Estate?

During the late 1990s, the traditional stock market changed dramatically. Traditional *P/E ratios* increased to 50 or more times earnings, with seemingly no upper limit. People no longer purchased stocks with the expectation that they would get an annual return on investment. They counted on the "bigger fool" theory to make money. This theory rests on greed as well as supply and demand, overriding investment considerations and turning people into speculators rather than investors. A modern-day holder of stock is counting on someone else to come along who will pay more for the stock than he or she did. Due to this increasingly insatiable demand for a place to put capital, the stock market of the new millennium has dramatically reflected the bigger fool theory.

In the new millennium, investors got a harsh awakening as they started to realize their stocks had become dramatically overpriced. The resulting bear market has helped to evaporate many a paper profit. The daily volatility and lack of clear direction of the stock market are indicative of this increasingly prevalent, unsound reasoning when buying and selling stocks. Ironically, the stock market does not reflect the real health and competitiveness of the companies involved. The country's indus-

Buzzwords

In the past, the price paid for a share of stock was a multiple of its per-share earnings. The price-to-earnings ratio, or **P/E ratio,** is the price divided by the earnings per share, either proven or projected.

tries are in great shape, cycles included; it's just that their stock value needs to be put back into an investment mode. Once we return to a real and sustainable P/E ratio, stocks will again become a viable alternative investment. People working in the market are constantly trying to hype the market values, but since the readjustment, stocks in the Dow Jones Industrial Average have been up an down between 10 and 11,000, with no appreciable long-term gain.

When individuals want to go back to being legitimate investors, they must take a good look at real estate as an investment; it still trades on a multiple of cash flow to establish value. It retains the added attraction of appreciation, with the interim tax benefit of depreciation. In short, it is a more constant and reliable vehicle for investment. In some cases, it can be a vehicle for speculation as well. One very poignant advantage that real estate has over stocks and other investment vehicles is that it is a finite commodity. Other than volcanic eruption at sea, there has been no real estate created for several million years. The continued growth of the world's population virtually ensures appreciation as the available land is absorbed.

Real estate investment can give you monthly income, tax shelter, and long-term appreciation. The stock market used to provide only income and appreciarion, but today it has lost sight of the fundamentals of value. Real estate is easy for most people to understand. Not only can you make money with it, but also you can see it, change it, and use it. You live, work, and play in it. It surrounds your entire life. Unless you are a cave dweller, you cannot go through a single day without using someone's real estate investment. Why not make it one of yours?

Housing—The American Dream

The single-family dwelling has been the average family's answer to how to get ahead and save for the future. As of 2005 over 69 percent of American families own their own homes, and home ownership is considered the cornerstone of the American dream.

After World War II, Congress passed a series of laws designed to encourage home ownership. The law creating the VA and FHA loan system has been further reinforced with government-backed home mortgage securities known as Fannie Mae, Freddie Mac, and Ginnie Mae loans. These laws enabled people to buy homes with as little as a zero-dollar down payment (in the case of the VA loan), and 3 percent down on certain FHA loans.

The banks that make these loans bundle them together and trade these securities on the market to investors, both large and small. There are even mutual funds that invest only in these government-backed mortgage securities. There are also REITs. (see "You Are Surrounded by Real Estate Investments," later in this chapter).

Purchasing Your Own Home

Individual home ownership has proven to be the most widely used and popular form of savings for the average family. Everyone needs a place to live, and paying a mortgage is not much different than paying rent; the only real problem for most first-time investors is the down payment. The government-backed mortgage has solved this to some extent by lowering the down payment from the 20 percent required by a conventional loan to as little as 3 percent for an FHA loan, and 0 percent for a VA loan.

The benefits are many; the interest is deductible from your gross income for tax purposes, and the house appreciates in value while you live there. The mortgage payment is designed to pay off the loan balance over the life of the loan. People are then free to use the resulting *equity* in their homes for any purpose they wish. It has become common to use it to purchase a college education for children, or to purchase cars and boats. Many people use it to pay off their accumulated credit card debt. In a similar way, income-producing real estate can be refinanced rather than sold to recapture *capital* for other uses (see Chapter 15 on financing).

The subject of this book, however, is commercial real estate investment; that will require a whole new set of tools for you to master. This book will provide those tools and the rationale with which to employ them.

Buzzwords

Capital is cash available for investment. **Equity** is the value evidenced by ownership.

The goal for any savvy commercial real estate investor is to create cash flow, shelter as much of it as possible with depreciation, and to build equity for ultimate sale or refinancing. The difference in building equity in your real estate investments and the growth of equity in your house is that someone else, through solid leases, is paying the mortgage—the note—on your investment property. In time, the building of equity will be the cornerstone of your net worth. Through timely refinancing or sale and exchange (1031 tax deferred exchange), your increase in equity will allow you to tackle larger, more potentially profitable properties. (A 1031 tax deferred exchange allows an investor to defer the payment of taxes if he or she rolls over the proceeds of sale into another investment equal to or greater in size than the one sold, and of like kind.)

Entry into the world of real estate investment is not confined to rich people. It is as simple as saving a few bucks and investing in a rental property.

Residential Rentals

People who have surplus funds often find that they can look at a modest investment in another house for rental purposes. Many a real estate empire has started with the purchase of a rental property. You pay the mortgage with the rent you collect, thus building equity in the second house. When this is parlayed into several more, it often leads to exchanging ownership in several houses for ownership in an apartment complex or small office building. Thus, step by step, a commercial real estate investment program can be grown into a significant real estate portfolio.

Make Your House Pay Your Way

To start with, most people have not realized that they can use their own house to create a greater wealth or make a living. How is this done? First of all, the tax law states that you can sell your house after having lived there for two years, and your profits are tax-free up to a limit of $500,000 per transaction. *Consult your accountant for specific guidance on all tax matters.* Second, you can build the house and make money by living there for two years before you sell. Or you can buy a fixer-upper and live in it for two years while upgrading the house and have the profits tax-free when you sell. There are many other solutions, and you can get more details by looking at *The Complete Idiot's Guide to Investing in Fixer-Uppers.*

Surrounded by Real Estate

Unless you are a cave dweller, you are surrounded by other people's real estate investments. People who keep up with the economic news are familiar with the names Donald Trump, Del Webb, William DeBartolo, The Rouse Company, Gerald Hines, and The Taubman Company. They have built some of America's most visible, well-publicized projects within the commercial real estate development industry. However, what these people do for a living is no different, except in scale and notoriety, than what local developers do, every day, in every city and town in America.

The entrepreneurs who build and/or own neighborhood bank buildings, office buildings, and local grocery stores are working at the same trade as Donald Trump and company, only on a more practical and local level. Without these people, our towns and cities as we know them would not exist.

Using Leverage

Commercial real estate development is defined as the creation of real property investments, "realty," as opposed to personal property, or "personalty." When buildings are built they become permanently attached to the land and, therefore, forever part of the real estate. Commercial real estate development is the business of creating this income-producing real estate. Why and how is this done? What prompts builder, buyer, and tenant to get involved is the attraction of using *leverage* to increase their profit. Leverage is the reason real estate investment can work for everyone.

A simple example of leverage occurs when people use a mortgage to buy a home. If you buy a property for $100,000, using a conventional down payment of 20 percent, you need to borrow $80,000 to complete the purchase (also known as 80 percent loan to value). Simplistically, if you sell the property in one year for $120,000, you have made a gross profit of $20,000. However, the deal is better than it appears, as you have used the leverage of the borrowed $80,000 to increase the rate of return from 20 percent on the gross price of the property, to a 100 percent rate of return on the $20,000 cash down payment you originally invested ($40,000 from $20,000).

Buzzwords

Leverage is the principle by which we use other people's money (OPM) to increase the rate of return on our capital investment.

Rate of Return Analysis

Item	Purchase Price	Sales Price	Yield	Rate of Return (ROR)
Price	$100,000	$120,000	$20,000	20% on price
Down Payment	$20,000	$20,000		100% on investment

Why is the use of leverage a good deal? First of all, without leverage, you would need $100,000 to buy the property. This makes it very hard for the average homebuyer. Second, by using the leverage of a loan, you increase the profit on your investment from 20 percent to 100 percent. If you are one of the fortunate and you have the $100,000, because of leverage, you could buy five properties and make another $100,000.

You Are Surrounded by Real Estate Investments

Real estate investors come in two varieties: the professional who does it for a living, and the investor who is looking to increase his or her net worth over a lifetime. Given a reasonable rate of success, the investor soon starts thinking seriously about turning professional.

As an example, seldom does the grocery chain own the grocery store. If it started out that way, it was most likely purchased at a later date by an investor group formed for the express purpose of owning quality, investment-grade real estate. Most companies in the grocery business need all of their money to improve and enhance the business of putting groceries in the hands of the buying public. Their emphasis must be on the volume of sales and the profitability of those sales. The buildings become leased investments whose desirability as investments depends directly on the creditworthiness and diversity of the tenants in residence on the real estate.

This process creates two types of real estate investors: those who develop the properties, and those who later purchase the properties as investments. In both instances, opportunity exists for profit. The profitability in each instance will be a function of the expertise of the party involved. In the case of the developer, his entrepreneurial talents will be involved, and in the case of the investor, her skill and knowledge will enhance the outcome.

Who Are These Mysterious Investors?

Since the advent of the REIT, the public has become more aware of the possibilities of real estate development. The notion persists to this day, however, that the real estate investor is, by necessity, a very well-heeled individual. This can be true in many cases, but it is by no means the rule anymore. Many people, primarily professionals, have pooled their pension plans and formed small self-directed REITs of their own. These groups have not really formed a publicly traded REIT, but rather, have formed partnerships and companies to own and operate these assets. They build, buy, sell, and exchange these investments regularly to maximize their portfolios, much the same way any investor does with a stock portfolio.

In every building project there are different functions for both owner and occupant. One person or entity may fill all the available functions in a transaction; however, in some cases, many different participants get involved in the various functions. The owner/investor may be the initial developer or someone who buys it after completion.

Buzzwords

Premises are legally defined pieces of real property that can be the subject of a lease or a sale.

Some buildings change hands many times during their useful life. The initial occupant can be the developer, the owner, or the tenant. In the case of multi-tenant buildings, the tenants may be, and usually are, unrelated to the owner. The tenant could be the developer, but not the eventual owner. There are many roles in any scenario for everyone. All involve real estate investment. For the tenant, the lease is also an asset as well as a liability. The right to occupy a specific *premises* can, under certain conditions, be assigned and, therefore, sold.

Commercial Real Estate

Commercial real estate is most often created by a real estate developer. It is usually that individual's primary occupation, and he must do it well enough to create a profit. Sometimes it is created by the occupant and later sold to an investor.

Where Is It?

Real estate investments are everywhere. The home you live in might have been created by a developer, and sold to you or the original occupant at a profit. In turn, if you purchased a lot and designed and built your house, then you have played the role of developer. The corner grocery store and the dentist's office building are other examples. Almost every structure not owned by the government can be classified as a real estate investment of one kind or another. Some public facilities such as stadiums, paid for by cities, are investments in the city's long-term prosperity, paying dividends in the form of increased sales tax revenues well into the future. Without real estate investment and development, we'd still be living in caves.

Who Creates It?

The general public is usually aware of the larger development companies in our country, but the small developer and investor create the largest amount of real estate investment. These people start out building one to six houses per year and graduate to apartment buildings and condominiums. They might start by building a small office building

The Straight Skinny

This is not rocket science; it's important to understand that anyone can do this. I have friends with an eighth-grade education who have made millions in real estate. If they can do it and I can do it, then you can do it!

for their own company, and add some extra, unneeded space for lease to help pay the mortgage. A group of local business people might pool their resources and build a building to house a new bank or automobile dealership.

These are all real estate investments, created by people who have never done this before and who have never invested in anything similar. Are they nuts? On the contrary, they are people who have seen the potential for profit. In the old urban areas of the Northeast and Midwest known as the rust belt, people are tearing down obsolete factories and building homes, marinas, and shopping centers.

In the West, the great American migration keeps fueling an ever-expanding real estate market for housing, retail stores, offices, industrial buildings, marinas, airports, and other real estate–oriented services. They are all real estate investments, owned by individuals, companies, REITs, banks, and partnerships. How do these people know how to do this? In the rust belt, abandoned industrial sites are being redeveloped to entice the suburban commuter to return to downtown. Old office and industrial buildings are being converted to loft apartments, and new sports complexes are sprouting in downtowns coast to coast. This reemergence of the downtown as a viable place to live and play is being fueled by a backlash against the ever-increasing commute time all across the country. You can take advantage of it by purchasing an investment property in the path of this new growth.

I have always worked with the theory that, if someone else can do it, then I can do it. By learning as you go, and not biting off more than you can chew, you can, too. What you don't know you can find out; what you cannot do, you can hire someone to do. You can find partners, consultants, employees, and experts to fill in all the gaps in your knowledge. All you need is the desire and some common sense, and you will be well on your way to becoming a real estate investor, or even a developer.

The business of development and/or investment is defined as the business of taking calculated risks, and the process is one of weeding out the list of unknowns to the point where you are comfortable making the go or no-go decision.

How Do I Learn About It?

Education is rarely more than paying better attention to what is going on around you. Since you are becoming more interested in investing, you will automatically become more aware of your surroundings. New buildings, new subdivisions, new tenants, and growth or change of all kinds will now catch your eye. Start taking an interest in your community and its processes. The planning commission and the city council or county board of supervisors deal with new buildings and growth on a monthly basis. Follow the monthly process in the papers and in the hearings if you have the time, and soon a clear pattern of growth and change will emerge right under your nose.

The Straight Skinny

If you're looking at a larger real estate investment or just want to get to know how it all works a little better, try subscribing to your local business journal (or check it out at the local library.) Also check the Wednesday real estate section of *The Wall Street Journal*. Just reading about the overall real estate investment market will give you an idea of how it all works together.

The Least You Need to Know

- ◆ Real estate is a hands-on proposition. You can make it work, and if you pay attention to your investment, it will prosper.
- ◆ There is a real estate investment for everyone; you simply need to locate some property you are comfortable with, and take it one step at a time.
- ◆ You are surrounded by real estate investments. When you start to notice them, you will pick up on some opportunities that were right under your nose all along.
- ◆ Real estate investments produce annual income in the form of rent you collect from other people.

Chapter 2

The Spectrum of Real Property Investment

In This Chapter

- ◆ Discover the many choices
- ◆ The one-time cash deal
- ◆ Take advantage of the long-term investment
- ◆ Compare credit with diversity
- ◆ Investments to absolutely avoid

What should you buy—a second home or a regional mall, an apartment building or a business park? Sounds like a meaningless question, doesn't it? In reality, what you buy will depend on so many variables, that no two people will come to the same conclusion. First is your budget; that in itself imposes certain constraints. Then, there is your background and your experience and training; that too will slant your view of the world and what is a good risk. Finally there is the market and your take on it—what the market is now, and what you think the future will bring. Mix all of this up and roll it around in your head, and up pops your decision. In the final analysis, you will buy what you are comfortable with, what you can afford, and what you think is a good risk over the long pull. Learn to trust your instincts; after all, they have taken you this far.

An important part of your approach to investment should be to incorporate your own background and experience in the process. If you are a teacher, a carpenter, a truck driver, an office worker, an engineer, or a stock broker, your background, education, and experience will have a great deal to do with how you look at and evaluate any potential investment. In addition, your ability to set aside some cash to make the investment will have a bearing on just what you can start with.

In this chapter, we'll explore your options for real estate investing and how your background and experience can influence your choices.

Who Are You, as an Investor?

The first part of finding your niche involves you, the investor. Are you a housewife, college student, full-time factory worker, nurse, businessman, or electrician? There is a place in real estate investing for almost anyone who is serious about investing and is willing to work at it. Part of finding your niche is understanding what your opportunity is, and what needs you can fill. A few examples:

- A college student may convince her parents to buy a condo that she can live in along with several of her friends, who would pay rent. The student gets free rent and will also gain an appreciation for the process of attracting quality tenants who can pay their rent and help maintain the apartment and pay the mortgage (build the equity).

- The full-time factory worker might buy a house on contract and then lease to a co-worker who has yet to establish a credit rating.

- A nurse might consider buying an old building and dividing up the space to rent to doctors for record storage, who therefore would save expensive hospital and clinic space for medical uses.

- An electrician might use his experience to rehab an industrial building that has suffered from deferred maintenance. He may end up leasing that building to other contractors with whom he has worked over the years, as well as using the space for his own shop and office.

- A college teacher could look at an old house and decide that, with a little renovation, it would make an excellent small apartment building to rent to students.

If you are looking for something to invest in, it is best to look at areas that are familiar to you based on your background.

The Many Choices

No matter what your situation, you must look at all aspects of real estate investment to find an area that is compatible with you and your goals. The potential areas of endeavor start with the simple purchase of a house or a vacant lot, and renting it out at a profit. From there the process progresses to normal, commercial income property investment, and on to the realm of full-blown real estate speculation. The range of potential involvement is limited only by the amount of money you have to invest, and the real estate market itself.

Consider the possibility of real estate as an investment for the long term, perhaps building a retirement portfolio that can be grown into a full-time proposition. If you entertain the idea of real estate as a career, then after you have gained some experience with investment property, you might also consider the possibility of becoming a developer, as an alternative to becoming an investor only. The obvious advantage of being a developer is that you will acquire all your real estate investments at wholesale, essentially creating them from scratch. For the eager and ambitious entrepreneur, this beats paying the retail price every time.

Buzzwords

A **cap rate** is a numerical representation of the risk perceived by a given investment. For an in depth look at cap rates see Chapter 9.

There is also the realm of the pure speculator. This area is both the most risky and the most potentially profitable. A way to get into this field might be the optioning or purchasing of a lot for later resale.

Each of these areas of real estate investing will be covered in the sections that follow.

If you look at an investment in a building that produces $100,000 in income before debt service each year, the difference between buying and building are shown below.

	Income	Cap Rate	Cost
To the investor	$100,000	8.5%	$1,176,470
To the developer	$100,000	12%	$833,333

The difference lies in the process of development. The risks are greater for the developer, and so is the rate of return. It is something to look forward to after you have acquired some experience.

As a Career

Unless you have a great deal of money to start with, real estate as a living starts with a job. If you have a well-developed entrepreneurial streak, you might become a developer right off the bat. Most likely, you will start with a job as a commercial leasing agent, initially as a runner (assistant, gofer, slave), working with and for an experienced agent until you get your feet wet.

After you become self-sustaining, 12 to 18 months into your chosen career, you should start to plan your long-term strategy. An agent is always on the front line when it comes to finding deals, so you have the immediate possibility of developing a network of investors, and creating small investment syndicates. With time, you could perhaps move into the development arena. Once you're in the industry, you can see more clearly the potential choices, fitting yourself into a niche that will suit your skills, goals, and ambition.

As an Investment

If you decide to continue with your current career and invest in real estate as part of your lifelong investment strategy, you will find that you're in good company, as most people fall into this category. The possibilities are endless and as varied as you can afford. By starting with a residential rental property, or a lot leased out for parking or Christmas tree sales, you're off and running as an investor.

By paying attention, managing the cash flow, and being alert to the possibility of trading up, you could grow this initial investment into something more substantial. Just the building of a home for your own use and selling it after two years of occupancy, rolling the tax-free profits into a new one, will probably have you living in a mortgage-free home in 10 to 12 years. Teeing off of this, use the built-up equity to buy some rental property, and you will be well on your way to becoming a long-term landlord. Somewhere along the way, you will find that when your portfolio becomes a certain size, you will have to pay more attention to it. This will prompt you to hire professional management or choose to do it yourself, thus mandating a career change.

As a Speculator

Why is speculation a possibility? It offers the most return for the least risk. Picture this: looking at your target community, choose a parcel in the path of growth, perhaps five to six years out. Make an offer to purchase it over a 10-year time frame, the logic being that you anticipate the value will double in the 5- to 10-year period. Offer

to pay $5,000 for a five-year *option* to pur-
chase the property at the current value, with
annual option extension payments of $2,500
each. This approach can then be compared
with purchasing the property with 20 percent
down and interest only for 10 years at 10 percent, with principal to balloon at the end of
year 10. With the option, you can reap a

Buzzwords

An **option** is a con-
tracted right to purchase a specific piece of real property at a
specific time.

greater profit by having the site appreciate only 25 percent over a two- to three-year
period. Remember, with a 20 percent down payment and a 25 percent gross appreciation over your period of ownership, your profit will be limited to much less. Look at
the chart below to see the effect at the end of the five-year period.

Speculation Profile

Transaction	Item	Year 1	Year 2	Year 3	Year 4	Year 5
Option	Option cost	$5,000	$2,500	$2,500	$2,500	$100,000
Option	Sale price	$100,000	$125,000	$150,000	$175,000	$200,000
Option	Profit	-$5,000	$17,500	$40,000	$62,500	$87,500
Option	ROI	loss	233%	400%	500%	78%
Purchase	Down payment	$20,000	$8,000	$8,000	$8,000	$8,000
Purchase	Profit	$0	$17,000	$18,000	$51,000	$68,000
Purchase	ROI	loss	61%	50%	116%	113%

Note: Land price at beginning $100,000. Escalation occurs on anniversary of contracts.

The land purchase approach, while less profitable, protects the investor's capital
investment. The option approach, while more speculative, and a total loss if not consummated or resold, is infinitely more profitable in any given year except the initial
year. With the proper research into your area's growth rates and patterns, as well as
historical absorption figures, how hard can it be to see where the growth of any area
is headed? This approach to real estate investment is best practiced in a growth environment; I don't recommend speculation in the rust belt states. The most classic kind
of real estate speculation is the "flip," one of several variations on the one-time cash
turnover transaction.

The One-Time Cash Turnover Deal

These transactions involve a quick turnover, sometimes without ever having to consummate the purchase. We all have read in the paper that during real estate booms in California, people were offered money, prior to closing, for their home purchase contracts. In late 1999 and early 2000, it again made the news in Northern California. When you execute a contract for a lot, a home, or any other type of real property, the possibility always exists that with plenty of time built into the contract, you might be able to resell it before having to consummate the original purchase. This is known as "flipping."

Buzzwords

Flips and rollovers involve selling real estate before you have to buy it.

The two most common transactions of this ilk are the *flip* and the *rollover* transactions. These are not necessarily well-known terms, but the principle behind them is widely practiced. I have sold over 60 percent of my projects at substantial profit without ever having had to consummate the original purchase agreements. Without exception, however, my transactions were rollover deals as opposed to flips. The difference between the two is that the flip involves no real added value to the land, whereas the rollover involves substantial added value to justify the increase in value. The added value will be in the form of specific project design, governmental approvals, and perhaps leasing and resale. Since you have not yet purchased the land, your improvements will all be on paper, altering the value through entitlements and marketing.

The Flip

The flip is a one-time turnover based on a lengthy closing time in the land purchase contract. Let's assume that you have spotted a nicely located residential lot on a main thoroughfare, and that it is, as yet, undeveloped. The area is slowly turning commercial, and you are able to acquire a 12-month option to purchase the lot. You may or may not initiate the process of rezoning, but you immediately advertise the property for sale as a potential commercial lot. It is quite common to find a buyer who will take it off your hands, subject to rezoning. With sufficient time to accomplish the rezoning, or at lease satisfy the buyer that the rezoning is feasible, you will find that most often you can even assign your option, taking your profit without ever having taken title to the property.

The flip can also be accomplished by "simultaneous closing" whereby you buy and resell the property simultaneously in escrow at the time of closing.

The Rollover Deal

This transaction is similar to the flip, but approached as a development deal from the beginning. Most development projects start with a 12- to 24-month escrow period. The time frame is intended to give the seller the best possible price for his land, and allow the investor/entrepreneur the needed time to pull the project together and petition for and get the rezoning. During the escrow period, you must accomplish all approvals necessary to build the project and lease the project to breakeven occupancy, while offering the project for sale immediately.

This three-pronged approach to all projects offers the developer/entrepreneur the flexibility of building out the project or rolling over her money without the build-out risk. My first project was a rollover transaction. I had $6,000 to my name and acquired a backer with some limited cash. In 19 months, we had optioned a site from the Boise Cascade Company, rezoned it, secured all the governmental approvals required to build a neighborhood shopping center, leased it to a 97 percent occupancy level, and resold it to an investor, assigning to him our original purchase contract, the plans, the leases, and the building permit.

At the time of sale, we had invested, to date, $13,000 in cash and two $25,000 letters of credit as well as two years of our time. We sold it without ever having taken title of the property to an investor who built it out, and resold it for a profit upon completion. We received our investment back plus $750,000 in cash. A fluke, you say. Using the profits from this first transaction, I repeated this at least six times over the next four years, and during the same time frame I also built out six projects for our own account. It can be done.

If you do a rollover, most likely you will only have to acquire the entitlements; you can find a developer to buy it from you to complete the project. The action of entitlement is a very well-recognized addition to the value of the property and will ensure you a profit for your time and investment.

Long-Term Investment

Investing in income property is the most familiar venue for most investors. They buy some property from a developer and hold it for the medium to long term, usually 5 to 10 years. When they have increased the value sufficiently through increased rents and good operations, they trade for another larger piece, or perhaps two, and start the process all over again. The most common type of investment property is known as income property.

Income Property

Income property falls into several different categories and variations. It is either a single-tenant or a multi-tenant property, and is either categorized as a "credit" transaction or a normal income property deal. (A credit transaction involves someone or some entity with a superior net worth and credit rating.) Typically, most income property is leased to multiple tenants. Single-tenant credit properties tend to be found in the larger, more conservative portfolios, often commanding very high prices. A timely example of this is Walgreen's.

Buzzwords

An **NNN lease** (a.k.a. triple net lease) is a lease in which the tenant is responsible for all operating expenses, taxes, and miscellaneous expenses associated with the real estate. It has been dubbed a triple net to differentiate it from all the old versions of the net lease. The use of the word "triple" emphasizes that the rent is absolute net to the landlord.

Walgreen's goal is having many smaller stores in every possible location with a criteria of being approximately three miles apart. Its method of doing this is to build the store itself, and then sell the building with a firm 25-year lease to an investor. Its asking price in the fourth quarter of 2002 was a 7.2 percent cap rate on the triple net (NNN) rental amount. These are considered the most desirable, both from a credit standpoint and a property management standpoint. The tenant's credit is what drives the deal. These leases, normally *NNN leases*, are generally for a sufficiently long period of time to enable the landlord to completely pay off the mortgage. When the tenant finally vacates the premises, the landlord simply sells the vacant building for the land value, and the cycle starts over again.

Appreciation and When to Sell

One of the most common debates among investors concerns the ideal time to sell the property. I believe the answer is simple. Sell the property when the investment goals have been met, and at a price that will persuade someone else to step in and carry it to another level. Most often I recommend that people sell when their initial equity investment has been doubled. This should be accomplished within a five-year time frame if the building is properly leased. In any case, you will make that decision when you begin a transaction.

Unforeseen events can, and will, occur, and if you are alert you might prosper by an unplanned action. Obviously, if you foresee a softening in the rental market, you might want to sell early before incurring an unacceptable level of vacancy.

Credit vs. Diversity

An argument can be made as to which investment is best, either the credit-tenant building or the multi-tenant building. The disparity in prices as determined by cap rates generally separates the people who are attracted to these two different investment types. People looking for rock-solid, dependable, no-management deals will pay through the nose for the credit deals. Entrepreneurs who want to maximize their profit and who believe in their own abilities to select and manage good investments will flock to the more profitable, lower-credit, multi-tenant deals.

Single-Tenant Credit Buildings

In a single-tenant credit building, the one tenant must carry the whole income load for the investor. When deciding to buy a single-tenant credit building, you must be convinced that the tenant's credit is bankable, and that the tenant has the operating know-how to survive the base term of the lease. The base term should also be sufficient to amortize the mortgage completely, rendering the building free and clear at the end of the base term of the lease. The building is likely to be a single-use structure, and, therefore, not readily releasable on the general market. The residual value to the investor will be the market value of the land and the salvage value, if any, of the building.

The other aspect of credit tenants is that, because of their superior credit, they believe that they deserve a lower rent than their less creditworthy brethren. This results in a lesser rate of return on investment than that achievable with multi-tenant buildings. This lower rental is generally accompanied by less frequent rent increases over the life of the lease. The typical lease would have a base term of 20 to 25 years with several five-year extensions at the tenant's option. The rent must be calculated using a 20-year, fully amortizing loan, plus a return on equity above that. The only reliable kicker to the lower yield will be the salvage value of the land and building when the tenant's lease is up.

In a perfect world, the location will have become so valuable over the lease term that the tenant will want to stay on beyond the option periods and will pay through the nose to do so. At that time, the landlord/investor will find himself in the catbird seat, having the delightful choice of selling at a great profit, or releasing the property at a greatly inflated rental, the tenant's excellent credit notwithstanding.

Multi-Tenant Buildings

In my opinion, multi-tenant buildings make the best investment for the average investor. The good news is that they are the most prevalent building forms in the commercial real estate marketplace. They are composed of industrial buildings, office buildings, retail buildings, mixed-use projects, miniwarehouses, apartment buildings, and anything imaginable in between. While there are many crucial components of a good multi-tenant building, the most important factor to the investor lies in the number of tenants. Essentially, the greater the number and diversity, the lower the risk. Admittedly, more tenants make for more management, but they provide lower risk of significant vacancy, steadier cash flow, and a better chance for increased rents through escalation and releasing.

These buildings come in a variety of sizes, types, and levels of desirability. They occur in all forms of development, from residential to industrial, office, and retail. They can be as small as 4,000 SF (square feet) and as large as 1,000,000 SF and up. Tenant-size buildings can vary from 500 SF or less, to hundreds of thousands of square feet.

The tenant's credit will vary from nonexistent to spectacular. The big question is how to sort the gold from the garbage. The best buildings will fit purposefully into the marketplace, but wherever they fit, they must be designed to fill that particular niche. A building designed for large tenancy cannot be successfully adapted or retrofitted for small tenants, or vice versa. Much of what will—and will not—work is determined by the sheer size of the marketplace. Even some oddball use can survive if the population is large enough, or concentrated enough. Shops that thrive in Manhattan, San Francisco, or Chicago will wither in suburbia where the population is less concentrated and smaller. Likewise, boutique-type shops that prosper in small towns can wither in the more competitive atmosphere of the discount urban marketplace.

The Straight Skinny

Do not get sidetracked and don't be persuaded to change your plans in the middle of the game. That having been said, the best operating policy is to make a plan, work hard to achieve it, and remain flexible.

Investments to Absolutely Avoid

Over the years, developers have tried many different innovations. Some did well, and some proved to be flops. The surprising thing is that many mistakes have been repeated over and over again, continually flopping. The old adage that those who ignore the lessons of history are fated to repeat them is true.

The most common example of this in the real estate business is the two-story neighborhood shopping center. I see a new one annually, and the second floor is always a flop. One of the less obvious flops is an office building in a small town with floors that are so large that they do not lend themselves to subdivision for the typical small tenant. These are failures of immense proportions, because, first of all, the developer is so obtuse that she has never noticed this type of failure before, and, second, the lender has to be equally lame for not having learned the lesson in Lending 101.

New generations must learn these lessons anew. Until they do, they will not become the establishment. This human propensity for learning the hard way is, sadly, not confined to the real estate field.

The Least You Need to Know

- There are endless numbers of investment types; find one that you're comfortable with, and go with it.

- If you decide that you like the real estate investing process, you can make a full-time living at it.

- If you follow the guidelines, real estate investment becomes a steady, reliable way to build future income for your retirement. It has cash flow, tax shelter, and capital gain; what more do you need?

- If you consider options, flips, and rollovers, you do not even have to buy real estate to make money on it.

- Avoid the deals that do not fit into easily defined stereotypes; they might not make you as much money, and they could break you.

Chapter 3

The Marketplace

In This Chapter

◆ How to research your target market

◆ Finding your slot in the big picture

◆ What do you want out of this investment?

◆ Creating a battle plan for your deal

Before embarking on your quest for real estate investments, I recommend that you look at the many choices of investment property available to you. The real estate market today is such that you can choose from available properties anywhere in this country and overseas. Wherever you decide to invest, it is prudent that you know the marketplace in which your potential investment will flourish. In this chapter, you'll learn how to research the market with an eye toward accomplishing your real estate–investing goals.

Know Your Market

Understanding any market requires detailed knowledge; you need to understand the implications of existing and future transportation corridors, where new residential growth is heading, the annual absorption of new homes, the size of the office, industrial and retail markets, and their respective absorption rates. Armed with these facts, you can then place any potential real estate investment into its proper context within the target marketplace.

Traditional Cycles

Another factor that affects real property and its market is the overall economy's cycles of growth and recession. Since the early 1990s, the U.S. economy has achieved a new pattern of growth that has, perhaps, put our old cycles to bed for good. In the past, our economy grew and declined in three-year cycles. Real estate markets have gone from scarce to overbuilt, in a fairly predictable pattern. The smart investors purchased land and buildings during the down cycles and sold at the top of the growth curve.

This is still good practice, but our traditional cyclical pattern may have changed forever. The 10-year growth cycle in the 1990s has been followed by a bear market in stocks and a warlike state of anxiety in the marketplace. It is unlikely that the stock market will stabilize in the foreseeable future, and America as we know it has changed forever since 9/11. This is not necessarily all bad. A more discriminating and aware population can make better choices in the years ahead. Perhaps we will learn from history after all.

The New Economy

What then, is this new economy? I cannot be certain that anyone knows for sure except, perhaps, God or Alan Greenspan. The Fed Chairman has slowed growth in an effort to keep inflation under control, and the economy, while suffering some higher-than-normal unemployment rates, seems to keep rolling along at a pace necessary for recovery from the short recession. My take on the situation is somewhat in line with Alvin Toffler's view that we have put behind us the Industrial Age, and have gone roaring into the Information Age. Alvin Toffler is the author of three books—*Future Shock*, *The Third Wave*, and *Power Shift*. I recommend that anyone who is interested in understanding our new economy read them all. Our government is always a step behind, as usual, attempting to apply Industrial Age solutions to a new era. I believe that …

- ◆ Growth is here to stay.

- ◆ Immigration to the United States will flourish as we completely dominate this technological era.

- The United States is and will remain the focal point of innovation and growth for the near future.

- Third-world countries will take over the manufacturing of almost all consumer goods.

- The United States will become a better place to live with an international presence beyond anyone's greatest expectations.

- Our sunshine states will evolve into meccas of living and recreation for the world's moneyed elite.

It is in progress as we speak. Our political stability is second to none, and breeds a climate of security unparalleled in the world, 9/11 notwithstanding.

With the recession supposedly in force, we see two opposing indicators that belie the traditional view of recession. Stock deflation from ridiculous highs toward the value mark is diametrically opposed by housing starts and home refinancing. The economists I know now feel that the value mark in stocks circa 2005 is a DOW average between 7,500 and 10,000. I believe the market will find its true value level again and stay there, increasing only as inflation and real increases in value occur. In other words, the stock market will return to its traditional range of values. When it does, we will again see real investment potential and long-term healthy prospects.

The housing starts show me that for once the public is ignoring the stock market and refusing to let that aspect of our economy convince them that all is lost. Nothing can be gained by believing that the stock market is a real indicator of our nation's economic health. The real companies that have experienced stock meltdown will keep manufacturing and servicing their clients, and their stock will recover to a value level. The rest of us need to keep doing what we do, and create some real value for our future. Real estate will help you in that endeavor.

The Straight Skinny

The U.S. government releases numbers for housing starts to the news media and on the web monthly. As you become more aware of the real estate–investing world around you, you'll also take an interest in leading and following indicators released monthly and quarterly.

Global Impacts

What effect will the rest of the world have on our economy? When China, Asia, and the third world start their inevitable growth spiral, the United States will start the wholesale importing of educated people from all over the world to fill our insatiable demand for technologically educated people. This will spawn opportunities for new styles of living to accommodate these people's traditional way of life.

Neighborhoods such as Little Saigon or Chinatown in California will proliferate all over the country, creating new opportunities for investment and growth. There will be new patterns of commerce, living, and recreation, and, therefore, completely new types of real property developments. It is exciting, and people with vision and entrepreneurial spirit should do quite well financially participating in this changing financial environment.

Where Do You Fit into the Puzzle?

This is not a light question. What you do for a living, how you invest, where you live all are pivotal facets of your economic lifetime. Experts agree that the average person born today will have three to four careers in a lifetime, necessitating retraining and re-education for each. Increased savings and astute investment will become an economic necessity for all who aspire to economic independence. You can no longer start out without a plan and hope for the best. You might find yourself washed up and out of work at 30. The one constant in life is change, and if you act and plan with that as a given, then you will have the required mindset for the future. Look at your investment pattern as part of your career and you should be able to make some clear, easily defined, and flexible plans for your future.

Your Financial Situation

Before launching your investment venture, chart your working career on paper to see what your financial realities are today, and will be in the near future. Chart both income and expenses to determine what your discretionary income is and will be. Be sure to add the projected income from your investments, as reinvestment will become an important source of new capital.

Money is a commodity necessary for investment. If your money is limited, you will need to be proactive and add some entrepreneurial capital to the equation. Perhaps you can become the motivating force behind an investor group composed of you and your contemporaries, thus earning your slice of the investment pie by being the one to seek out, and select the investments, manage them, and play the required proactive role.

For years, people have started businesses and other investment projects with little or no money. I started with $6,000 and found a partner with quite a bit of money, but no time to invest. You can take whatever you have and pool it with friends, or take out a loan, or, as some people do, evaluate the feasibility of using the cash availability potential in your credit card accounts. No matter how you do it, you can make an investment commensurate with your means. You can buy a lot with 20 percent down and make payments on the rest. By selecting a lot in the path of growth, and perhaps changing the entitlements, you can add significant value to your purchase and realize a nice profit.

The important thing about limited capital is not to overshoot your capabilities. Make sure that you can pay the carrying costs (interest) if you are buying leveraged. If you cannot make the carry, you could lose your initial investment.

Resources

Other resources needed for this enterprise are the skills that are required for the real estate portion itself. The disciplines required to successfully invest in real estate over the long term are the following:

- ♦ Accounting
- ♦ Brokerage
- ♦ Management
- ♦ Negotiation and salesmanship
- ♦ Legal advice
- ♦ Construction
- ♦ Architecture and engineering

All of these disciplines are required, but are not necessarily embodied in your own repertoire of skills. How do you acquire them? You can include individuals with these skills on the ownership side of the investment, or you can hire the required consultants. You will probably do a bit of both. Over the years, as you gain experience, you will find that you use consultants less and less as you gain the required background, experience, and skills for the tasks ahead.

Define Your Goals

The foundation for any journey is a plan, a road map of sorts, showing where you're starting from and where you want to end up. The important ingredient to any plan is flexibility. The best test for judging the validity of your plan is to determine the worst things that can happen along the way, and develop strategies for coping with these potential setbacks. Allocate part of your income to this plan, and create an emergency fund for those times when the unforeseen occurs.

Better Believe It!

Remember Murphy's Law: "Whatever can go wrong will go wrong." Then add O'Reilly's postulate, which states: "Murphy was an optimist!"

In real estate investment, it's important to select a type of investment that you can relate to, and one that, to you at least, makes perfect sense. It is vital that you understand the process required for successfully managing the property. If it is industrial, you should know something about the type of tenants who will be using the property.

If it is residential, you should know something about the population that will be the target market for the apartments. Are they singles, empty nesters, transients, or families? All these considerations will come to bear on the process of successfully managing the property.

Good management will increase the income over time, giving the property a better resale value than when you purchased it. Your goal will be to have the rate of increase of your annual net income before debt service (NIBDS) outstrip the annual rate of inflation. By having your income exceed the inflation rate, you will realize a net gain in the net asset value of your investment over time.

Primary and Secondary Goals

Part of your goal setting should be primary, with some secondary considerations for the long term. For instance, you might have a primary goal of building a portfolio of industrial properties (manufacturing or warehousing facilities), and a secondary goal of consolidating your investments in one city or state. The most important part of this type of goal setting is to understand the rationale for the goal itself. If you choose to invest in industrial property, it should be because you are comfortable with this type of property and understand its current and long-term role in the overall economy of the region.

For example, Reno, Nevada, has become a warehouse hub for the state of California due to California's hefty annual inventory tax. To minimize the tax's impact on business, California companies store their inventory in Reno, where there is no inventory tax. To invest in warehousing in Reno you should, therefore, know all you can about the California tax situation and its potential longevity. Should California decide to repeal the tax, then the Reno investment might be jeopardized. If, however, it is clear to you that the cost of inventorying goods in Reno will always be competitive with warehousing them in California, due to land prices, cost of construction, and transportation, then the outlook for your Reno investment should remain golden for the foreseeable future.

Long-Term Goals

Part of your plan should address immediate goals and concerns, and then place them into a longer-term strategic context. A short-term goal could be the accumulation of enough capital to make your first investment.

The short-term solution could be to invest in some form of mutual fund or REIT (see Chapter 2) until there is enough capital accumulated to swing the down payment for a building of your own. Another short-term goal could be to form an investor group to make the initial investment.

Longer-term goals might encompass owning your own building without partners, or creating a portfolio of similar or diverse properties. Another goal could be the realization of greater geographical diversity in your portfolio. Whatever the plan, have reasons for your choices, and have a realistic way to get there. If you can only save $5,000 a year, you will not accumulate that $100,000 down payment needed for your first building in five years.

Make a Plan

What does a plan look like? I'm not sure what anyone else's plan would look like; I'm only sure what mine looked like when I started. It has been modified over the years as I progressed, as unforeseen circumstances necessitated some agonizing reappraisals from time to time. The key elements, however, are probably similar in everyone's plan.

First, I believe you should chart your available and foreseeable financial resources. Extrapolating your career path, and charting it against industry norms, can accomplish this. You should know where you fit into the scheme of things, and, being realistic, be able to outline this fairly accurately.

Second, start with the desired end result and back into a program to get there. If, for instance, you want to own a building worth $3,000,000 by the time you're 40, then you know that you will need approximately 25 percent ($750,000) of the purchase price as equity to make that purchase. How do you accumulate this by the age of 40 with your available resources? Your solution could be to invest $25,000 per year until you have a down payment for a smaller investment, then, through astute management, roll this over with your ever-increasing capital pool until you can exchange into the property you want.

Your plan may be too ambitious, or a little too shortsighted. Don't worry about it. As along as you set your resource goals realistically, you can fine-tune the plan as you go along.

Where to Start

Start today, looking at what you have accumulated so far. Is it enough to start with? Do you need to readjust your lifestyle to accommodate a pattern of investment? Do you need to sell the Ferrari and buy a Chevy to have the money to accomplish your goals? Are you married? Do you have children? Do you plan to have any, and, if so, how much will they cost? What about saving for their education? Does your wife or husband work? Will he or she continue to do so?

These questions and the corresponding answers will have a vital bearing on your plan and the probability of its successful fruition. If you are married, you will have to get the wholehearted cooperation of your spouse. You will have to agree on the program, and, further, will have to formulate a plan of dissolution should you face a divorce in the future. It would be pointless for you both to successfully implement an investment strategy only to find that you will both lose it to attorneys in the event of a divorce. Be realistic. These things happen. Plan for the worst, and you can safely enjoy the present and whatever happens in the future.

Better Believe It!

Your first deal is similar to a hunter's first kill. The agony and the ecstasy are all part of the deal.

Stay Local

Unless you live in Farmtown, U.S.A., you should start your investment program by selecting an investment locally. Chances are that you are fairly familiar with your local environs, and with a little work can get an accurate handle on its potential for real estate appreciation.

If you live in a small town, chances are that you are part of a larger *SMSA (Standard Metropolitan Statistical Area)*. Any SMSA can be divided into quadrants that can be charted almost uniformly throughout the United States. The NE (northeast) quadrant usually contains the most expensive residential areas, the SE (southeast) quadrant the medium-priced homes, and the SW (southwest) quadrant the "starter" or "blue-collar" homes. The remaining SE quadrant is composed of the old core city area and/or the industrial area of the SMSA. Why is this, and is it consistent throughout the country? The simple answer is that wealthy people do not drive to and from work with the sun glaring in their faces through the windshield. This rule holds true all across America unless there is some natural barrier such as a mountain, ocean, or a river to prevent it. Obviously there are exceptions, and your community may be one of them. The important thing is that if you intend to invest your hard-earned cash in a community, you had better know what is where, and how and why it is growing or shrinking.

Buzzwords

An **SMSA** (Standard Metropolitan Statistical Area, a.k.a. Metropolitan Statistical Area, or MSA) is composed of a core city and its surrounding suburbs, usually referred to in terms like the New York, Chicago, or San Francisco Metropolitan Area. **Sunbelt** states are so-called because of their conspicuous lack of economically debilitating winter weather. Sunshine will outdraw a blizzard any day of the week. You can book on it!

Draw a financial and real estate map of your area, and check your assumptions with the local real estate professionals. Talk to real estate brokers about your program. After all, they will be the ones looking for properties for you to buy.

Enlist the aid of a good investment broker, and take him into your confidence. Convince him that you will stick with him throughout your program if he will commit to giving your portfolio preferential treatment when buying and selling investment properties. You will have to pay a broker anyway, so get one on board early, and get him on your side for the long haul.

If you live in a rural farming community, there will be little or no opportunity for investment, and you will have to compete with the local movers and shakers for what limited opportunities there are. You are better off searching in areas of growth and consistent demand. The best examples of this type of area are found in the *Sunbelt* states, as they are the ones experiencing consistent, annual, net immigration.

Other areas of opportunity lie in states that experience high rates of population turnover, transient areas such as Arizona, Nevada, California, and Florida. Change breeds demand for diverse real estate products.

How to Get There

Having made your plan and done your research, the next step is to actually do it. The first step is the hardest, and the uncertainties are rampant. Remember, real estate investment is the business of taking calculated risks, and the process is the elimination of as many uncertainties as possible, so that you enter your comfort zone. When you feel comfortable with the resulting facts, understanding the potential problems to the extent that they may be foreseen, then you will be able to pull the trigger with confidence.

The Least You Need to Know

- Do the research, as there is no shortcut to knowing firsthand what the shape and texture of your market feels like.

- Make a realistic plan, based on your resources, background, and abilities.

- Work like mad, keeping in mind that success is a mixture of sweat and common sense.

- Stay loose. Don't become too narrowly focused; the ability to think on your feet and adapt will put you ahead of the competition.

- At all times, keep looking for innovative ways to enhance your investment.

Chapter 4

Timing Is Everything

In This Chapter

- ◆ Organize your resources
- ◆ Start with research
- ◆ Find and consult with some experts
- ◆ Locate an investment you can be comfortable with
- ◆ Do it over if necessary

As with most things in life, timing is everything. To be involved in real estate investment should be a logical next step in your financial evolution, rather than a wrenching and traumatic event. If you were going to become a developer, I would tell you that the proper ratio between planning and execution is two to one. I believe that the better and more thorough the planning of a project, the easier and more trouble-free its execution.

There are many things to prepare before you launch a career or make a significant financial commitment. The areas that need to be examined are as varied as your life. You must make sure that all your existing and future commitments can be met without jeopardizing your plans, and you must have a clear understanding of why and how you are embarking on this significant commitment.

It is pointless to go through all the steps, start down this road, only to have to abandon your plan halfway through the process. If you set up your plan with a built-in, fail-safe plan from the beginning, then you should suffer few, if any, losses. The worst consequence of this scenario will be that you only failed to complete the plan, not that you have lost any money. In this chapter, you'll learn how to prepare a sound real estate–investing plan.

Prepare Yourself

There are several aspects to self-preparation. Set up your lifestyle, prepare your finances, and do the research. A lifestyle does not just set itself up. You and your spouse must have clearly defined goals for your life together. I realize that this sounds quite anal-retentive and lacking in spontaneity, but a careless approach to life will be reflected in a careless approach to investment or any other endeavor. Having children is a large commitment in terms of time and money. Your personal life needs to be as organized and well thought out as your professional and financial life if you are to be successful at either.

Likewise, regarding your overall lifestyle, you must choose between the flashy car with large payments and the Chevy with no payments, the large home early in your life together or a gradual transition into a practical home when needed. International vacations are more costly than family vacations to the local lake or Disneyland.

Why bother to ask, "What am I working for?" If you look at your career and your lifestyle as a whole, you will find that during your child-rearing years, you will be naturally restrained from exotic living by the demands, responsibilities, and activity characteristic of the process of parenting.

You will need a lot of money 18 years into the process for education and preparation of your children for their independent lives. It should happen around that time of your life, when your career or careers are starting to mature into the peak years. This will be the time when you will need some of the fruits of your investment program for the children, and, at the same time, you should have more disposable income to invest in your plan.

Money

How do you arrange the money? I have used a rule of thumb during my life that has worked for me, and you will have to create one that works for you. My financial plan is simple, and I have never deviated from it. I have broken my financial responsibilities into four categories; likewise, I have broken my take-home dollars into fourths to cover them. Twenty-five percent of my take-home pay covers each of the following categories:

- ◆ Mortgage or rent payments

- ◆ Utilities, household expenses, home and car insurance, car payments, medical costs

- ◆ Discretionary spending, clothing, entertainment, food, miscellaneous, cash savings for emergencies

- ◆ Life insurance, investments, education fund

Obviously, this type of budget requires some discipline, but if you wish to get ahead, you cannot start out in adult life having everything up front. Indulging in instant gratification is not a characteristic of successful people.

Young couples who want to start their lives together with a new home and two new cars will most likely never achieve an investment portfolio of any kind. Their burden of debt will preclude any meaningful investment program, and preclude a long-term accumulation of wealth.

Better Believe It!

True financial independence requires discipline and planning. Save now so that you can enjoy a carefree tomorrow. Constant credit card debt is the kiss of death to any serious financial planning.

Instant self-gratification is the antithesis of planning and discipline. If something is worth doing at all, it is worth doing well. Building wealth is not an accident. Look at the statistics. Over one third of American families are only one or two paychecks away from homelessness, and the cash savings of the average American family is less than $10,000. You can see that the people who achieve financial independence are the exception, rather than the norm.

Plan

Once you've established your financial plan, and the fund in which you wish to invest, you then must devise an investment strategy to implement your plan. How soon will you have enough cash to make a significant purchase? What should you do with the cash until you purchase your first investment? Will it be a rental house, or an existing income property? Will you go it alone or look for partners and fellow believers? All these considerations must be included in your plan. You don't have to reinvent the wheel; you can find good ideas and information from many sources. Use all the sources you can find: friends and family, investment counselors, bankers, brokers, and reference material at the library. Use the Internet; it's an incredible resource.

Do the Homework

The research is the function of planning that sets the successful apart from the average. Here's how you get to really learn something about your future. Most commercial real estate brokerage companies have reams of information about the marketplace available for their clients. They are only too happy to educate you in the ways of the market, as a means of cultivating you as a client. Talk to as many good brokers as you can find. Take their statistics, facts, and trends, and make your own extrapolations. Compare the data you have acquired from the different firms for accuracy and consistency.

It is not too hard to examine the historical absorption rate for, say office space, with the economic history of the area to determine the consistency of the trends shown in the data. Check the facts given to you by randomly verifying them yourself. Don't take their rental rates, occupancy rates, and current inventory figures as gospel; check them out. Talk to builders, leasing agents, other investors, and property managers. Look at all different types and sizes of potential investment properties.

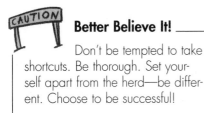

Better Believe It!

Don't be tempted to take shortcuts. Be thorough. Set yourself apart from the herd—be different. Choose to be successful!

By doing all of this, you will find that you are naturally drawn to a particular segment of the industry because something about it makes sense to you. There are as many types of investments as there are developers, and even within any category, there will be specialties.

Market

The market is composed of developers, investors, and tenants, and their interaction is facilitated by hosts of consultants. Tenants are either residential or commercial—that is to say, they are either private citizens or businesses. Residential real estate deals with individuals and families, and commercial real estate deals with the businesses. These markets are quantifiable. Each SMSA, town, or area has a basic population statistic against which all the real estate products can be measured. Real estate products are incredibly diverse. The following is a *partial* list of the types of property in the major categories of residential, industrial, office, retail, and recreational.

Residential	Industrial	Office	Retail	Recreational
Lots	Single-tenant buildings	Single-tenant buildings	Single-tenant buildings	Amusement parks
Condos	Public warehouses	Multi-tenant buildings	Multi-tenant buildings	Marinas
Patio homes	Frozen food warehouses	Suburban low-rise buildings	Strip centers	Cinema complexes
Apartments	Mini-storage	Mid-rise buildings	Neighborhood centers	Golf courses
Time share	Incubator office buildings	High-rise buildings	Power centers	Time share vacation homes
Single-family homes	Manufacturing plants	Office condos	Regional malls	
Subdivisions	Distribution facilities			
Master planned communities				

Investment property classifications.

Type

In the residential field, investment opportunities exist in both the rental and for-sale areas. Investments can be made in creating and selling residential products such as lots, houses, condominiums, and time-share vacation property. These investments will yield short-term profits, which can increase your capital base for use in long-term, income-producing investments, or larger cash-flow projects. Other opportunities in the residential field call for investment in income-producing rental property, such as apartments and single-family houses. Residential properties, other than apartment buildings, are very management-intensive and I don't recommend them for the long haul.

Commercial development has similar cash-flow versus income investment opportunities, the difference being that rather than investing in a completed project for income, you might choose to become the financial partner of a developer to build properties for sale to other investors. Investing with a developer is both risky and smart. By buying in at the beginning, you will be acquiring your investment property at a wholesale price, versus buying a completed project and paying the going investment rate.

The difference between the two is the developer's entrepreneurial profit. The risk lies in the developer's ability to successfully complete the project as planned and on time. Since all investment entails some calculated risk, this is a viable choice, especially when you need to build up your capital base for the larger, long-term, income-producing investments. You might consider backing a local house builder. Most lenders require a builder to have the lot paid for when building a *spec* home.

This form of spec building runs through all the building types, from residential to commercial building. It is, however, most common in residential. In commercial building, to get conventional financing, most lenders today require that multi-tenant buildings be leased to *break-even* occupancy prior to the funding of the construction financing. (See Chapter 15 on financing.)

Buzzwords

Spec is the term for a speculative venture. A spec home is built without a buyer in hand, on speculation of acquiring one at, or before, completion. **Break-even** is defined as the point at which the net income from rents will be sufficient to pay the mortgage or "debt service."

This precludes the pure spec building so common during the 1970s. The normal form of investment with a developer is a joint venture, evidenced by a partnership, a corporation, or a limited liability company. These different forms of ownership agreement will be covered later in detail in Chapter 17. The standard deal is a 50/50 split of profits between the developer and the investor. As a developer, I have completed 45 joint ventures to date, with no two exactly alike. The business deal and the structure are 100 percent subject to negotiation between the parties. As a point of departure for you, I will say that a rather typical deal for building a house is that the investor pays for the lot and the net proceeds from the sale are distributed as follows:

1. First to the *construction loan*

2. Second to the investor to return her capital

3. Third to the builder, a negotiated fee

4. Finally, the profit is divided 50/50

The size of the builder's fee, and whether the investor is paid interest on the capital invested, is negotiated as part of the transaction.

Investing in income property involves purchasing a property or an undivided share in a property that is full of tenants paying rent. It will be purchased based on a multiple of net, before debt service earnings NIBDS (net income before debt service).

The NIBDS is capitalized at a certain rate and a value is agreed upon. The resulting price is a function of the rate of return calculated on a cash basis. For example, if a property with an NIBDS of $100,000 per year were sold at a *cap rate* of 10 percent, the price would be $1,000,000. This price is set so that the buyer will realize a return on the investment of $1,000,000 of 10 percent ($100,000) per year. The investor or investors then manage the property, slowly turning over the rents during their ownership, and resell it later at a profit or *capital gain.*

If the investment has been a successful one, properly managed, the gross income should at least keep pace with inflation. The bottom line (NIBDS) will have appreciated substantially in five years to a level of approximately $130,000 per year. Simplistically, if the property is sold again at the same 10 percent cap rate, the investors will have accomplished the following during the investment period:

- ◆ Received a 10 percent return on their cash per year
- ◆ Made a capital gain of $300,000 on the sale

Buzzwords _____

A **construction loan** is a temporary, short-term loan, entered into for the construction of the building (see Chapter 15). The **cap rate (capitalization rate)** is the process of valuing an income stream by assessing a numerical factor to the probability of risk (see Chapter 9). **Capital gain** is a category of income defined by the IRS as short term (no less than 6 months, but less than 12 months) and long term (over 12 months). All other income is taxed as "ordinary income."

Select the Team

It takes knowledge, skill, and determination to accomplish this type of goal. The skills involved are accounting, brokerage, construction, management, legal, and entrepreneurial. Does your repertoire include all these skills? If it does, then you are qualified to proceed as a "one-man band." If not, you are like the rest of us. Your choice is to hire consultants, or to recruit fellow investors as partners. Either way, these bases must be covered or the investment will not prosper. Just purchasing the building involves market knowledge of comparable sale prices, rents, and trends in the specific building type.

One-Man Band

Individual ownership (just the investor and her wallet) offers the most risk and the greatest opportunity for gain, as well as total control over the project's destiny. This is the most common form of investment, ranging from owner-occupied buildings to individual real estate empires. It's do or die alone.

One of the great advantages of being the Lone Ranger is autonomy. Partners tend to rely on consensus and/or "conventional wisdom," making innovation difficult. Going it alone enables individual investors to "go where no man has gone before." Inherent in this is the potential for great profit through innovation or unique vision. The opposite is also true. The pitfalls are many and all too visible. Almost every year I see another two-story strip commercial building go up, and the results seldom vary. Except in specific locations, these projects always fail. If an investor does not know that, or does not have a partner who knows that, then he might be the person serving as an object lesson to others.

Partners?

Besides the obvious advantage of splitting the financial risk, the advantage of having partners is both practical and convenient. Having partners, fellow stockholders, or fellow members, adds more experience with which to tackle the problems, as well as providing someone to cover for you should you need a vacation. There are so many disciplines involved in the investment process, and a wealth of individuals working in the industry, that it should not be difficult to find someone with a complementary background and set of skills. The other important consideration for taking on partners is the raising of additional equity capital. More money means a larger, more diverse, and, therefore, safer project.

The Product

Having selected the players and done the research, the next step is to select the product. You alone, or you and your partners, must evaluate your chosen marketplace and decide which type of product looks to be the best bet for investment in the near future, remembering to consider its income potential and its residual sale price potential. I recommend looking for product that is well located, but perhaps poorly managed, and, therefore, underpriced. By buying on the low side of the market, and through astute management, improving the cash flow, you will have the opportunity to make a larger-than-normal profit. This will also result in a better sale price when you dispose of the property.

Buy?

Having targeted the product, and the general area within the marketplace you prefer, your next decision involves buying versus building. The marketplace generally dictates the cost of buying an investment property. Certain investment types, with perceived risks and potential, are selling for a certain cap rate, and others are selling for another cap rate. The big trick is to do better than the market. This is accomplished by having a better handle on the market than your competitors (other investors). Knowing more means spotting trends in advance of others, and capitalizing on them. For example, the first person to buy an apartment complex and turn it into a condominium complex made an inordinate profit, as condos generally sell for two to three times the cost of apartments.

Build?

Should you choose to build, you should spend a great deal of time looking for a fledgling developer, but one with good experience as a builder or leasing agent. These two skills are essential to successful development of multi-tenant properties. Perhaps you can find a company that has built homes for owners by bidding the work in the past. By providing the capital for the first lot, you could enable him to become a spec developer, rather than just a contractor. You might even form a new development company with the builder. He does the work, and you provide the capital.

Make Your Selection

Ultimately, it will boil down to making a selection. To do this properly, you need to make sure that you have identified some viable choices from which to pick. Don't get into a situation where you have only one possible choice—at least, not at the start of your investing career. If, for example, you choose to buy a strip retail center in the $1- to $1.5-million price range, make sure you call as many investment brokers as you can find and get their submittals. Look at all of them, and prepare a spreadsheet and a checklist to see how they compare.

Soon it will become apparent which ones should emerge as the front-runners. Eliminate the others and start the process all over in greater detail. Make a personal, detailed inspection of the properties, and compare the results. Look for deferred maintenance, and mismanagement. You can capitalize on these aspects when negotiating your purchase price.

Offer

In Appendix B is a sample purchase agreement, which is designed not to be used as a specific purchase contract for your deals, but as a point of departure for you when writing a purchase agreement. When you get it done, give it to your attorney to clean up. Do not let him or her start from scratch, it's too costly.

Better Believe It!

The purchase contract is the most important risk-limiting document in the investment process. Draft it with care, and get it right!

Don't worry about making the contract too tough. Put into the contingency clause all of your concerns, and give yourself enough time to eliminate your most pressing concerns. Make their elimination a condition of continuing with the transaction. Give as

The Straight Skinny

You make money when you buy, and you collect it when you sell. In between is a lot of hard work and attention to detail. You cannot recapture any overpayment. Do not lose sight of this.

many chores as possible to the seller to accomplish for your approval. People are slow about paperwork, and this will buy you time to eliminate your concerns. Take care to write the contract in plain English, resist "legalese," and take the time to articulate your concerns to the seller or the seller's agent. If she understands your concerns, then she will be less likely to view them as unreasonable. Try to get them to look at it from your point of view. Point out that you are new to the property, whereas they have been working with it for a long time. Convince them that you are just a little guy, not an important investor, and stress that this is a big move for you and you are nervous.

Flexibility

Realize that, if you follow my advice to the letter, you are going to experience rejection from some sellers. After all, the seller thinks the terms offered, and the material furnished, are both reasonable and sufficient for you to make a decision. Do not be offended by rejection. It's your hard-earned money that is at stake here, and mistakes can be very costly.

Try to understand the seller's objections or rejections. Negotiate and compromise as needed, while keeping your vital contingencies in the agreement. If it becomes too hard, consider walking away and going to the next property on your list. Rome was not built in a day, and buying is the most important part of the investment.

Do It Again If Necessary

There is a saying: "If at first you don't succeed, try, try again." This is trite, hackneyed … and very true. This is not the time to be in a hurry. Old clichés are old clichés for a good reason. More often they prove to be prophetic. Act in haste and repent at leisure. You can write your own clichés for this sentiment. The important thing is that you take the sentiment on board and don't make mistakes that you will have to pay for later. Take your time and get it right.

Buy It Right

The concept of "buying it right" means that your goal is to maximize the property's potential at the inception of the transaction. You cannot recover money spent in excess of value. Always look for the undervalued project. It will be the one with poor leases, bad maintenance, and upset tenants. You and your team can fix these problems, creating greater economic value through the process. This is entrepreneurial effort, and it pays well.

Avoid poorly constructed buildings. Do not be concerned about cosmetics. They are inexpensive to improve, and have an immediate and profitable effect. Ugly, well-built buildings can be dramatically improved with some cosmetic changes, but ill-conceived structures with inadequate services and design elements can never be rectified economically.

Have the Courage to Say No

In any given transaction, the moment may come where you seem to be trying too hard. You're not getting a good feeling about the way things are coming together. This is the time to walk away from the transaction. The only failure I ever experienced in my 24 years as a real estate developer occurred when I proceeded with the purchase, ignoring my misgivings.

Things that start poorly generally do not improve. They get worse. The time to walk is when you have little or nothing to lose, before your money becomes committed. There will always be another deal, another place, and a better time. The only caution to this advice is that there is no perfect deal, so do not fall into the trap of attempting to create the perfect investment. It does not exist.

The final gut-level criterion for anything in this business is: does the project work the first time and every time? If the answer is yes, then it is safe to proceed.

The Least You Need to Know

- Preparation is everything; do not move until you're ready.

- Hire and listen to the experts, but make your own decisions based on what you have learned.

- Select investment property with care; buy it right. Do not stretch too far for any deal.

◆ Walk away if necessary; you can start over. Sometimes it takes several tries to buy the "right" property correctly.

◆ Have patience and be persistent.

◆ Successful deal making require an "attitude"; create your own.

Part 2

Types of Real Estate: The Good and the Not-So-Good

Real estate encompasses many different property types and opportunities—from single-family housing to apartments and condominiums, from vacant lots to new communities, from strip centers to regional shopping malls, from single-user buildings to business parks, and from one-tenant buildings to high-rise office buildings. How do you choose where to start? This part will guide you to the answer.

Consult your budget, check out the various types of real estate investments available to you within your means, and find something that fits your personality. You need to feel right about it, and somewhere, among all the alternatives, there is the right one for you.

Making a selection means more than understanding the choices. You will also need to know the marketplace, select some good consultants, and do the research. Then, you are ready to pick a good investment.

Chapter 5

Investment Types

In This Chapter

♦ Speculation as an art form

♦ Compare the cash flow project versus the long-term investment

♦ The value of short-term investments

♦ Amazing opportunities in long-term investment

So far you've had a look at some of the choices available to you in the world of commercial real estate investing. In this chapter, you will see how they work, and how rates of return on the same dollar investment vary from project type to project type, as well as how these returns relate to risk and commitment. You'll see the difference between $100,000 spent on a speculation deal versus the same amount invested in a cash flow deal. Finally, the same analysis applied to a long-term income property will give you some idea where to start looking for your comfort zone.

Speculation

The fact that speculation is the most potentially profitable transaction type is offset by the very nature of speculation itself. The word "speculation" implies risk and reward, and it is no different in real estate than in any other field. The risk taker and the conservative both have their place in the real estate industry, because without them, very large companies would dominate the business.

The reality of the industry is that the large companies make less money per dollar invested, and the small entrepreneur makes more per dollar invested, but takes the greater risk. Most large developments—such as new communities, large housing tracts, urban office buildings, and regional malls—require so much capital that only large companies tackle them because they have access to large amounts of capital. For the most part, they are public or semipublic companies, answering to stockholders. The nature of large companies is that they attract employees, not entrepreneurs. Their judgment of the validity of a project is based upon a consistent rate of return over a long period of time.

Small companies or individuals are the hard-core entrepreneurs. These people are always on the cutting edge, filling the niches left by the large companies. Eventually, if they are successful, they, too, grow into large companies and start losing their entrepreneurial edge. In effect, they become the establishment, and a new generation of entrepreneurs emerges to fill the vacuum. The cycle never ends, and is much the same as in other industries. Real estate is, in reality, no different a business than other industries; its primary difference is that it deals in a finite commodity, and is, therefore, going to be subject to increases in value. We have all seen the price of computers go from $10,000 each to $500 in less than a decade. When have you seen the price of housing go down, or when has the rent for office space fallen for less than a year or two?

Let's examine a speculative venture, using a million-dollar budget. The main difference in speculation versus other forms of investment is that we are not setting out to build anything. We are going to speculate that by buying a property correctly, and manipulating it astutely, we can create a greater value, perhaps without taking title to the property at all.

Buzzwords

A **balloon payment** is the balance of the principal of the loan, due in one lump sum (a.k.a. the balloon) at the expiration of the loan term.

The two types of speculation are the option and the long-term purchase, funded by the seller. In the option transaction, we are going to pay the seller a nonrefundable fee for the right to purchase the property at a given later date, at a specific price. The time frame may be extended by additional payments, and the purchase price may be escalated over time, but all these variables will be structured into the deal at the outset. The other scenario is to purchase the property with a small down payment, say 20 percent, and pay the balance of the purchase over time, with a substantial *balloon payment* at the end of the contract. A typical time frame for this type of transaction is 7 or 10 years. We shall look at both transactions in the same time frame, a 10-year period.

The Benefits

When looking at the option scenario, we will assume that the time frame is 10 years, and we will, for the sake of simplicity, also assume that we are going to sell the project to one or more buyers at the end of the term of the deal. With a budget of $1,000,000, we must decide on how to allocate the money and how to manipulate the property to secure the best advantage.

Since we are going to secure an option, we can assume that we will have to make a decent initial payment, and regular, annual additional payments through year five, and then larger payments annually if we want to extend the option exercising date. A typical cost and income spreadsheet involving the optioning of 640 acres of land would be as follows:

(Cost) and Income Items	Yr. 1	Yr. 2	Yr. 3	Yr. 4	Yr. 5	Yr. 6	Yr. 7	Yr. 8	Yr. 9	Yr. 10
Initial Option Pmt	-$150,000									
Annual extensions		-$35,000	-35000	-$35,000	-$35,000	-$50,000	-$50,000	-$50,000	-$50,000	-$50,000
Engineering		-$25,000								
Legal		-$25,000				$20,000				
Total cost / yr	-$150,000	-$85,000	-$35,000	-$35,000	-$35,000	-$30,000	-$50,000	-$50,000	-$50,000	-$50,000
Cumulative costs	-$150,000	-$235,000	-$270,000	-$305,000	-$340,000	-$370,000	-$420,000	-$470,000	-$520,000	-$570,000
Sales										
Residential 560 acres @ $25,000 / acre						$14,000,000	$14,000,000	$14,000,000	$14,000,000	$14,000,000
Commercial, 80 acres @ $ 100,000 / acre						$8,000,000	$8,000,000	$8,000,000	$8,000,000	$8,000,000
Total land cost						-$3,200,000	-$3,200,000	-$3,200,000	-$3,200,000	-$3,200,000
Net Income						$18,430,000	$18,380,000	$18,330,000	$18,280,000	$18,230,000

Notes: Assume 640 acres @ $5,000 per acre
   Improvements - Subdivided into 4 parcels
   All sold in same year

Land-option scenario.

If you examine this scenario, you will determine that it is quite risky, and even though you have not spent the full million, you might need the unspent balance to hang on to the property until something sells, no matter what the price. The prices shown are for example only and are not necessarily indicative of any particular transaction or any specific area of the country.

By purchasing a property that is likely to be needed for housing development within the 10-year period, we can realistically just buy it and hold it. If the property was closer to the urban area, and more immediately developable, say within five years, the land would cost more, and require subdivision, necessitating a different budget, and a smaller purchase. If we look at the numbers then, we are going to purchase 320 acres of land, at a price normally paid for agricultural land, and lease the land back to the seller, allowing him or her to keep farming. This is the farmer's bonus, paid up front. The land value will be about $5,000 per acre in most places. This creates a financial breakdown as follows:

Costs	Yr. 1	Yr. 2	Yr. 3	Yr. 4	Yr. 5	Yr. 6	Yr. 7	Yr. 8	Yr. 9	Yr. 10
Cash down	-$640,000						-$2,560,000	-$2,560,000	-$2,560,000	-$1,280,000
Interest		-$204,800	-$204,800	-$204,800	-$204,800	-$204,800	-$204,800	-$204,800	-$204,800	-$204,800
Cumulative interest							-$1,228,800	-$1,433,600	-$1,638,400	-$1,843,200
Total costs							-$3,993,600	-$4,198,400	-$4,403,200	-$3,328,000
Sales price	$0	$0	$0	$0	$0	$0	$27,878,400	$27,878,400	$27,878,400	$27,878,400
Gross income	-$640,000	-$204,800	-$204,800	-$204,800	-$204,800	-$204,800	$23,884,800	$23,680,000	$23,475,200	$24,550,400
R.O.I.								598%	564%	533%	738%

Notes: 640 acres @ $5,000/acre = $3,200,00 total purchase price
Interest at 8% annually in arrears
Assume land sale in year 7, 8, or 9.
Land value at sale is assumed to be $1.00 per foot or $43,560 / acre

Ten-year speculation analysis.

The Downside

Looking at the table, you will clearly see the appeal of the speculative venture, as the rate of return is very good, approximately 80 percent per year. Why then isn't everyone in the speculative business? Referring back to the table, you can clearly see that in year eight we have run out of money, our million dollars is gone, and if we cannot sell this year, we lose it all.

Buzzwords

Absorption is a term used to describe the amount of space leased within a given time. It is defined empirically as the absorption rate (e.g., 100,000 square feet per year). A building built without any significant preleasing is being built on speculation, a.k.a. "spec."

In stark economic times this would very likely happen. If we guessed wrong on the projected *absorption* in the area, or if a recession hit the housing industry during this time frame, we would be in real trouble. Can these obstacles be overcome? Sure. It takes someone who can see it coming, and raise the required money in a timely fashion, perhaps renegotiating the deal with the farmer, cutting him or her into the profits in exchange for some interest forbearance. There are many ways to solve problems. That is where your entrepreneurial talent comes into the picture, and if it is successful, you can earn good money.

The Cash-Flow Project

The cash-flow project is the simplest form of equity builder for the average investor, and every area is full of homebuilders short on cash. With another lot, they can make more money, so there will always be one who will be open to an investor and a profit split. Should you have more money to invest, you could try your hand at buying some acreage and subdividing it into lots for sale to builders, or build some homes yourself. The possibilities are endless.

Land and Lots

Creating lots for builders is generally a good investment. Using the numbers from my home area, unsubdivided land sells for approximately $40,000 per acre for houses considered starter homes. The particular prices may vary in your area, but the relative ratios between wholesale and retail should hold true in any area.

For example, let's assume a development with four units per acre. In this case, finished lots sell for $40,000. Improvement costs—road and utility construction (the "hard costs")—will total approximately $10,000 per lot. This brings the land and hard costs up to $20,000 per quarter acre lot. With other "soft" costs—engineering, overhead, insurance, and selling expenses—your finished cost per lot should be around $25,000. Since the gross sales price per acre is $160,000 (four finished lots at $40,000), and your cost per acre is $100,000 ($40,000 for the land and $60,000 for hard and soft costs), your gross return would be $60,000 per acre. Depending on how you pay for the improvements, and the absorption rate, your return would be in the 40 to 60 percent per year range on invested capital.

When considering a lot creation project, remember that carrying the debt can always be a burden if sales do not meet your schedule. Be prepared for a worst-case scenario. I always recommend when dealing with land-improvement projects, to keep your leverage to a minimum. This will increase the need for cash, and increase your yield.

Housing

A typical investor/builder partnership involves the investor buying the lot and then splitting the profits of the sale of the house with the builder. It is a fairly simple scenario. For example, houses in an area might sell for $100 per SF (square foot). The finished cost of the house to the builder is $80 per SF, yielding a gross profit of $20 per SF. Typically, the lot cost is 20 percent of the cost of the average house. In this case, the lot would cost $16 per SF (20 percent of $80/SF). The profit of $20 per SF would be split with the builder. In this case, the investor's return would be half of that, or $10/SF. Since most homes take about six months to build, an investor could, theoretically, turn over the investment twice a year.

The Short-Term Investment

There are many types of short-term investments, but there is a common thread running through all of them. They are properties purchased for resale in 12 to 24 months. The properties can range from a house, purchased as a fixer-upper (see my book *The Complete Idiot's Guide to Investing in Fixer-Uppers*), and resold at a profit, to a new retail center, built and fully tenanted and sold to an investor at completion. Developers who build and sell are known as merchant developers, and they make a very good living, even on a small scale. The ones who build and keep are the ones who can build considerable wealth over the span of their careers.

Flipping

The speculation shown before in Chapter 2 is a prime example of flipping, but the practice has broader implications. A property can be placed under a purchase contract, and be treated as a development deal. It can be resold prior to the purchase date simply because the price in the original contract was very low, or the investor has made material changes to the value and entitlement of the land during the period it was under contract to the investor. The key to flipping is that the original purchaser never takes title, essentially flipping his or her interest in the contract to another through the right of *assignment*.

Buzzwords

Assignment is the transference of your rights to another. You may, in the absence of any agreement to the contrary, assign any beneficial interest in real property to another.

If assignment is precluded in the agreement, then the flip must be accomplished by a simultaneous closing of the two escrows, wherein the original buyer takes title and resells it simultaneously in the same escrow transaction. Similarly, if you find yourself in the process of building your dream home, you can explore the opportunity for profit by merely listing it for sale at a substantial increase over your cost. If you get a buyer before you move in, you will have created your first speculative development.

Development

The merchant developer is the typical short-term investor, taking raw land and converting it into income-producing investments. I have spent 25 years doing this, and have, between flips, rollovers, and build-outs, 45 deals under my belt. The typical transaction could be illustrated by my last office building, shown in the tables below. It was a small building, only 16,000 rentable square feet, and therefore, not as profitable as my typical project, which is around 40,000 SF. Economies of scale always make larger projects more profitable, until the law of diminishing returns takes hold around 100,000 SF.

In comparing the costs and the sales price, you can see that the rate of return for the merchant builder is 103.5 percent. Spread over the two-year life of a project like this one, it boils down to approximately 50 percent per year.

Better Believe It! ___

The right to assign the contract is very important, because it means that you can take capital gain treatment on contracts assigned after one year. The double escrow results in ordinary income. Negotiate hard to have the right of assignment, even if the seller must approve. If the seller must approve, make sure that approval cannot be unreasonably withheld.

Buzzwords ___

One acre is equal to 43,560 square feet of land. A&E is an acronym for Architecture and Engineering.

	Total Budget
LAND	
Land 1.67 Acres 72745 SF	$364,640
Closing Costs	$9,500
TOTAL LAND	$374,140
SOFT COSTS	
A&E	$60,000
Survey / Staking / Testing	$7,500
Leasing Commissions @ $3.00 / SF	$38,400
Insurance / Taxes / Legal / Acctg.	$7,000
Governmental Permits	$15,000
Loan Points $ 1,300,000 @ 3 Points	$39,000
Interest @ 10 % (1/2 outstanding for 6 mos)	$35,000
Misc. & Contingencies	$10,000
TOTAL SOFT COSTS	$211,900
HARD COSTS	
Landscape Area 19,025 SF @ 2.00	$40,000
Paved Areas 31,710 SF @ $ 2.25	$78,264
Building Shell @ $32.00 / SF, 20,000 SF [OH&P NIC]	$622,508
Tenant Allowance @ $ 25.00 /SF., 16,064 SF	$401,600
Taxes @ .0675 x 65% on shell only	$32,501
TOTAL HARD COSTS	$1,174,873
TOTAL PROJECT	$1,760,913
Value at completion from Chart 5.3	$2,337,000
Gross profit	$576,087
Cash equity	$460,000
ROI	125.24%

Cost breakdown.

Income and expense recap.

Income	Annual
Rents	$225,400
Less 5% Vacancy allow	-$11,270
Gross Potential Income	$214,130
Expenses	
At $4.75 /SF x 16000 SF	$76,000
Less recapture from tenants	-$72,200
Net expenses	$3,800
NIBDS	$210,330
Value @ 9% cap rate	$2,337,000

The Long-Term Investment

Who follows the merchant builder around? The long-term investor. This is the position most passive investors take. They look for a project that suits their needs and pay the retail price for it. In the above example, they would have purchased the project at the market rate of 9 percent based on NIBDS (net income before debt service). This price would have yielded them a gross return on cost of 9 percent, or, as we refer to it, the *cash-on-cash* return. Seldom, however, do investors buy for all cash. They usually assume the developers take out a loan, or they secure new financing based upon the purchase price of the investment. Most lenders today would loan 75 percent of the purchase price on that type of deal.

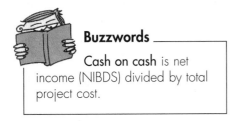

Buzzwords

Cash on cash is net income (NIBDS) divided by total project cost.

Buying

How, then, does this deal stack up? If we look at the financing, and assume that the buyer secures permanent financing for 10 years at 8 percent, with a 30-year constant payout, then the investment breaks down as follows: cash = $584,250, and loan dollars = $1,752,750. With this as an assumption, and assuming that the leases were as I executed them, with a 5 percent annual increase, let's look at the long-term investor's return on investment.

By analyzing the table above you will see that the investors did quite well over the long haul. Obviously, during this period there were capital requirements to replace departed tenants, and there may have been periods of vacancy greater than the projected 5 percent, but the final result in year 10 should not be far from the mark in a well-managed project.

Income	Yr Purchased	Year 2	Year 3	Year 4	Year 5	Year 6	Year 7	Year 8	Year 9	Year 10
Rents	$225,400	$236,670	$248,504	$260,929	$273,975	$287,674	$302,058	$317,160	$333,018	$349,669
Less 5% Vacancy allow	-$11,270	-$11,834	-$12,425	-$13,046	-$13,699	-$14,384	-$15,103	-$15,858	-$16,651	-$17,483
Gross Potential Income	$214,130	$224,837	$236,078	$247,882	$260,276	$273,290	$286,955	$301,302	$316,368	$332,186
Expenses										
$4.75 /SF x 16000 SF	$76,000	$79,800	$83,790	$87,980	$92,378	$96,997	$101,847	$106,940	$112,287	$117,901
Less recapture from tenants	-$72,200	-$75,810	-$79,601	-$83,581	-$87,760	-$92,148	-$96,755	-$101,593	-$106,672	-$112,006
Net expenses	$3,800	$3,990	$4,190	$4,399	$4,619	$4,850	$5,092	$5,347	$5,614	$5,895
NIBDS	**$210,330**	**$220,847**	**$231,889**	**$243,483**	**$255,657**	**$268,440**	**$281,862**	**$295,955**	**$310,753**	**$326,291**
Value @ 9% cap rate	**$2,337,000**	**$2,453,850**	**$2,576,543**	**$2,705,370**	**$2,840,638**	**$2,982,670**	**$3,131,804**	**$3,288,394**	**$3,452,813**	**$3,625,454**

10-year cash-flow projection.

The average annual rate of return on cash invested ($584,250), with an annual debt service of $154,417, is 19 percent before tax considerations, and the increase in value of the project over the 10-year holding period would be $1,288,454 before deducting capital expenditures. Assuming that unreimbursed capital expenditures would be approximately $150,000, then the real capital gain, taxable at the 20 percent rate, would be $1,138,454, or an additional 195 percent return on capital, before taxes. Not too bad, I'd say.

Building

If you wish to look at the equation from the point of view of the developer/investor who builds and retains the projects for a reasonable period, say 10 years, then you add the merchant builder's return, and the buyer's return outlined above, together. To see the total impact over the long run, refer to the table below.

Income	Yr Purchased	Year 2	Year 3	Year 4	Year 5	Year 6	Year 7	Year 8	Year 9	Year 10
Rents	$225,400	$236,670	$248,504	$260,929	$273,975	$287,674	$302,058	$317,160	$333,018	$349,669
Less 5% Vacancy allow	-$11,270	-$11,834	-$12,425	-$13,046	-$13,699	-$14,384	-$15,103	-$15,858	-$16,651	-$17,483
Gross Potential Income	$214,130	$224,837	$236,078	$247,882	$260,276	$273,290	$286,955	$301,302	$316,368	$332,186
Expenses										
$4.75 /SF x 16000 SF	$76,000	$79,800	$83,790	$87,980	$92,378	$96,997	$101,847	$106,940	$112,287	$117,901
Less recapture from tenants	-$72,200	-$75,810	-$79,601	-$83,581	-$87,760	-$92,148	-$96,755	-$101,593	-$106,672	-$112,006
Net expenses	$3,800	$3,990	$4,190	$4,399	$4,619	$4,850	$5,092	$5,347	$5,614	$5,895
NIBDS	**$210,330**	**$220,847**	**$231,889**	**$243,483**	**$255,657**	**$268,440**	**$281,862**	**$295,955**	**$310,753**	**$326,291**
Value @ 9% cap rate	**$2,337,000**	**$2,453,850**	**$2,576,543**	**$2,705,370**	**$2,840,638**	**$2,982,670**	**$3,131,804**	**$3,288,394**	**$3,452,813**	**$3,625,454**
ROI On Cash $460,000	**21%**	**23%**	**26%**	**28%**	**31%**	**33%**	**36%**	**39%**	**43%**	**46%**
Additional Annual Capital gain	**$576,087**	**$692,937**	**$815,630**	**$944,457**	**$1,079,725**	**$1,221,757**	**$1,370,891**	**$1,527,481**	**$1,691,900**	**$1,864,541**
ROI on Cap gain if sold	**125%**	**151%**	**177%**	**205%**	**235%**	**266%**	**298%**	**332%**	**368%**	**405%**

Builder/investor 10-year analysis.

While you can clearly see that the original developer/investor has a better rate of return based on the entrepreneurial profit derived from the development process, it is due to the fact that the debt burden is $1,300,000 on the original investment rather than the buyer's $154,417. This yields a greater annual return, averaging 33 percent per year as opposed to the investor/buyer's 19 percent. However, the purchaser/investor still has a very respectable return on cash invested, without having taken two years to create the investment.

The Least You Need to Know

- There are many different ways to invest your money; your job is to find one that you can be comfortable with.

- Your choice must make sense to you. You must believe that the building is useful and will have a sustainable economic life for the reasonably foreseeable future.

- It is essential that you do not get in over your head. Make sure the investment fits your resources.

- Once you launch, it is imperative that you pay close attention to the investment. Follow through!

- Proceed with caution.

Chapter 6

Real Property Products

In This Chapter

- Raw land
- Industrial properties and business parks
- Office buildings: suburban versus high-rise
- Retail, from neighborhoods to malls
- New communities and regional malls

The difference between the various types of real estate investment properties goes far beyond the budget of the individual investor. If you have little background in finance and accounting, a multi-tenant project may be too overwhelming. You might prefer a single-tenant building, or you may be annoyed with dealing with families and therefore be unsuited to apartment management. If you are a person who runs a welding business, you might feel more comfortable when investing in industrial properties rather than downtown office buildings. Conversely, if you are a banker, you might prefer something in an urban environment. People like myself want to work 9 to 5, Monday through Friday, so we are attracted to commercial properties, tenanted with businesspeople. Suffice it to say that there is literally something for everyone.

In this chapter, you learn about specific real estate products that have demonstrable market value. You will be able to tell the difference, and select a type of property that "speaks to you."

Land

When you look at land as an investment, you will find that the veritable smorgasbord of possibilities can overwhelm you. The choices available to you range from thousands of acres of unentitled land down to ¼-acre residential lots. The size of the land in question, and its zoning condition or condition of entitlement, will dictate the price and the immediacy of development. In general, if you are investing in land, and you do not intend to develop it yourself, you have only two logical buyers: the developer and the bigger fool. Since we have covered the bigger-fool buyer (see Chapter 1), you know that for this buyer, you will need to be in a growth market and boom time. These conditions must always be present to attract another buyer who is willing to pay more money for unimproved land. The developer, on the other hand, looks at land as needed raw material for his or her business, and is always on the lookout for more land in the right place. *A great place to invest is in the path of growth.*

The size of a given parcel, and the condition of the entitlements, if any, attached to the land will dictate the number of possible ways to make money on that specific parcel.

I break down land into three arbitrary size categories: small, or remnant parcels (¼–20 acres); medium-size parcels (20–100 acres); and large tracts (100–640 acres). Anything over 640 acres is a very large parcel, and, by default, falls into the realm of the large development company or speculator.

Small Parcels

When you are starting out in the business and have chosen land as your venue, small parcels are most likely your best bet for an investment. The "buy and hold" scenario is a safe plan, relying on the passing of time and the increase in development activity to create a greater value. *Remnant parcels* occur in the wake of development for various reasons.

In a subdivision, there are always parcels that are not as desirable or as well located, and are therefore passed over by buyers who have a good selection to choose from. When the wave of development has moved on and time has passed, these parcels are generally disposed of by the developer at a discount. The passing of time will cause the surrounding properties to appreciate, along with the remnant parcel.

In expanding markets (such as Phoenix), growth is constant and there are many people in the speculation business. Sometimes these people overpay for a speculative parcel. This overpriced purchase is a prime example of the bigger-fool theory. This buyer has, in fact, become the biggest fool, because the purchase was over market value.

Buzzwords

Remnant parcels are those skipped over during the normal process of development. They are the "missing teeth" on the street.

In states where the growth is not as prevalent, you will find these gaps in development represented by obsolete properties, such as abandoned factories or slum residential property. These can be redeveloped and put to good economic uses if the market is there to support these upgrades. Unfortunately, blight exists where market conditions do not support a higher and better use. Most often, complete demolition and redevelopment is necessary to achieve an effective turnaround. In situations like this, a certain critical mass is required to have the desired impact. (Critical mass implies that you have enough building or tenants to afford services such as management and maintenance to enhance the quality of the deal and maintain and grow its value.) Unfortunately, there are no rules or guidelines to determine what constitutes critical mass, so I do not recommend this type of project/investment for the novice.

Since time is money, the imputed costs (interest and taxes) of carrying the parcel just compounds the problem. This parcel will remain undeveloped until one of two things happens. The first possibility is that the buyer decides to cut her losses, discounts the price, and moves on. The second possibility is that a new wave of market demand will elevate the end-user price (rents) and cause the overpriced parcel to become viable at the newly established rental rates. To capitalize on this, the buyer will most likely have to find a way to build it out to realize any profit on the original investment.

Medium-Size Parcels

Some other ways to ensure making a profit, enlarging that profit, and, at the same time, making the parcel easier to sell, are to improve the land so that it becomes more valuable. This holds true for all parcels. There are various improvements that can be made to real estate, but they all fall into two distinct groups, tangible and intangible. The tangible improvements are the traditional ones: bringing utilities to the site, grading the site in preparation for development, and enhancing the site with landscaping.

The intangible improvements lie in the area of entitlements and development; entitlements range from zoning to final recorded subdivision maps, while development improvements range from planning approvals to leasing and financing. Improved parcels represent immediate opportunities for developers, and are readily saleable. This form of land investment is invariably profitable, and the resale is virtually guaranteed if the improvements are done properly. The test of the viability of the entitlements lies in the feasibility of the development project created by the change in entitlements you have accomplished. If they can justify the new land price, then the sale is assured, and a good profit will result from the effort made.

Large Parcels

Large parcels are inherently longer-term propositions, and should be treated with caution. Because of their size, they are only available well ahead of the path of development, and, consequently, require greater amounts of money and time. The advantage of larger parcels is that they lend themselves more readily to subdivision and resale. Since there are more buyers for smaller parcels, large parcels are a good bet to zone, master plan, and subdivide. This is always a profitable investment plan, and some companies do nothing else. They are essentially in the business of creating inventory for other developers. A typical section of land (640 acres) will be broken up into several residential tracts, and as many as four commercial sites. The smaller, more affordable-sized parcels are then easier to market.

Industrial

Industrial properties, both subdivisions and buildings, are reliable investments in many communities. Since many of the traditional, Industrial Age businesses have been phased out, the demand for industrial property is now segmented into different areas. The traditional heavy industries, such as steel and chemicals, are generally restricted to areas where they already existed for decades. These neighborhoods have accepted these "dirty" industries, such as steel mills and chemical plants, learned to live with them, and are in the process of making sure they clean up their act. Gaining governmental approval for the building of a new plant for such an industry in an area not used to the associated pollution and "dirt" is all but impossible. Most communities looking at industrial development are looking to the new "clean" industries such as computer and electronic manufacturing.

Growth areas for industry are primarily centered in the South and the West, relegating the old industrial uses to the rust belt. As in all types of development, industrial development has areas of specialization and general uses. Most industrial uses today are concentrated in so-called "parks," because communities have insisted that these areas have a better image, and fit better into the communities they serve. Parks, almost uniformly, all fall into two categories today, industrial and business. Industrial parks tend to house manufacturing and distribution facilities, while business parks tend to attract the clean industries of high-tech manufacturing, distribution, and offices. Most often there is a healthy mix of uses in each park, with the business park becoming the more expensive of the two environments. Business parks also include commercial areas such as restaurants and banks to serve the higher concentration of office population they attract.

Special-Purpose Buildings

Within industrial and business parks, buildings fall into several categories, the most risky of which, for investment purposes, being the special-purpose building. This category consists of structures designed only to house a specific use (such as a bank, restaurant, or factory), and not readily adaptable to more general uses.

The investment opportunity in this type of building lies in the credit of the tenant in occupancy. Since the building is not readily adaptable, the lease must assure the investor that he can recoup the original investment. Most often the length of the lease will be tied to the length of *fully amortized* financing available for the building. The theory here is that the residual land value will be sufficient for the

Buzzwords

Fully amortized means that the loan payments, made for the full term of the loan, are sufficient to repay the entire principal of the loan as well as the interest.

investor to recoup his initial cash investment and realize a decent profit if, and when, this special purpose building becomes vacant. The obstacles to conversion can be special construction such as too-high ceilings, odd floors, or as in the case of banks, odd-shaped and highly reinforced rooms. In addition, the location may be an impediment, such as a factory located next to the railroad. It was ideal for the factory, but would make for a noisy location for loft apartments.

Multi-Tenant Buildings

General-use structures, such as warehouse buildings and multi-tenant structures, have the same appeal in industrial areas as they do in office or retail areas: the more general the use, the greater the demand. The larger the number of tenants, the lower the risk of significant vacancy. Multi-tenant industrial uses are not as common as in office and retail development, and are usually found in what I describe as incubator/office buildings in the business parks.

An incubator/office building is one where there is a glass exterior in the front and a truck access in the rear, and the building area in between can be improved to provide 10 to 100 percent office space. This enables a user to start with a small office and an assembly area, or some form of warehouse area, and expand the office to the point that both operations need a new home. This flexibility allows for uses ranging from 100 percent office to 100 percent warehouse. It is very flexible and usually in constant demand in expanding markets.

It is the predominant spec development in business parks across the country. One of the best types of multi-tenant industrial buildings is the miniwarehouse. They are all over the country, capitalizing on the fact that people who live in apartments and small homes need additional, temporary storage space. These projects make excellent investments, but are hard to finance when under development. Established miniwarehouses, however, if well occupied, can be readily financed. The rents for this type of product have normally equaled those of apartments and make, therefore, a very attractive development project.

Office

Office developments parallel the same range of opportunities as the other types of development, from special use to multi-tenant facilities. The principal divisions peculiar to office buildings lie in the size of the buildings and the size of the tenant that can lease them. This is not as simple as big buildings for big tenants. The real difference lies not in the size of the building, but in the size of the floor plate, the area of any floor in a building devoted to tenant space and common areas. The floor plate will include all uses on the floor, including access (stairs and elevators), public areas (corridors and rest rooms), and tenant spaces.

If the distance from the corridor, or entry point, into the tenant space to the window wall is greater than 40 feet, the building cannot be economically planned for small tenants. Tenant spaces as deep as 60 feet can be configured for medium-size tenants (2,000–10,000 square feet), and tenant spaces deeper than 60 feet can accommodate the larger tenants.

The size of the floor plate will tend to influence the class of building constructed, on the theory that the larger tenants are better financial risks than smaller tenants. Therefore, the larger buildings will be found on more expensive land, and in areas of greater urbanization. These buildings are usually mid- or high-rise, and are referred to in the industry as "class A" buildings. The buildings require large amounts of money to buy and maintain. The owners are most often institutional investors or REITs, as mentioned in Chapters 1 and 2.

Large Buildings

Large buildings are not necessarily better investments than smaller ones. Their relative attractiveness lies in the type, size, and quality of the tenants. An investor looking for a large building to buy considers not just the quality of the building as an investment, but the ease or difficulty of disposing of the investment once the investor's goals have been accomplished.

The number of entities wealthy enough to purchase a large building is limited. In boom times, there is often no problem finding a ready buyer, but in times of recession, the larger investors generally have their hands full managing their existing portfolios. When dealing with large tenants, greater capital reserves are required for reinvestment whenever significant vacancy occurs.

Better Believe It!

When it comes time for lease renewal, don't kid yourself that that 10 percent tenant does not know how important he is to your bottom line! If you can anticipate this situation, you might be able to replace that tenant with several smaller ones. If you have that opportunity, then you can use it as leverage to make a better long-term deal with the larger tenant. Perhaps the new term of the lease can be extended beyond the period of your ownership. This handily transfers the current problem tenant to your successor.

Small Buildings

Small office buildings break out into two types: single-tenant buildings and multi-tenant buildings. As in the larger buildings, the floor plate will be the driving force behind the tenancy.

As a general rule, the large tenant in a small building has a disproportionate impact on the property. I would caution any investor away from a small building where any one tenant occupies more than 10 percent of the leasable space. Look closely at this tenant before purchasing such a building, because if you have a normal mortgage (75 percent of value), the cash flow to your investment is tied up in tenants representing 20 percent of the office space. If you look at a traditional vacancy allowance of 5 percent, then 15 percent of the tenants are responsible for 100 percent of your cash flow. Should you lose that 10 percent tenant, you have lost two thirds of your cash flow. If you believe that that tenant is well capitalized and is going to stay around for a while, then proceed, with caution.

Retail

The size of the building and the size of the tenant hold true for retail projects as well. Retail buildings run the gamut from single-tenant buildings to regional malls. If you are an investor looking to buy or build a regional mall, you need to have several hundred million to invest. The rest of us have to look at the balance of the available product. Single-tenant buildings are, as an investment, mostly a function of the tenant's credit and longevity. They are no different than single-tenant buildings in any use category. Look at them in the same fashion.

Strip Centers

Strip centers are a classification of shopping center characterized by both size and tenancy. They are most often 5,000 to 25,000 rentable square feet in size. Most are "unanchored," that is to say, they do not contain a national chain store or a tenant with "bankable" credit. Due to their awkward size and their lack of significant credit tenants, they are a riskier proposition for an investor than a conventional neighborhood or power center. Please refer to the discussion of cap rates and risk in Chapter 9.

Buzzwords

In-fill projects are those built on land that was passed over during the first pass through an area by developers. They are like the missing teeth in a smile.

This inherent risk is two-sided. The increased risk brings with it a greater potential for profit. Strip centers tend to be *in-fill projects* on heavily traveled thoroughfares and are, therefore, quite visible. Small tenants like these centers, as the visibility and accessibility are the key to their survival. The characteristics enable the local or "mom and pop" tenant to compete with their better-heeled, national chain competitors.

Neighborhood Centers

Everyone lives near a neighborhood center. They are so-named because they are designed to serve the immediate (generally assumed to be a 3-mile radius) surrounding residential neighborhoods. It traditionally takes over 15,000 people within this 3-mile radius to support a center of this size and tenancy. This center has a supermarket, a drug store, and a bank as the main attractions. The balance of the tenancy is composed of smaller convenience stores, most of which are owned by local merchants.

Over the years, these centers have grown to 200,000 SF or more and are referred to as community centers. They are, however, merely a variation on the neighborhood center, serving more highly concentrated populations. This center is always an attractive investment for anyone. Its size lends itself well to resale, and the type of tenancy tends to remain stable with little or no turnover during the life of the center. It will become obsolete only if the residential neighborhood falls into slum conditions, or if it does not stay up-to-date and competitive with its nearby contemporaries.

Power Centers

These centers are composed of discount stores, known as "box stores," and range in size from 200,000 SF to over 1,000,000 SF. The tenants are the same all over the country. They are the recognized discount stores typified by Wal-Mart, Home Depot, and Office Depot. They are everywhere, and have become the staple of American shopping. These centers range in value from $15 million to over $100 million. These shopping centers are most often owned by sophisticated investors who stay in constant touch with the tenants, and who are adept at anticipating changes in the public's shopping trends. These types of investments are recommended only for experienced real estate investors.

Regional Centers

Regional centers—such as the Galeria in Houston, Metro Center in Phoenix, or Sun Valley in Walnut Creek, California—are so large and expensive, that they create an economic environment of their own, totally independent from the rest of the community. They draw from populations in excess of a quarter million people, and the owners are few and very large, and are usually restricted to developers and institutional owners, or combinations of the two.

It takes huge amounts of capital to build and maintain these centers, so the few companies that do it seldom face any new competitors. Every regional center that will be built over the next 20 years has already been identified, and is most likely in the planning stage. It is a closed industry to all but the super-rich.

Mixed-Use Projects

These projects are hard to quantify, and are generally a one-of-a-kind investment. While they are usually built to capitalize on some unique local need or custom, the most common type of mixed-use would be found in centers that mix retail and office uses in an urban setting. Other forms of mixed-use projects are not recommended for novices, and I have deliberately stayed away from them over the years, as they are hard to finance.

Very Large Projects

There is not a great deal of opportunity for the average investor in large projects unless you can pool your money with other investors interested in this type of development/investment. Most very large projects are composed of residential properties around some sort of new community core, or urban renewal projects, where the city has decided to demolish an old, run-down section of the city and open it up for the development of new buildings.

New Communities

New communities are referred to as master-planned communities, and usually comprise at least 1,000 acres. They can, however, be as large as 20,000 acres, and involve a time frame stretching from five years to decades. The large master-planned community is becoming more visible around the country as developers seek to capitalize on the retirement habits of the population. There are even new communities today for family living. A prime example of this would be the new Anthem communities of the Del Webb company, springing up in the late 1990s in several different states.

Urban Renewal

Since the East Coast of the country was the first to be settled and continues to be the most heavily populated, the cities are much older than those in the western part of the country. These old urban cores have lost most of their residents to the new suburbs surrounding the old core city. Some downtown areas have fallen into disrepair and become hosts to many of the country's social problems. Several methods have been promulgated to combat this problem, the two most common of which are metro government and urban renewal.

The traditional solution to urban blight has been urban renewal, wherein a city condemns and demolishes sections suffering from economic obsolescence, clearing the way for new development in an attempt to revitalize the city. Investment opportunities in these areas abound. The federal government and individual cities have many programs to stimulate growth and urban renewal at the local level.

Sadly, while these opportunities exist, the blighted neighborhoods seldom take advantage of these programs. Experience has shown that government-supported development does not have the same success as private, more experienced development. These potential investments—while available and needing entrepreneurial talent—are seldom a good investment for someone who does not intend to work at the real estate business full-time. Even more than conventional development opportunities, these investments require the experienced care and feeding of a seasoned professional, preferably one with extensive urban redevelopment experience.

In urban areas where the city core has proven to be resistant to the suburban erosion, inner-city industrial properties have successfully been converted into "loft" residential units. Currently there are 12 such conversions going on in downtown Phoenix. This form of entrepreneurial investment has proven itself as a good investment. Typically, though, the lion's share of the profits go to the early bird who acquired the properties before the trend caught on. The latecomers have found their profits eroded by increased prices.

Commercial Centers

The bulk of commercial real estate opportunity lies in well-recognized commercial areas, along well-traveled transportation routes, and surrounded by an established residential population. These areas breed the types of investment choice that you should be looking for. If you need that speculative ingredient in your investment portfolio, then look a little further out, on the leading edge of the city's expansion, or even beyond. Good investment does not have to entail inordinate risk, and the ordinary garden-variety investment should, if well managed, bring satisfactory results to the average investor.

The Least You Need to Know

- Don't be swayed by your prejudices. Often, preconceived notions can cause you to overlook a good deal.

- You must decide, after all the input, where to place your dollars; look carefully, select conservatively.

- You must be able to relate to and understand the investment yourself. Do not rely on someone else's interpretation of the facts.

- With so much to choose from, pick substance over image every time.

Where to Invest— Locational Factors

In This Chapter

- ◆ Deciding where to invest is the important first step
- ◆ Researching the markets available to you will tell you where to invest
- ◆ What do statistics really mean?
- ◆ Now that you have the facts, what should you do with them?
- ◆ Comparing the experts' opinions, and making your own decision

Real estate investment is an art. There are no absolute rules that you can apply to every possible scenario. The most important part of the mix is good judgment based on common sense. It is a profession that is difficult to define. If you decide to become an investor or developer, you must have the strength of your convictions. Anyone can gather the facts—a few do it well and thoroughly, but when the final bell rings, you must make the decision.

One of the first decisions you will have to make is where to invest. In this chapter, you'll learn how to go about answering that question.

Decide Where to Buy

The most basic approach to any real property investment is to answer the question, "Where?" The two obvious answers are your own home ground, or somewhere else. If you live in the western part of the country, you are probably in or near a growth area, and could therefore easily choose to stay put and stick to the area you know.

Better Believe It! _____

Becoming astute in this business largely depends on three factors: observation, intuition, and common sense. The final ingredient is being smart enough to realize that you are in the right place at the right time. The essence of entrepreneurship is having the resolve to do something about it.

If you live in a very rural place, or somewhere where there is net annual out-migration or population stagnation, you might want to consider looking elsewhere. No matter what your circumstances, you must approach each possibility as if you had no knowledge of the area at all. In point of fact, until you made the decision to invest in real estate, you will have, most likely, never looked at your area or any other area with any consideration for its investment potential. When you look at the world through analytical eyes, it becomes an altogether different place. Places that were beautiful become interesting, or not, for totally different reasons.

Places that were eyesores start to look intriguing for their turnaround potential. Mundane places start to look like targets of opportunity. The vacant lot opposite the Safeway, the undeveloped parcel in your neighborhood, the farm at the edge of town, the factory near the waterfront that closed several years ago. You are suddenly able to look at all these places that you have driven past countless times in the past from a new perspective.

The abandoned factory can become loft apartments, the lot across from Safeway might sprout a gas station/car wash, the empty lot down the street may be ready for a spec home, and the farm at the edge of town is probably going to be the next subdivision. Why let someone else do it when you are right there with money to invest?

Home Town

There are inherent problems with any decision. When evaluating whether to invest your money locally or out of town, you must be able to deal with your own reality. If you live in a locale for any length of time, you will acquire some opinions about this locale that are based on living there, rather than investing there. If you look at an area that is new to you, you start with a clean slate. Personally, I get the best results when selecting projects by changing cities and even states every six years. My particular type of investment and development strategy requires a fresh look every so often, and I often need to be where I work. When you are prejudiced for or against an area, it will color your judgment.

No matter where you look, you must start over with a new perspective. Is this place economically healthy? Has employment risen over the last 10 years? Has the level of income risen over the last 10 years? Are companies locating new facilities here? Are they building freeways? What is their 10-year plan? Who are the largest employers, and is this a one-industry town, perhaps vulnerable in the future? Remember, the only constant is change. What is the local government like, and is it pro-business?

These are questions that you will probably never have pondered before. If you have a specific career path and a long-term economic game plan, you most likely have already given some consideration to the area in which you live and work. If you are not, then you should start doing so. Your economic future will depend on the answers.

Big City

It is likely that you will (and I recommend that you do) make your first investment in an area that is within an SMSA (Standard Metropolitan Statistics Area) that is growing, and that has a diverse and dynamic employment base. It would be preferable if it were in an area where commerce can thrive throughout the year rather than on a seasonal basis. If you choose an area that is constantly closed down by bad weather, or if the port is closed for three months a year, you might find that eventually this area succumbs to the *rust belt syndrome*. This is not a given; rather, it is a consideration. Do not be swayed by qualities that do not contribute to growth or economic health. Concentrate your research in areas that will make a long-term difference in the market. Resist using the criteria of others. Decide for yourself what factors really contribute to long-term economic health and continued growth. Make your own list.

Buzzwords

The **rust belt syndrome** is evidenced by the increasing abandonment of obsolete industrial properties, and the accompanying decline in residential values around these industrial centers..

Research

Research is a two-part process. The first step is deciding what data is meaningful, gathering the data, and then tabulating that data. There are some overall demographics that most of us in the industry can agree are important to research, such as the following:

- Population size and annual growth

- Net in or out middle-class (middle income) migration

- Median income and the 10-year trend

- Level of education of the population

- Type of industry prevalent in the area—old style (heavy), or new style (light), or electronic

- Number of building permits and the 10-year trend

All of the above should be held side by side with SMSAs of comparable size in the country. No statistics can be considered meaningful unless they are compared against their peer SMSAs.

In 1973, I made a formal statistical summary of the top 50 SMSAs in the country, using my own criteria, and I found some interesting results. Chicago always came out ranked number one in the nation. It is logical, because it is the economic hub of the country. If, however, I dropped out the SMSA size criteria, Minneapolis/St. Paul surged to the top. Consistent winners in the top 10 were Sunbelt cities, and I'm sure that if I did the same study today, the same cities would be in the top 10, the only changes being that the ranking may have changed.

You and the Facts

There are many ways to gather the data you will need to make your decision. I strongly recommend that you gather your own data. There are many sources to pull from:

- The U.S. census

- Local chambers of commerce

- Industry group publications

◆ Appraisers

◆ Brokerage companies

◆ Mortgage bankers

◆ Banks and other lenders

◆ Tax roll information

The list is endless. Take the obvious sources and add some of your own, developed from your own point of view. There are many criteria that can be meaningful for analysis. Some are obvious, and others are obscure. The big trick is to be discriminating in your information gathering. You must concentrate on data that you consider meaningful and accurate. Authenticate the data personally by random checking. Examine the source for reliability, rather than self-serving promotion. Finally, compile it into a statistical model that meets your needs.

Hire It Done

I'm sure this sounds like a lot of work, and if you have a full-time job, you probably don't have time to pursue this to the level of detail required. There are many market research companies that will do it for you for a few thousand dollars. If you go this route, I suggest that you guide the research personally to establish what you want to know, rather than taking their canned feasibility study approach (which is the process of evaluating a deal). Any reputable firm will be able to get you the facts, and for an additional fee, make a recommendation based on your criteria. It is not a bad idea to get a recommendation, but remember this: A feasibility study is the process of evaluating a potential investment property. When a research firm or an appraiser makes a recommendation, its primary modus operandi is covering its own butt. It will err on the side of caution so that you cannot seek redress for errors at a later date.

There is nothing inherently wrong with this approach. It will tell you where the mindless herd is going, and if you keep in mind that its recommendation is available to all that pay for it, then you are armed with reality.

The best approach is to then take the data, which will be accurate, and interpret it for yourself. It's your analysis and your unique spin, oriented to your plans, which will set you and your investment program apart from the herd.

The Straight Skinny _____

If you have any illusions about what a herd instinct can do, just look at the gyrations of the stock market from 1990 to the present. It started with a strong upsurge in almost all sectors, for no reason except the bigger-fool theory. Everyone was a genius, and industry pundits predicted the market would go to 30,000. Everyone forgot that an investment must be based on real earnings and nothing more. The current market, stuck in the 10,000 range, is undergoing a healthy dose of reality. The market's swings were primarily dictated by the press and the pundits rather than any fundamental change in corporate earnings. The market reacted to perception rather than fact. Investors are now paying the price for their lack of forethought and analysis. If you refuse to think for yourself—or are too lazy to—then you must pay the price.

How to Read Between the Lines

Part of the interpretive process involves asking the right questions of the right people. For example, if you ask lenders what they are lending on retail buildings in your chosen market, and they respond $75 per SF, then you know that the competition is spending approximately $100 per SF to produce their projects. Lenders today like to lend approximately 75 percent of cost rather than 75 percent of value. Look for the averages, not the exceptions. Experienced, professional developers can do better if they have a good track record with the lender. Concentrate on the lender's average deals.

Projections

Part of the market research is extrapolation of the conclusions drawn from the data and the creation of some credible projections for your chosen market and your proposed investment. While it is acceptable to ask a market research firm to do this for you, remember, its orientation is not necessarily in your best interest. In the final analysis, you must exercise your own best judgment. If you are satisfied with the accuracy of the facts, and you think your criteria are valid, then you should be on firm ground when making your decision.

Facts, Title, and Documents

Once you are past the point of deciding where to invest, you must deal with a specific parcel of land. Other than location, your first point of analysis is the preliminary title report. This occurs in states that use the title and escrow system. Other states use an attorney-facilitated closing method, wherein an attorney researches the chain of title and pertinent facts regarding your particular piece of real estate. Whichever system is used in your chosen locale, the process must be exacting and thorough. You must ascertain the legal and physical condition of the real property. The legal condition is the first concern, for if there are built-in restrictions or insurmountable problems, you need to find out fast.

If there are liens, if there was a gas station on the property, if there was a PCB spill, if the property is cross-collateralized, if the ownership is unclear, if there are restrictive covenants, if there are *easements* in the wrong place, you might be unable to implement your plan. Some of these problems have a solution, and under the title and escrow system, you have an ally that can help. When all is said and done, the title company can insure a problem that they are convinced is harmless. I'm not sure what relief is available under the other system, but your title attorney will have all the answers. This is a necessary step, and I recommend that you make sure the preliminary title report or abstract contains *legible* copies of *all* the documents referred to in the report. This will enable you and your attorney to make a speedy and thorough analysis of the legal condition of the title.

Buzzwords

Easements are portions of real property reserved for use by the public or third parties. For example, all public utilities run through private property for the benefit of the property and that of its neighbors. The individual property owners are not permitted to build over these easements, as they need to be accessible for service.

What Do the Facts Mean?

Drawing conclusions from the facts is different from making the decision. Conclusions are subjective, and they are fraught with human frailties. People tend to look at things through the filter of their own self-interest. When you are relying on the advice of others, it's good to keep this in mind. A broker making a recommendation, or interpreting the facts, is using the occasion to sell you something. He wants to convince you of two things. First, he is the broker you need to use, and second, this piece of property is the best choice. Do not be upset by this. The broker, mortgage banker, or marketing consultant is just doing his job. He is trying to give you his best guess while protecting his rice bowl. Take the information on board and run it through your own self-interest filter. This is the enlightened approach.

The Expert Opinion

The key element of the so-called experts' opinions is the law of averages. Their best guess, to be in your favor, is to go with the law of averages. They will always recommend that you play it safe. They want you to take the middle road so their projections and recommendations will appear conservative and prudent.

This is a good role for them, and it protects their professional reputations, while doing no harm to their clients. You must take this fact, and look at the other possibilities, searching for the road less traveled. If everyone is aiming at the same product, there must be a niche that lies unfulfilled somewhere. If you can find it and fill it successfully, then you are on your way to being successful as an investor. For example, an old urban office building in Houston might be turned into a miniwarehouse at a very good profit, and many an abandoned store could be successfully converted to other uses.

Your Take

In conclusion, it should be apparent to you that you must become an independent thinker. Your take on any deal will be the determining factor in its success. In this regard, you will always be the Lone Ranger. If this bothers you, then you should stick to playing the percentages and following the herd. Index funds were created for people who cannot, or will not, think for themselves. They go along, playing the averages. There is nothing wrong with this, but it will not make you rich and independent. This book assumes that you do not want to settle for the middle of the road and that you intend to do something about it.

The Decision

If you find that the theme of this section is repetitive, you are correct. It is deliberately so to hammer home the fact that you need to become a rugged individual to be effective in this endeavor. The difference between life and death in a crisis situation is often mindset. If you are easily defeated, you die. If you are continually discouraged, you fail. If, however, you are determined to succeed and are undeterred by obstacles in your path, you are already way ahead of the pack. Front-runners avoid the pitfalls of the many following in their wake.

Start the Plan

It all starts with your well-crafted plan and the realization that with any plan, once set in motion, the unforeseen will always surface. The elements of your plan should be kept simple. First and foremost is your objective; second is the map of how to get there. If your goal is realistic and your map conservative, there should be no obstacles that you cannot overcome. The normal, day-to-day setbacks of dealing with tenant turnover, maintenance problems, and occasional legal hassles are to be viewed as all in a day's work.

The key element in launching your plan is the irrevocable commitment of your funds to the project. Once your money is invested, you are stuck with the decision. There is no buyer's remorse; get on with it. Once you have taken this step, there can be no more second-guessing or hindsight. You are forced to work the plan for all you are worth. The constant attention to detail and the proactive response to possible future problems will make the difference between success and failure.

Better Believe It!

Make a good business plan, work it diligently, keep your eye out for changes in the market or opportunities to innovate, and stay flexible. As in the art of war, the plans become almost irrelevant after the first shot is fired.

Stay Flexible

As in any plan, flexibility is your best ally against disaster. One person's problem is generally another's opportunity. Turn your own problems into opportunities. During the late 1980s, the Great Recession occurred, and in California, there was more office space brought on to the market through corporate downsizing than was ever produced by developers in a boom year. Was this a disaster? For some it was, but for others who could see it coming, and who took immediate proactive steps, it was not necessarily so. They successfully converted large tenant space into smaller spaces, increasing the number of tenants in their building, albeit at lower rents, and through greater diversity improved the quality of their investment. When the recession was over, they were able to again escalate their rents to get their investment program back on track.

Sometimes there are problems that have no immediate solution, and you need to survive so that time will solve the problem. If you can hang on during a recession, time will bail you out. If, however, you can see another avenue ahead of others, then you might be able to finesse a solution before everyone else jumps on the bandwagon. Some of the best tools for remaining flexible are a cash reserve for recapitalization (renovation and redecoration), good dialogue with your tenants, and attention to trends in the marketplace.

The Least You Need to Know

- You must choose where to invest—in your own backyard, or in some far away "hot" market. There are many plusses and minuses for both venues; your understanding of both is key to your decision.

- Again and again, research will produce the facts you need to decide.

- If you are attracted to the hot market, ask yourself why it is hot, and how long it can sustain that heat. Take an unbiased look at your own backyard. Is it the boonies?

- Once the decision is made, do not forget the process. Take it one step at a time.

Chapter 8

Using Professional Help

In This Chapter

- ◆ Evaluate what you can and cannot do
- ◆ The real estate broker's job
- ◆ The architect/engineer—who they are and what they do
- ◆ The attorney—the good, the bad, and the ugly
- ◆ The contractor: the nuts-and-bolts guy
- ◆ The manager, a.k.a. the "bean counter"

With your decision made to invest, your research accomplished, and your target deal identified, it is now time to marshal your resources. If you are fully qualified to assume all the roles required of any deal, skip ahead to Chapter 9, but if you are not, this is when you will identify your potential team. In this chapter you'll learn what and who you will need on your team to identify an investment, purchase it, and successfully manage its growth.

The Team

You will probably need to hire market researchers, brokers, architects and engineers, attorneys, contractors, and building managers. This is not as daunting as it might appear. These disciplines have their place in any real property building and management plan. The costs are built into the budget, and the tenants expect to pay rent based upon these costs.

The typical list of expenses from any standard pro forma cost breakdown is as follows:

- Land
- Architecture
- Engineering
- Surveying and testing
- Brokerage commissions
- Legal and accounting costs
- Interest and loan points
- Overhead
- Permits
- Insurance
- Real estate taxes
- Building costs for shell, site preparation, parking, and landscaping
- Taxes on construction costs (and miscellaneous expenses)

These costs are a part of any building, and the rents are calculated as a percentage return on the costs plus all operating expenses for the building.

If you buy an existing building, you are paying all these costs plus a profit to the original developer. If you buy from a subsequent owner, you are paying the appreciated value accrued to the building from his stewardship as well. The rent you set for your tenants will be based on your costs paid, plus the additional costs you incur in the process of owning, managing, and leasing your property. In addition, over the time you own the property, you will raise rents at a rate to keep ahead of inflation to assure you a capital gain when you sell.

Your Role as an Entrepreneur

Assuming that you are not an experienced real estate entrepreneur, you must decide whom you will need and why. What is your role besides picking up the check? See yourself as the coordinator and the central communicator. Your job is to assemble the team and motivate them to do the job well enough to show a profit on your invest-ment. In essence, you are the professional nag. Other than doing the things you are qualified to do, you make sure that everyone else does his or her job on time, the first time, and every time.

Active

If you opt to take an active role, you will be required to coordinate and check the work—generally following through on everything done by your consultants. You will have to chair meetings, arbitrate disputes, solve problems, hire and fire consultants, and negotiate all the agreements. You will, if you are astute, take an active role in liaisons with your tenants, as well as personally oversee the leasing and renewal of tenant spaces. Do you have the time for this? If not, then you need to find the perfect property manager.

Passive

When you decide to take a passive role in the process, you start to consider an invest-ment in a REIT or larger properties where one of the partners takes the responsibil-ity for the day-to-day management of the investment. Normally, the manager takes a fee for this service. Managing partners and managing members have to be qualified to do the job, and their fees are justified by their performance. In many cases, the man-ager will earn his or her equity in the property through the hands-on process of development or management. At the very least, he or she will extract a fee for the service. If you intend to take a passive role, the choice of manager becomes a pivotal decision.

The Brokers

Before you can manage either an existing income-producing property, or land on which you can develop an income property, you must purchase it. This most often requires the services of a professional real estate investment broker, or a raw land broker. Once

Buzzwords _____

A **facilitator** is one who serves as the "third party" in a 1031 exchange. He or she takes custody of your money when you sell, purchases the new property, and exchanges it for your money.

the building or lot is under your control, you will need the services of a leasing agent, another brokerage function.

Finally, when you have manipulated the property to its highest and best value, you will require the services, yet again, of the investment broker to dispose of the property. If you further elect to delay payment of the capital gain upon sale of the project, you will need the investment broker and a *facilitator* to find another investment for you to consummate a tax-free exchange.

Buying

The real estate brokerage function is usually a specialized practice. Most commercial brokers start their careers as leasing agents and gradually develop a specialized practice after a few years. They most often gravitate to areas that they feel most comfortable with, or areas they perceive as most profitable. In growth areas, the land specialist makes a very good living, and the investment broker is always in demand.

From a per-transaction viewpoint, the investment broker is selling the most expensive commodity outside of large land tracts, but, because of the size of the transaction, he or she earns the smallest commission. The raw land broker usually charges 6 to 10 percent of the sales price as a fee, while the investment broker charges 1.5 to 3 percent of the sales price. The leasing agent's commission is calculated on a lease-by-lease basis, where the commission is a function of rental rate, type of lease, and term of the lease.

Long Term

Once you have made the decision to start down the road of real estate investment, you might want to (and I strongly recommend that you do) recruit some consultants/ partners for the long haul. Obviously, your first choices may prove to be incompatible with your long-term goals, but you should always have the long view in mind when recruiting talent. This has advantages for both parties, especially the role of the broker. The more he or she knows about you and your goals, the better she can meet your needs.

Once the broker gets a feel for your style of business, he or she can better represent you and your properties to prospective buyers and tenants. The other aspect of creating a long-term relationship is to save money. If the broker knows that he or she is locked into your operation, the broker might be willing to come up with a program that gives you some discounts on the various fees involved. Knowing that each transaction will result in a commission when you buy, leasing fees while you own, and sales commissions when you sell, the savvy broker will most likely either give you some special service or a discount on the fees as a package.

As part of your long-range plan, you should consider getting a real estate license, but be cautioned, if you routinely step on the broker's commissions, they will stop bringing you the best deals. A license is most useful when selling, or when you have enough experience to do without a broker; then you can use it to buy as well. After 30 years, I'm still using brokers, and I have been licensed since 1973.

The Architect/Engineer

Depending on the type of acquisition you're interested in, you eventually will need the services of an architect or an engineer, and maybe both. If you're going to build an investment property or if there is a building involved at all, you will need an engineer. Should you purchase an existing investment property, releasing and replacing tenants will require the services of an architect or space planner or both. A space planner is an architectural specialty, dealing exclusively with the documents pertaining to tenant improvements, rather than the building shell. If your tenant renovation entails changes to the structure as well as the tenant work, then you definitely will need an architect and most likely a structural engineer. Most busy architectural firms have all the services except engineering in their practice, and they can hire and supervise the engineer as needed.

Building

Should you decide to go the route of building the investment, you will need architects and engineers for the entire process. A surveyor will produce a boundary survey and topographic map, the civil engineer will design the site improvements and foundations, the structural engineer will design the building structure, and the architect will design the exterior, the building components, and coordinate all the above functions. There are several ways to manage this process.

The simplest—but most expensive—way is to hire the architect and make him or her responsible to engage and supervise the others as part of his or her scope of work.

CAUTION

Better Believe It!

Too often I have seen an attorney, in a well-meaning manner, guide an owner toward a business decision. The attorney's sole function is to point out the potential pitfalls and benefits of a legal issue, and it is your job to make the decision. Do not abdicate your business decision—making power to your attorney. Ever!

The less costly approach is to hire the architect, and with her cooperation, hire the other functions directly. This will put you squarely in the middle of the process, and in my mind, that is the place to be. As the focal point of all the work you will, by default, have to keep up with what is going on and coordinate all the moves. As the central communicator, you will be the first to know what's what. This will expand your knowledge of the building process and make you a more enlightened and effective owner. It is worth doing at least until you have acquired a firm grasp of what is going on, and a thorough understanding of the building's many components. Once you get too busy, you will probably be able to afford to delegate this chore.

The Attorney

The attorney can be, and often is, a pivotal player on the team. Due to the nature of his function in preparing contracts and other documents, the attorney necessarily becomes involved in all facets of the investment's acquisition, operation, and disposal. You must focus very carefully on the role you wish the attorney to play. Hire an attorney who is experienced in the field of real estate law and practice, as well as one who may have experience in the particular product you will be dealing with.

The key to successfully working with a good attorney is to, at the outset, clearly define the scope of work between the attorney's job and your own. Remember, an attorney is supposed to be an expert in the law, not necessarily in business or real estate development and ownership. The attorney's proper function should be to protect your interests, seeing to it that you have the legal tools to implement your investment plan.

Should you find the attorney wanting to make these decisions, suggest that he or she put his or her money on the line along with yours. In effect, you're saying, "Put up or shut up." You might also require flat fees for different services where appropriate. In general, the attorney should not be reluctant to do so, since she is supposedly an expert in the preparation of these documents, and should completely understand the scope of the work. If the attorney does not understand the scope of the work, or if she is reluctant to commit to a flat or a not-to-exceed fee, you should consider acquiring a more qualified and confident attorney.

Planning and Building

When planning a development project, you will need to manipulate or create a variety of documents. In order of their appearance, they are the following:

- Purchase agreement

- Title report

- Property documents (such as operating agreements or reciprocal easements between abutting properties)

- The ownership document (corporation, partnership, or LLC)

- Entitlement and application documents

- The brokerage agreement (leasing contract)

- Architect's contract

- The engineering contracts: civil, structural, surveying, and testing

- The utility agreement and easement documents

- The building lease

- Loan documents and *Estoppel agreements*

- The property management agreement and its attendant subcontracts

Buzzwords

An **Estoppel Certificate** is a document stating that the tenant is not in default, is in possession of the premises, is paying rent, that the lease is in force, and that the landlord is not in default.

I'm sure there will be others not listed here. There always are. The key to successful documentation in any project is enforceability and accountability. Wherever possible, the documents need to be cross-referenced and interlocking, linking the accountability between the consultants to the owner. You want them to be checking on each other's work and to be responsible for undetected mistakes. It is not your job to properly design the building, but to pay for the design, and make sure the people involved do an adequate job in a timely and professional manner.

Managing

If you charge your attorney with the task of creating and manipulating documents for an existing property, you will have to contend with the following, as a minimum:

- The purchase agreement
- The title documents
- The existing leases
- Estoppel agreements from lenders and tenants
- New or old loan documents
- Ownership documents and operating agreements
- The property management document
- Your new lease
- An exclusive leasing agreement
- The exclusive listing agreement for sale
- The sales document
- The exchange documents (maybe)

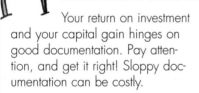

Better Believe It!

Your return on investment and your capital gain hinges on good documentation. Pay attention, and get it right! Sloppy documentation can be costly.

Sounds like a lot of paper, doesn't it? It is. Pick your attorney carefully, and make sure she does a great job. You do your job correctly, and your attorney will automatically do her job correctly also.

The Contractor

Another key player in your plan is the construction company. It will be involved whether you are building or buying. If you are building from scratch, you will need a larger, better financed, and more experienced contractor than if you are purchasing an existing property. The difference lies in the scope of work. Sometimes, when a substantial building is involved, some owners use one contractor for the site work, another for the building shell, and still another for the tenant work. As the owner of an existing income property, you will, most often, need only an experienced tenant improvement company.

Building

When you set out to develop any investment property, the selection of a good contractor should hinge on several factors:

- ◆ You will want the building to be as good quality as the budget can afford.

- ◆ You need to have it built within a specific time frame.

- ◆ You will want it built within budget, with few, if any, cost overruns.

- ◆ You will want to be able to enforce the warranties on the construction.

To accomplish these four factors reliably, I strongly recommend a negotiated contract. The process I favor is to select several highly qualified contractors at the beginning of the design stage, furnish them with the preliminary plans and outline specifications, and have them bid the project on a not-to-exceed basis with a fixed fee. Assuming that the successful bid is within my budget, I then execute a contract with the chosen bidder, adding him to the design review process to ensure that we stay within budget throughout the working-drawing process. This procedure will guarantee that you will not be over budget as far as the building shell is concerned.

The budget for tenant improvements will be a test of your negotiating skill with the tenants. The contractor should further guarantee the cost of the individual items on the standard tenant improvement list for a 24-month period starting on the date of commencement of the construction.

Managing

When you decide to purchase an existing investment property, you will want to have an expert's opinion regarding its condition at the time of sale. The lender will generally require an expert opinion, and I strongly suggest that you accompany the architect/contractor/inspector during the inspection.

If you can arrange it, have your proposed tenant improvement contractor selected and under contract at this time. It would also be a great idea for her to participate in the inspection of the building to gain a first-hand idea of the location and the condition of the major building components. Time and energy spent at this time will serve you well.

Most often, the agreement of purchase will contain a clause that requires the seller to repair any deficiencies in the building or areas of accumulated deferred maintenance. This inspection will also provide you, as the new owner, with a list of ongoing maintenance items to be included in your annual operating budget. The contractors involved can help you establish prices for these items, often suggesting innovative ways to improve the maintenance at a lower cost.

The Property Manager

One vital player at this time, especially when purchasing an existing building, is the proposed property manager. He should be involved in the selection and inspection process from its inception.

The Straight Skinny

Don't be afraid to ask questions. There are no stupid questions, just stupid owners. No one involved in the process will expect you to be an instant expert, and most people will be willing to do a good job for you if they are treated fairly, and compensated adequately.

The property manager will most likely *not* be you. The skills required of a good manager are not those required of an entrepreneur. A good property manager needs to be part diplomat and part bean counter. You do not want your manager to take risks with your money. You want him or her to preserve and enhance your investment in the property, enforce the leases, and collect the rents on time. You do not want him or her negotiating terms for your new leases, but you do want him or her to present your ideas to the tenants, acting as a buffer when there are disagreements. This allows you, as the owner, to intervene and save the day whenever the inevitable conflict occurs.

Planning

The astute use of the talents of a qualified property manager should start, in a development project, when you hire the architect and contractor. If you allow the property manager to participate in the design process, you will find that he can eliminate many costly and impractical design flaws. Neither the architect nor the contractor has to live with the finished product. Their ideas, while potentially aesthetically pleasing and well built, can become management headaches over the sustained period of ownership. A prime example is the use of water features in some urban projects. In areas that have severe weather, the presence of water freezing and thawing can wreak havoc with the improvements around it.

A good manager will diligently strive to eliminate these items while they still exist only on paper. Erasing them and redrawing the detail is infinitely cheaper than demolition and reconstruction. Most often, paid managers will spec their time at this point to ensure that they have the management contract when the time comes. For the professional manager, it is sound salesmanship, and a chance to demonstrate his or her knowledge of that particular building type.

Managing

Likewise, if you intend to purchase an existing income property, a manager can be a great resource. A new investor might not be aware of all the building choices available for purchase. You will be very unlikely to know which are the most management intensive, and which lend themselves to rent escalation over the period of your projected investment plan. Likewise, he or she can help you examine the seller's rent roll and expense breakdown to determine if the figures are reasonable or if the expense items can be improved upon. She or he can help set up your management machinery and provide guidance in the areas of leasing and tenant selection. She or he is in a position to evaluate your new building's rent roll to spot potential problem tenants. The manager might even be familiar with some of the tenants from other properties under her or his care.

Having reviewed this section, you are now aware of the potential complexity of the selection and recruitment process. You need to look within to evaluate your skills and potential for contribution. Try to be realistic. There is no profit in kidding yourself, and it could prove to be disastrous down the line. Your role is first, last, and always that of the final decision-maker. Start from that premise, and build up your skills through experience.

The Least You Need to Know

- You must plan to take an active part in the management of your investment.
- There are many experts in all the fields. Find some good ones and use them astutely. Do not abdicate your prerogatives.
- Every consultant has a role to play. Decide what you need, and ask only for what you cannot do yourself.
- Listen to your attorney, but make your own decisions.

Part 3

Stepping Up to Your First Deal

Here's the truth of it. You make your money when you buy; you maximize the profit when you manage; and you collect your earnings when you sell. This section shows you how to systematically select a property to purchase, how to determine whether it is a good deal, and finally, how to make your first offer.

It takes you through the process, the consultants, and the documentation, so that you can become thoroughly comfortable with your first purchase. You will be fully prepared to close the transaction and set up the property for a long-term profit.

The Components of Value

In This Chapter

- ◆ Cash flow: cost and value
- ◆ Buildings and their role in the investment
- ◆ How leases determine value
- ◆ Growing your investment
- ◆ How to find the money you need
- ◆ Determining value

When you buy a piece of investment real estate, what exactly are you buying, and what is it worth? Where land is concerned, you are purchasing a commodity that you know will become scarcer, and whose location will become more visible. Where income property is concerned, the answer is not as clear. In this chapter, you'll learn about the components of value.

The Basics of Value

There are two elements to any purchase, and both have a value. First, you are purchasing an existing cash flow, and second, you are purchasing a building. I have always joked that when I am finished with a development,

I sell the leases and throw the building in for free. This is not far from the truth. You will note that when an appraiser examines a building, he looks at the leases to establish value, and the comments in the report that pertain to the building address its replacement value.

When buildings cost $100 per SF or more to build, how can we dismiss their value when making an appraisal or an offer to purchase? The answer is, quite simply, something is only worth what you can get for it. The real estate market is no different than any other market. The laws of supply and demand and the current market price of an income stream govern the price of income-producing real estate. We will take up the subject of capitalization rates later in this chapter, but, for now, the simple explanation is that the valuation of any building for sale as income property is priced based on a multiple of its NIBDS (net income before debt service). It is similar to purchasing an annuity, but with one subtle difference. You can change the rate of return (ROR) through astute management. The unknown element in the transaction is you, the buyer. If you can find a property where the leases are under market, or where the building is ready for an upgrade, you might be able to dramatically increase the income stream, resulting in a significant increase in value.

Cash Flow

Since you are purchasing cash flow, let's examine the income side of any income property. What are the elements that will appear on the prospectus (a.k.a. the pro forma) for evaluation? First is the GPI (gross potential income), which represents what the building produces if it is at 100 percent occupancy. Since a multi-tenant building will always have turnover, the industry demands a nominal vacancy factor be added to the pro forma to reflect that reality. It varies from 5 to 10 percent depending on the market and who is evaluating the building. Subtract the vacancy allowance from the gross income and we are left with the EGI (effective gross income). EGI equals GPI less the vacancy factor.

Next, we must examine the operating expenses of the building. They include, but are not limited to, utilities, insurance, repairs and maintenance, taxes, reserves for replacement, window washing, janitorial, landscape maintenance, parking lot sweeping, and management costs. If the building is leased on a gross basis, the tenant's rent will include provisions for these expenses, and the cost of operations will be deducted from the GPI to determine the NIBDS. If the building is leased on a net basis, the tenants will reimburse the landlord for these expenses in addition to their monthly rent. The only charge against the GPI in a net leased building will be the cost of the expenses that pertain to the imputed vacancy factor shown above. This is then subtracted from the GPI to determine the NIBDS. This is what you are buying. It will look like the table shown below.

When you examine the income stream of a specific property, the pro forma will be more elaborate. It will list all the tenants and provide detail on expenses that pertain specifically to the building in question. It should, however, be verified against the owner's tax return for accuracy.

INCOME	Current Yr.
Gross Potential Income [GPI]	$490,000
Vacancy Allowance @ 5 %	-$24,500
Effective Gross Income [EGI]	$465,500
CAM EXPENSES	
Real estate Taxes	$48,000
Maintenance/Repair/HVAC	$3,600
Insurance fire / liability	$14,400
Elect	$7,200
Water & Sewer	$4,800
Refuse	$1,200
Janitorial	$31,200
Windows / sweeping	$4,800
Security	$8,640
Pest Control on demand	$1,800
Yard Maint & Common Area	$4,800
Subtotal	$130,440
Management Fee @ 10% exp.	$13,044
Total Common Area	$143,484
Tenant reimbursed CAM	$136,310
landlords Expense	-$7,174
Net Income Before Debt service [NIBDS]	$458,326

Pro forma income and expense breakdown (net leases).

Existing

When you buy a building, you are buying an existing income stream at a multiple thereof. What you should look at and examine closely is the potential built into the leases for increases in the rental rates. In my leases, there is always an escalator, but since all leases, mine included, are subject to negotiation, the escalation clauses may vary all over the lot. Some leases may be flat for three to five years and escalate every five years thereafter. Some may be escalated annually, based upon the consumer price index or a fixed figure or percentage. Whatever the case, you need to examine the leases one by one, creating a spreadsheet, which will show you the built-in increase in cash flow and the lease expiration dates.

This built-in rate of return increase will portray the cash flow potential before you bring your management talents to bear. It should also indicate when the leases expire, helping you plan your strategy.

Future

You should never buy an income property for the existing income stream. The existing income stream is only used for setting the asking price. You should purchase the investment for its potential increase in income and long-term appreciation and staying power. A well-located, multi-tenant building, properly built, is an asset that can pay an ever-increasing return for the foreseeable future.

Key elements to look for are, as outlined previously, the built-in increases, the lease expiration dates, and the size and configurations of the tenants. The potential for tenant expansion at lease renewal time should be examined, along with the likelihood of tenants having to vacate because you cannot accommodate their future expansion needs. Interestingly enough, you might want to encourage a tenant to vacate at renewal time, rather than create a situation where the tenant becomes an overly significant part of your cash flow.

Building

Since you are also buying a building, it is important to ascertain exactly what the building is, and how it fits into the marketplace. Can it be modernized when needed, and can it be maintained economically? What is the level of deferred maintenance? What will it cost to bring it up to snuff? It is prudent to have an expert help with this evaluation. If it is a relatively new building, there may still be warranties in place; ask for them, and make sure they can be transferred to you at the time of purchase.

Sometimes older buildings have been updated with new air-conditioning units that may be under warranty. If the parking lot has been resurfaced, there may be a warranty. Examine the maintenance contracts and talk to the contractors and repair people. Talk to the contractors who have been building the tenant improvements. If the seller was the contractor, talk to his subcontractors. Find out anything you can about the building. Set up a spreadsheet for maintenance and refurbishing. Add to the budget the cash necessary to accommodate lease renewals and releasing. Existing tenants usually want new carpet and paint to extend their leases. Gladly pay it for a good long extension at an increased rental rate. It is a good investment.

What Do You Have?

When examining the building, look at the structure, the ceiling heights, the utility systems, and the roof (especially the roof). Leaking roofs can cause more damage than just the cost of repairs. Water can damage your tenant's equipment and files, causing them to lose a lot of money. Guess who gets to pick up the tab? It would be prudent to solicit the opinions of an architect and a contractor when performing this evaluation, because these are the professionals to whom you must turn for solutions to any of these building problems. Their opinions can be evaluated in terms of dollars and lost tenancy, should the need for extensive renovation arise. One of the ongoing problems of management is that you must keep the other tenants happy and in business while you renovate a suite for a new occupant.

What Can Be Done with It?

When you look at the building, you must attempt to put it into its proper niche in the marketplace. Its entries, ceiling heights, and utility systems will determine whether the building can remain competitive during your ownership. Sometimes, when the market upgrades, your building may slip from a *grade A building* to a *grade B*. Is this cause for concern? Not really. Your concern should center on your ability to continue raising rents and maintaining occupancy. I have never built a grade A building, as I believe that the rate of return on a grade A building is less than it should be. My grade B buildings have always been great performers, starting out at a minimum of 12 percent cash on cash and improving annually ad infinitum.

Buzzwords

A grade "A" building is one that is generally considered to be the best located and most costly to construct, commanding the best rents in town. A grade "B" building will be the second tier in quality.

Leases

The most significant part of your purchase is the pile of leases attached to the building. These documents will spell out what you can and cannot do as a landlord. Sometimes good buildings have very poor leases, and sometimes the reverse is true. This will not cause you any sleepless nights unless the economy turns sour or your tenants start acting up.

The key to managing a building successfully lies in the enforceability built into the leases. The landlord's options to compel a tenant to honor her obligations are as necessary as an escalation clause. The ability to penalize late payment of rent, enforce the rules and regulations, and regulate the tenant's behavior are paramount to managing a successful building.

You will need to control maintenance, parking, signs, noise, and a host of other actions in addition to being able to enforce the timely payment of the rent.

The Document

You must take the existing lease to your attorney and compare it to the lease you want to use in the future. The problem is that if you hit a renewal tenant with a completely new lease, he will feel betrayed, get defensive, and strongly consider moving out. The tenant will feel that you have broken the trust established by the old landlord. You must avoid this at all costs! Like it or not, the tenant is the most important person in your life when it comes to managing your investment.

You must satisfy your tenants' needs at all costs if you wish to keep them. Moving is expensive, and unless there is an overbuilt market, the tenant will have to pay the costs of moving and new documents, such as stationery and business cards, not to mention down time, employee productivity losses, and communication relocation. This can be, and is, a startling and ever-increasing number. Unless the tenant requires more lease space, the tenant wants to stay in your building. To smooth things over when you ask for more money and a better lease, you must offer the tenant incentives that will placate, and make the tenant feel that she is not only important to you, but that she is receiving preferential treatment.

Shortcomings and Improvements

The most common shortcomings you are likely to find in some existing leases are as follows:

- They are generic, pre-printed, one-size-fits-all in quality. This is not good, because no preprinted form can address all possible considerations.

- There is no penalty clause for late rent payment.

- The default clause is not sufficient to evict in a timely manner.

- There are no rules and regulations, and if there are, they have no enforceability.

- There is no escalation built into the lease.

- There may be concessions granted that affect your ability to lease to other tenants, such as exclusives or options on contiguous space.

When you take over an existing property, you must catalog all these problems and eliminate them forever when the lease comes up for renewal. Don't be tentative about this. Insist that these changes must be incorporated into any new lease agreement. There is nothing wrong with explaining why you need to do this. If the tenant insists on keeping a clause that is not going to be standard in your new program, offer him or her the opportunity to pay extra for it. If you have to live with a restriction, at least be compensated for it. Most tenants will back down. The single exception might be a tenant who feels that the option to expand is necessary. You can live with that with the proper notice provisions.

How to Change It

The best way to make substantive changes in the lease is not to issue a completely new lease immediately, but to use the old lease, substituting only the clauses that you feel you must have. Don't try to slide these past the tenant. Go over the changes with him or her, explaining that your investors, or your lender, require them.

Future

Why are you going to all this trouble, revamping leases and manipulating rents? The simple answer is that this is how you profit while owning property. By increasing the lease rates over time you increase your ROR, and by improving the quality of your leases, you make the project more saleable. You need to develop an organized, long-term strategy over the life of the leases you have inherited, to not only clarify and strengthen the leases, but also to improve the bottom line. These things don't happen by accident. You must make a plan and be persistent.

Long-Term Plan

Your long-term plan might look like this:

- Rewrite the lease to clarify rental payments and penalties, and add rules and regulations.

- Eliminate all exclusives or restrictive covenants.

- Change the lease structure completely from gross leases to net leases. Gross leases include the landlord paying some or all of the operating expenses of the building, and triple net a.k.a. NNN leases have all expenses as a "pass through" to the tenants (see Chapter 19).

- Budget some improvement money to convert the electrical system, which will accommodate individual metering for your new net leasing program.

- Modernize the lobby and common areas, and revamp the landscaping to create a better atmosphere.

A strategy such as this, implemented over a 10-year period, will result in a better cash flow, a more attractive property, and a higher resale value.

Exit Strategy

You must start planning your exit strategy the day you take title to the property. If, for instance, you buy an office building that has gross leases, your plan to convert them over your tenure as the owner will result in a minimum improvement in your bottom line by $2 per SF. If you sell at the same cap rate you purchased it for (9 percent), that increase in your bottom line, independent from any other increases, is worth $22.22 per SF at the time of sale. If your building was a 50,000 SF building, you have made a profit of $1,111,000 by converting the leases.

The passage of time, inflation, and other factors will provide you with another boost. You may not be 100 percent successful in all that you plan, but if you accomplish most of the plan, you will find that owning and operating income-producing real estate can be very profitable.

Financing

Another element in the buying and selling of investment property is leverage, using other people's money to increase the return on your own cash. You will find that most income property has a mortgage attached. Mortgages are sometimes assumable and sometimes not. In some cases, you might want to assume the debt, and sometimes you will need to find new financing. Terms built into the financing may preclude assumption, or require that you qualify for the assumption as if you were taking a new loan. Older financing that has 30-year terms, is often assumable, and if there are no restrictions to secondary financing, might be advisable to assume.

When purchasing an investment, use financing to your benefit, arranging for as much as you think you will need. If you place all your cash in the deal, you will have no reserve for emergencies and recapitalization. Only you can determine the right mix, and it will be predicated on your game plan.

Existing Loans

What do you need to avoid when considering assumption of an existing loan? The most important item is the amount of the loan as a percentage of your purchase price. If the loan amount is low, and the terms preclude *secondary financing*, you might find yourself in a cash bind at some later date. Older loans commonly did not have this clause.

A due-on-sale clause is common in new loans and shows up frequently in some of the older loans. This will be a problem for your seller, and maybe for you, too. The due-on-sale clause is the lender's tool to have a voice in who assumes the loan. The lender does not really want to have the loan paid off, because he or she will have to immediately find a new loan, and that costs money. The real goal is to have a look at the buyer, and perhaps extract a one-point fee from the transaction for its paperwork. The newer loans have, most probably, been bundled with other loans and sold on the secondary market, and will therefore, not be assumable. The seller will have to pay off these loans at the time of sale, often having to pay an early-payment penalty to meet the original lender's *yield maintenance* conditions.

Buzzwords

Secondary financing is a second loan, junior in priority to the primary mortgage. A **yield maintenance** clause provides that, in essence, the lender gets the interest owed to maturity even if the loan is retired early.

This is the clause that enables the bundling and resale of loans on the secondary market. The buyers are assured of their yield even if the loans are retired before maturity.

New Money

If you need financing (most buyers do), I recommend that you seek new financing. The reason is simple: You can shop for money on your own terms, setting it up to coincide with your game plan. If, for instance, you plan to own the property for 10 years and then move on to bigger things, you can set the term of the loan so that you will not have any penalties to pay when the loan is retired. Most yield maintenance clauses in new 10-year loans are written so that you cannot prepay the loan for at least the first five to nine years. In essence, you are locked in for that period. Thereafter, they will stipulate a decreasing penalty in years six, seven, and eight, finally allowing you to prepay without penalty in the last two years. This should dovetail nicely with your game plan.

Capitalization (Cap) Rates

How do people determine what to pay for a piece of real estate? For many years the calculation of cap rates has been the purview only of the lender, and most people have gone along with it. You may also be forced to do so because of the market. I believe, however, that you should know how to calculate a cap rate and you should do so, at least, to determine the spread between the asking price and what you think the property is worth. It is also helpful when you are ready to sell the property. A proper cap rate calculation can help you justify your asking price.

How to Calculate

Buildings acquire value by capitalizing the income stream, the NIBDS. No one disputes this method, but at the same time, few people understand what a cap rate is and how it operates. Traditionally, a cap rate is an expression of risk. How is it determined, and who says it is right or reasonable? In financial circles, a cap rate of 10 percent is considered average or optimum. A cap rate over 10 percent denotes a higher-than-normal risk, while a cap rate under 10 percent indicates lower-than-normal risk.

Theoretically, with a cap rate of 10 percent, an income stream of $100,000 per year is worth $1,000,000. It is calculated as follows:

$100,000 divided by 10 percent (0.1) = $1,000,000

In popular theory, this is considered a reasonable return on capital with a "normal" amount of risk built into the deal.

Each individual or entity should determine the relative risk of any deal and its relationship to her or his capital for each deal contemplated. How should this be done? Most people say that if it looks risky, ascribe an 11 percent to 13 percent cap rate to the deal. If it is really off the wall, then go higher. I have never encountered a real estate deal with a 20 percent cap rate, but it might be possible.

There are several methods used to come up with a cap rate, and I have found the following to be a reliable estimate of risk:

C = Y – I followed by R = Y – (MC)

- ◆ C is a constant or a coefficient
- ◆ Y is the desired yield to equity (cash invested)
- ◆ M is the percentage of loan to value
- ◆ I is the interest rate of the financing
- ◆ R is the resulting cap rate

Let's see how it works. Assume the following:

- ◆ You want to buy a building.
- ◆ There will be a 75 percent new loan in place at closing.
- ◆ The new loan has an interest rate of 8.5 percent.
- ◆ You are willing to buy the building *only* if you can yield 13 percent on your capital (equity).

What, then, is the cap rate?

C = Y – I or C = 13 – 8.5

Therefore, C = 4.5

Then,

R = Y – (MC) or R = 13 – (.75 4.5)

Therefore, R = 13 – 3.38 or 9.62 percent (cap rate)

The value of the investment to you will be determined by taking the NIBDS and capitalizing it (dividing it by) at the rate determined by you to produce the desired yield (the cap rate). This has been calculated above to be 9.62 percent.

This formula basically ignores amortization, and therefore, is somewhat an approximation. Over the past 30 years, I have not found a formula that works any better, but if you have one, please e-mail it to me for evaluation. (For my e-mail, check the front matter of the book.) No matter how you calculate the risk of buying any specific property, you are always the sole factor in deciding what it is worth to you. One of my readers, Peter Anastasiadis of Philadelphia, who can be reached at peterana@ix. netcom.com, submitted the following formula to me for evaluation. It seems to have equal if not better merit than my own. Try both and make up your own mind:

> LTV (loan to value) Ratio = .75
>
> % Equity (e) down (cash invested) = .25
>
> Desired rate of return on equity (ROE) = .25
>
> Annual mortgage constant (MC) 7% 30 years = 7.98

The formula works as follows:

> LTV x MC = C1.75 x .0798 = 5.99
>
> E x ROE = C2 .25 x .15 = 3.75
>
> Cap rate = C1 + C2 = 9.74%

Set the Price

Armed with this insight, you are now ready to determine both the price you will be willing to pay for an investment property, and the sale price of the property when you are ready to sell. If you create a sales package correctly, itemizing things about the property that set it apart from the herd, you may get a superior price for the property when you sell. Use it as a way to justify the price.

The Least You Need to Know

- ◆ Scrutinize the building. Determine its condition and its potential. Document and cost out all deferred maintenance and potential upgrades.
- ◆ Dissecting the leases will provide you with specific objectives to enhance the future cash flow.
- ◆ Make a plan based on the examination of the potential investment that will allow you to see how to achieve your long-term objectives.
- ◆ Decide what the building and its attached income steam is worth to you, and craft your offer accordingly.

Chapter 10

Dissecting the Deal

In This Chapter

- ◆ What are the tenants worth?
- ◆ Check the paperwork, that's where the value is
- ◆ Establish a management framework
- ◆ Inspect and evaluate the building
- ◆ Review your cash requirements
- ◆ Trust your instincts

When you invest in a piece of real property, you must determine for yourself that your contemplated purchase is a good deal. There are two factors in this determination: one external, the comparison with similar properties and their sale prices; and one internal, the evaluation of the property itself.

The external comparison is one that you will have made before you make an offer to purchase, and the second will be performed during your *due diligence* period, also known as the *free look* period. In this chapter you learn how to set up your deal from the beginning, creating tools that will allow you to evaluate the deal's feasibility and manage it once you have completed the acquisition.

Evaluating the Purchase

Comparable prices can be obtained from brokers, verified by the public record, and from appraisers. Most buyers who are going to get new financing will need an appraisal anyway, so the money is not wasted. I would, however, not order the appraisal until I had determined for myself what the comparable selling prices are and have an acceptance of my offer in hand. Appraisals are expensive.

Before you have a formal acceptance of the purchase offer, you can often get an estimate of value, informally, from an appraiser in expectation of the appraisal contract. This is sometimes referred to as a *bench appraisal.* This expression of value is not binding and cannot be used to establish value with a prospective lender. The appraiser is extending his or her informal opinion as a courtesy as part of the appraiser/client relationship. Once you've gone through this process, you will, at least, have a pretty good idea how the building you are considering relates to its competitors. Ideally, the building should be for sale at a lesser price than its competitors. If you can determine that, physically, the building can compete, then by working the leases (see Chapter 9) you should be able to bring it up to par.

Buzzwords

Due diligence is the process of discovery of all the pertinent facts about a piece of real property. The **free look** is the time period in a real property contract during which the buyer's deposit is fully refundable. The **bench appraisal** is an estimate of value informally given by an appraiser.

Look at the Tenants

Part of the internal examination is to carefully evaluate your prospective tenants. What should you look for? The answer to this question is ultimately a subjective one, as everyone has different criteria for evaluation of other businesses. There are, however, several common threads that run through any analysis process. Most people will want to know about the business itself. What is it? Is it legal? How long has it been in business? Another obvious yardstick is its financial statement.

Some other items I tend to evaluate are the size of the company and its expansion capabilities. This analysis gives me some idea of its potential for providing tenancy for other investment opportunities in the area. Small tenants can grow into larger ones, and they are good prospects for any new investment you might undertake. If the tenants are large, are they too large? Do they represent too much of my bottom line? If so, how do I get them out of the building, and in doing so, can I stand the expense of re-leasing and recapitalization? You should develop criteria such as these for yourself over time until they become second nature to you when evaluating or developing property.

The Financial Statements

How do you get a look at a tenant's financial statement? The seller should have, in the tenant's file, a copy of the original financial statement furnished during the initial leasing process. While this is most likely out of date, it will give you a good idea where the tenant was at the time of the original lease. Other sources are the credit agencies and Dun and Bradstreet. You can always request an updated statement, as some leases have provisions for that purpose built into the boilerplate. It is quite common in retail leases, but less so in office and industrial leases.

My criteria for leasing to a locally owned business whose financial condition is not a matter of public record, is to evaluate its ready cash against its short-term obligations. For me to allow it tenancy in my building, it must be able to meet its short-term obligations and pay the rent for a full year without any further income. I apply these criteria uniformly to new businesses and those with little established credit history. If it is a business that is established, but privately held, then I also look at its operating income history for the five preceding years.

The Business

Another subjective evaluation is applied to the business itself. Again, I have several criteria. Is the business good for your building's image? Will it hamper further leasing efforts? Does the business use an inordinate amount of parking? Government tenants are notorious for this as their employee density is most often twice that of private businesses. A lack of parking will inhibit future tenants from entering the building. Is the tenant a good neighbor, or is he or she messy or loud? This might cost you some existing tenants as they move away from the offender.

Another important criterion is the building's overall character, established by the tenant mix. Is the building a financial building, a real estate building, or a medical building? The synergy between tenants can establish a building's character and help to establish a long-term positive image. Likewise, imprudent leasing can create an image of a second-rate building. Tenants to avoid like the plague are telephone solicitation companies, judo schools, beauty schools, and the like. They will not add to a building's image. In retail buildings, too many restaurants signal a shopping center in the final stages of economic or locational obsolescence.

Tenants who are in similar fields, or who represent various segments of a common industry, will create a synergy for a building that will establish it as a destination for the businesses' customers. If the tenant mix has been carefully crafted, it will be a big plus when re-leasing. You will find this condition instrumental in maintaining a bright economic future for the building. If the tenant mix has been put together haphazardly, without regard to impact, it can ruin the building for future prospects. Since it is your investment, the tenant mix is strictly subject to your own judgment.

Look at the Lease Documents

One of the basic tools for successful management is created by the proper analysis of the leases. You must know the basics and have the answers at your fingertips. You need to know, at a minimum, the following criteria:

- The tenant's name, phone, fax, and e-mail addresses
- The size of the tenant's demised premises
- The lease execution and expiration date
- The number and condition of renewal options, if any
- The rent per square foot and the total rent
- The rent escalation dates
- Any nonstandard concessions granted to the tenant

When assembled, it will look something like the following table.

Tenant Spreadsheet

Square Footage	Tenant Name	Suite No.	Security Deposit	Original Rent	Rent Bump	% Increase	Commence. Date	Expiration Date	Renewal Options
35000	Office Building								
2560	Tenant # 1	100	$2,987	$12.00	07/01/98	5.00%	08/01/97	02/28/02	1x5
6600	Tenant # 2	300	$7,700	$12.00	08/01/98	5.00%	08/01/97	07/31/02	1x5
5120	Tenant # 3	120	$5,973	$12.00	07/01/98	5.00%	08/01/97	07/31/02	1x5
4000	Tenant # 4	200	$4,667	$12.00	07/01/98	5.00%	08/01/97	03/31/00	1x5
1280	Tenant # 5	220	$1,493	$14.00	08/01/98	5.00%	08/01/97	05/31/00	None
4000	Tenant# 6	400	$4,667	$13.00	08/08/98	5.00%	08/01/97	07/31/02	1x5
1280	Tenant # 7	240	$1,493	$14.00	10/01/98	5.00%	10/01/97	09/30/00	None
2560	Tenant # 8	450	$2,987	$14.00	12/01/98	4.00%	12/01/97	11/30/02	1x5
1280	Tenant # 9	250	$1,493	$14.00	09/01/98	3.00%	09/01/97	08/31/00	1x5
1280	Tenant # 10	230	$1,493	$14.00	12/15/98	5.00%	01/01/98	12/31/00	1x2
5040	Tenant # 11	420	$5,880	$14.00	05/01/99	5.00%	04/01/98	03/31/01	1x5
50	Covered Parking Spaces	1-50	$0	$1,250.00					
35000	Total Security deposits		$40,833						

Lease analysis, all leases NNN Total GLA, 35,000 SF.

Requirements

Every landlord has a favorite lease, and, good or bad, the landlord seems to be able to make it work. In general, the lease shown in Appendix B as a sample commercial lease has all of the tools that I deem essential to my style of management. You will note that the lease is not in a standard lease format. In 1995, I abandoned my traditional 30-page lease set up on legal-size paper and re-created the lease in plain English, wherever possible, in a format that has proven to be easy to use and tenant-friendly. In it are three sections, the first two of which are shown in the Appendix. I have eliminated the "Exhibit" section for brevity's sake. The fact is that each project will have a custom set of exhibits.

The resulting lease has proven to be a hit with small tenants, because it is written in plain English. They seldom feel the need to spend a lot of money on attorneys, and negotiations have become fairly straightforward.

Lease Breakdown

The first section I have labeled the "Main Body" of the lease. It is in this section that all of the business points of the lease are assembled, and all, or at least most of this section, is negotiable. This gives the tenant all of the business deal in one section. The major areas are: The Summary, Premises, Term, Possession, Rent and Rent Adjustment, Additional Rent, Assignment and Subletting, Insurance, Services and Utilities, Holding Over, Default, Remedies Upon Default, Covenants to Operate (in retail leases only), ADA (Americans with Disabilities Act), Brokers, Disclaimers, and Signature Blocks.

The second part I call the "General Provisions," and it is in this part that all the necessary boilerplate resides. Most tenants do not realize that the lenders involved with the building mandate the bulk of the boilerplate. The lender's position is that, in the event of something happening to the landlord, the lender must assume that role. Therefore, the lender wants the landlord's position to be well covered. When tenants want to negotiate with this section, I refer them to the lender's attorney, and I save a lot of money on legal bills.

I have seldom seen a lender make a substantive concession in the boilerplate language. They have a take-it-or-leave-it attitude. The only concession in the section occurs when the landlord grants an exclusive use to a tenant. These clauses contain: Use, Compliance with Laws, Alterations, Additions, Surrender, Repairs, Liens, Hold Harmless, Subrogation, Property Taxes, Rules and Regulations, Hazardous Substances, Entry by Landlord, Reconstruction, Eminent Domain, Estoppel Certificate, General Provisions, Building Planning and Employee Parking, Discrimination, Authorities of Parties, and the Signature Block.

Finally, the "Exhibits" will contain, for the most part, the following documents:

◆ The property description with a legal description, a site plan, a floor plan, and, to be attached later, a copy of the tenant's improvement plans.

◆ There will be an exhibit entitled "Construction," delineating the landlord's work and the tenant's work, who will pay for what, and when the money will be paid. Customarily, all costs of construction to be done by landlord and paid for by the tenant are paid up front.

◆ Usually, there will be an "Acknowledgment of Commencement" document to be executed by both landlord and tenant stating that the tenant has taken occupancy on a specific date and establishing the commencement of the rent.

◆ There will be an "Estoppel Agreement," executed by landlord and tenant for the benefit of the lender or another party, stating that the lease exists, and is in force, and that neither party is in default.

◆ There should be a copy of the rules and regulations attached.

◆ There may be a "Special Provisions" exhibit attached, spelling out any special agreements between landlord and tenant, such as options, rent escalation, and so on.

◆ If there are CC&Rs (Covenants, Conditions, and Restrictions) recorded on the property, there will be an exhibit showing the recorded document. Most often, in retail development, there is a document referred to as the REA (Reciprocal Easement and Restrictions) that spells out the uses and restrictions of the common areas, such as parking and signs and spelling out any exclusives granted to tenants by the landlord.

The leases and the clauses included in the leases provide the basis for your authority to manage the building. The leases will form the legal framework for their enforcement and the preservation and enhancement of your investment.

Management Tools

The most important area in any lease or management tool lies in the document enabling a landlord to collect the rent. This is obviously spelled out in the lease, the essential elements of which can be, and usually are, scattered throughout the lease in the Main Body and in the General Provisions. They spell out when and how the landlord is entitled to collect. Attorneys like to scatter them so that they are not so blatant. They are, for the most part, completely in the landlord's favor, and the lenders require it to be so. If they were all in one place, they would seem onerous to anyone. As it is, they are bad enough.

Collecting Rent

To reliably collect the rent on time, the landlord must have in the lease the following elements:

- A clear statement of the rental amount and how it is calculated

- An unequivocal due date, late date, and default date

- A specific notice provision with a short fuse

- A clear definition of default by the tenant

- A detailed list of the landlord's remedies upon late payment, nonpayment, or default, including, but not limited to: late charges, interest, acceleration of the lease, repossession and eviction, and additional damages, including the cost of re-leasing and refurbishing

If these provisions are written in plain English without the benefit of legalese, the tenant will generally pay on time, every time.

Redress of Grievances

This doesn't mean to buy your tenant a new wardrobe; *redress* is a legal term meaning to compensate for or to resolve problems. Even with the proper tools in place there can still be problems. In almost every case, the landlord needs to work with the tenant, even in a bankruptcy situation. The real nightmare occurs when you have to go to court. If the tenant is bankrupt, you will almost never collect. It is better to do what you have to do to get the tenant to vacate expeditiously.

The one thing you never want to allow in the lease is *right of offset.* This clause gives the tenant the right to pay for something and deduct it from the rent. The tenant may be proven wrong at a later date, but in the meantime, he or she has legally withheld your rent. Agree to go to binding arbitration, mediation, or court, but never agree to the right of offset in a lease.

Buzzwords

Right of offset is the ability to offset expenses against monies owed. **Redress** is a legal term meaning to compensate for or resolve problems.

Evaluate the Building

Having thoroughly worked over the leases, you now get to examine the other part of your proposed purchase—the building. Use the following questions:

◆ How is it built?

◆ What is the floor plate, and how does it relate to the tenants?

◆ What are the mechanical systems, and are they adequate for the reconfiguration of tenant spaces?

◆ What is the condition of the roof and the parking lot?

◆ What is the level of deferred maintenance?

Physical Plant

Other than the structure and the exterior, the main areas of concern are the HVAC (heating, ventilation, and air-conditioning), the roof, and the parking lot. These items are not designed to last 30 years. They will wear out, and your lease might have a provision for excluding capital costs. That is why I recommend a budget item in your common area expense called "reserves for replacements," and the amount is set, annually, at one-10th the cost of replacing these items.

Better Believe It!

You will get a lot of flack from the tenants on a reserves for replacement clause. Do your best to establish the reserve, because you will surely need it.

You need a good inspection, as mentioned before, using your architect or space planner and your contractor to create a realistic budget. You want these expenses to appear above the line. This means in the expense breakdown, before the NIBDS (net income before debt service).

Unfinished Space and Budgets

If you are purchasing a new building from the original developer, or any building with vacancy, you are buying an income stream based upon occupancy of the entire building. If there are vacant spaces, you must insist that the seller deduct the cost of tenant improvements for the vacant space from the price. If the seller refuses, then you can legitimately say that the rent for that space cannot be included in the NIBDS for capital-ization purposes. This can be a significant amount of money, and if you cannot get this concession from the seller, you will have to pony it up yourself when the space is leased.

Economic Obsolescence

Some buildings can appear underpriced, and you need to examine them carefully. Hope-fully, the underpricing is due to poor leasing, which astute management can rectify, but it may also be due to the onset of economic obsolescence. Sure indications of this are ...

◆ Low ceilings in the corridors and tenant space.

◆ Small and unattractive lobbies.

◆ Inadequate or inaccessible parking.

◆ Inadequate HVAC.

◆ Structural problems (foundation settlement).

◆ Inadequate restrooms and elevators.

The easy one to fix is a cosmetic problem, such as short entry doors, bad decor, poor window coverings, old carpet, and dirty paint. You will also score big points with the tenants when you upgrade the building. If the lower rent is due to this, you might have acquired a bargain because the seller did not budget for continued modernization. Capitalize on his or her mistake, and do not make the same mistake.

Capital Requirements and Intuition

Whether buying or building, you will need enough money to ensure the success of the venture. The building cost is only part of the equation. When you are building, you should have a sufficient capital base to pay for the building up through the lease and to establish a working fund for re-leasing and refurbishing. When you are buying an existing building you must not only pay for the building, but you must also set up the re-leasing and refurbishing fund, as well as eliminate the deferred maintenance imme-diately after closing. This will sit well with the tenants and get you off to a good start. Often, the transition time will become the most important circumstance to influence the tenants when it comes to renewal time. If the last landlord was popular, you had better follow in his or her footsteps.

Your sources of funds can be as varied as the deal. They can be, but are not limited to, the following:

♦ Your cash

♦ Partners' money

♦ Existing or new mortgages

♦ Secondary financing

♦ Hard money loans (bad choice!)

♦ Resale of part of a large project (spin-off)

Whatever the combination, make sure you have what it takes, then add a fudge factor for bad luck.

Gut Instinct

The final part of the evaluation of any deal boils down to your gut instinct. How are the vibes? Are you trying too hard to make the deal? Does it feel uncomfortable? Why? If you have any nagging feelings of doubt, you had better look into them before proceeding with your purchase.

The Least You Need to Know

♦ Your tenants are money in the bank. Get to know them.

♦ You must understand and improve on the documents you inherit from the purchase.

♦ Management tools will make your life easier or harder. Create them carefully, and make sure they are securely grounded in your rights under the leases.

♦ Make a capital plan and use it to good advantage. Do not waste money on non-income-producing items.

♦ Trust your gut reaction. It has taken you this far.

Chapter 11

The Purchase Contract

In This Chapter

- ◆ Who writes the purchase agreement?
- ◆ Hedge your bets—use contingencies
- ◆ Enable your objectives—build in your schedule
- ◆ How to use the free-look period to your advantage
- ◆ Get a jump on the purchase

Contracts and other legal documents are the primary tools in the real estate–investment business. The leases establish value, and the initial purchase agreement sets the schedule for the investment. *The purchase contract is the single most important risk-limiting document in any real estate contract.*

The purchase contract sets the stage for the purchase, setting out the details of the transaction. What is the contract about? Money! It states how much is to be paid and when it is to be paid. Most important, it also states under what circumstances the price can be reduced, or the agreement canceled without the loss of your deposit. There is a lot of work ahead in becoming comfortable with consummating the purchase. You have to do considerable research and examine both the building and the documents, and each and every step along the way may provide a valid reason to cancel the escrow. In this chapter we explore the necessary documentation for an informed purchase. The purchase agreement itself will allow you to properly set up the project for a profitable acquisition.

Who Should Draft It?

By now you should be answering this type of question in your sleep. You should draft it, in plain English, and have your attorney tweak it so that it clearly states and enables your intentions, regarding the timing and contingencies in the transaction. Why should you write it? So that you know every clause and nuance in the agreement without having to look at the contract. After you've done a few of these, you will have the deal structure in your head, and you will be able to administer the agreement without constant reference to the document. When you have finished drafting, you should have an agreement that closely parallels the timeline outlined in your plan. A timeline can be as simple as a list of key dates, reinforced with a come-up file (a calendar of upcoming crucial events such as lease expirations) that you refer to daily. That way, there will be no missed dates during and after the due diligence period.

Inputs

What should be in the contract, and whom do you look to for these items? People to discuss the timeline with include, but are not limited to, your broker, your attorney, your property manager, your contractor and architect, and your lender. They will be happy to provide you with guidance relating to what they think needs to be examined, as well as how long it will take them or another consultant to accomplish the task. Most of these people will be examining the purchase themselves as part of your overall management strategy. You might find the need to consult someone like an independent mortgage banker or an investment broker about the market as well.

Length and Tone

Address the issues and the timeline in a simple bulleted list, indicating who is to do what and how long it should take. At the same time, there will be items to be accomplished by the seller, and this should be incorporated into the timeline. Sequencing is important. Most often, you as the buyer cannot proceed with your examination until the seller or the lender has furnished you with the items to be examined. Leave plenty of time to produce the data or documents, and leave ample time for review.

The Contingencies

The list of contingencies is relatively the same for the purchase of all properties, from land to income property. The major differences lie in the number of documents. Leased investments will have the added list of loan documents and leases. The basic list will be as follows:

- The title report
- All documents referenced in the title report
- The ALTA survey
- A topographic map for land, an as-built survey for income property (showing the location of all easements and utility lines), as well as the precise location of the buildings in relation to the required setbacks and other restrictions
- Any pertinent contracts
- The loan documents
- The leases
- Estoppel certificates
- Any new loan documents

Contingencies are for your protection. They allow you to back off before your money is irrevocably committed.

Why Have Any Escape Clauses?

Two reasons. First, to buy you time to get comfortable with the deal, and second, to finalize everything necessary to close the escrow. The research and examination is done for obvious reasons. Buying something on someone else's say-so is a risky proposition. The nature of any real estate deal is such that the transaction can be complicated and fraught with problems. The mere fact that a property exists does not make it necessarily a good deal.

Flaws in the leases or a problem loan could signal potential disaster down the line. If, for instance, you were to assume the existing financing, and the term of the financing is due to expire within 12 months, you had better be certain that a new loan can be had within that period of time. Often, new loans for existing property can take up to six months, and sometimes they are not available at all. Sometimes a lender will require the property to be modernized as part of the transaction, so you had better have the renovation money in your budget.

What the Outs Should Be

Let's take a look at the list of contingencies and see what each one is designed to tell you.

- The title report will let you know whether there are any liens or restrictions on the property that can affect current or future plans for the property.

- All the documents referenced in the title report will provide you with specifics about the reason for recording them in the first place. There can be restrictive covenants, design guidelines, or occupancy requirements that are not apparent from the leases or the building itself.

- The *ALTA survey* will show the property boundaries and all existing improvements, as well as all easements and restrictions of record.

- A topographic map ("Topo") for land will show the contours and enable an architect and civil engineer to determine the feasibility of building on the land within the confines of the local planning ordinances. An "as-built survey" for an existing building will show the building's precise location in relation to the streets and setback requirements, as well as the location of all easements and utilities.

- Any pertinent contracts will let you know who is involved with the property, such as managers, contractors, and utility companies. Some of these you will want to inherit, and some you will want the seller to terminate at or prior to the closing. You will also want the seller to indemnify you from any obligations due to these agreements and their cancellation. This indemnity must survive the closing.

Buzzwords

The **ALTA survey** is a survey that includes the results of a physical inspection of the property.

- Examination of the loan documents will help you determine whether to assume or replace the current financing. It will also give you a good indication of the project's original cost, as most loans are for 75 percent of the construction cost or purchase price.

- The leases have been covered in Chapter 10.

- ◆ The Estoppel certificates will reveal any problems between the seller and the tenants or the lender.

- ◆ Any new loan documents will need to be scrutinized by you and your attorney to determine whether they will enable you to do what you need to do when managing your investment.

How to Get What You Need

The only way to meet your requirements in the purchase agreement is to negotiate with the seller point by point. The seller will have a similar agenda, and your job is to get his agreement with your program, while honoring his needs in the process. This is a tall order, but in any marketable, fair, and equitable contract, there should be enough common ground for both buyer and seller. The seller did not get to be an owner without sharing most of your concerns, and you will have to put yourself in the seller's shoes someday when you sell. This is why most transactions work out. They must be inherently fair to be executed at all. In as much as you are a new buyer, you might find that you will lose your first deal due to an excess of caution.

Your Role

The easiest role to play as the buyer is the questioner. Ask as many questions as you can think of. There are no stupid questions, only stupid people who forgot to ask a vital question. The more you ask, the more you learn. If you are a good listener, people will talk to you. You will be surprised how a seller can fill the silence with information.

Remember that when you are a seller and you let your broker do the talking. As a buyer, you must attempt to question anyone who knows anything about the building, especially the owner, the manager, the lender, and the tenants. Often, you will learn more through casual conversation than you can glean from the documents. For example, you may discover

Better Believe It!

Do not be discouraged. Learn from rejection; slowly get the feel for what you can obtain. Be patient. You will own this investment for a considerable length of time. Do not rush into it!

Buzzwords

Consideration is money or actions, taken at a cost, as compensation to the seller for your acquisition of the beneficial interest in the real property.

existing oral agreements. Even though they are unenforceable, you would be surprised how many oral agreements there are in real estate. To be enforceable, any contract involving real property must pass four tests:

◆ It must be in writing.

◆ It must be executed by competent parties.

◆ It must be of lawful intent.

◆ *Consideration* must have passed between the parties.

In general, you can choose to ignore any oral agreements made by the seller to any tenant. It is, however, imperative that the purchase agreement states that the seller indemnifies you against any matters not of record, or presented to you for your approval in writing prior to closing the escrow. Remember, the seller has to do this to make a sale, and if he or she is not willing to do so, walk away.

The Seller's Role

The seller's role in the transaction is to satisfy you that all is as represented. The seller must disclose any facts pertinent to the transaction. Do any sellers do this? Not many. There are always things that are forgotten, conveniently or not, and things that are deliberately left unsaid. If you are clever, you will ask your questions in writing and demand written answers. The seller's written answers, referenced in the purchase agreement, become representations that survive escrow closing.

The Broker

In reality, there will be two brokers in the transaction: the listing broker and the selling broker. In residential sales, this is almost always the case. The commercial end of the business does not yet have the multiple listing services, so there are many transactions listed and sold by the same broker.

When you are looking to buy, get your own broker, and have him represent your interests exclusively. Brokers are the front-line troops in the real estate business, and their knowledge and resourcefulness are assets that you need on your side. You should attempt to find a broker who specializes in your preferred investment type. It is also important that the broker is a member of a company that has a leasing agent as well. From time to time, you will need a leasing agent to keep your building full. It is better to keep it all under one roof, if possible.

The Contingency Period

The contingency period is your free-look period. This time starts when the purchase agreement is fully executed, and escrow is opened. During this time you get to examine the specifics of the investment. You should have, prior to making the purchase offer, made sure of the market and the particular investment type. Once you have the building in escrow, the meter starts running.

The most typical scenario is that the seller has a fixed amount of time to deliver documents for your inspection and review, and you then have a specific amount of time to accept or reject these documents. If you have an objection to anything presented, then the seller will have a specific deadline to cure the problem. Once the time has expired, you will have to *go hard* on your deposit, and prepare to close or walk away from the transaction.

Buzzwords

Going hard on the deposit means that it becomes nonrefundable at a certain point, and that, should the buyer not consummate the transaction, the seller is legally entitled to keep the deposit.

The contingency period is designed to give you the opportunity to examine the specifics. Should you discover anything that is not as represented, or find something that will prevent you from pursuing your game plan, you may decline to approve the deal, retrieve your deposit, and walk away.

How Long?

The contingency period varies from about 60 days to 6 months. The period will depend on the types of contingencies encountered. Take, for example, the purchase of a multi-tenant office building with a provision for new financing. I would estimate that the contingency period would be at least 90 days, and perhaps as long as 6 months. Once this period has passed, the closing could be another 30 days or more.

The sequence of events should go something like this. After the escrow is opened, the seller will have a specific amount of time, usually 30 days, to produce the following:

- The preliminary extended coverage title report

- An ALTA survey or an as-built survey certified by the title company

- Copies of the leases

- Copies of any contracts, such as property management, contracting, subcontracts, utility agreements, and so on

- Loan documents

The seller typically has to produce executed Estoppel Certificates within 60 days of the opening of escrow, but not less that 30 days prior to closing.

The buyer then has 30 to 60 days to evaluate and question the seller about the documents. If there are any serious objections, the seller has 30 days to cure the problem. The whole process, if it goes smoothly, should take at least 120 days.

Who Pays for What?

This is not an inexpensive proposition, so who pays for what? Cost follows function. The seller pays for the documents that verify his or her position, such as copies of documents, title report, and surveys. The buyer pays for his or her independent examination of these items. Accountants and attorneys and other experts paid to review the data are the buyer's expense.

When it comes time to close, the seller pays for the title policy, any costs incurred to provide clear title (paying off any liens, and so on), and one-half the cost of the escrow closing. The buyer then pays for one-half the cost of closing, any costs involved in assuming or obtaining the financing, and the full purchase price of the property, less the original deposit already paid.

The Least You Need to Know

- Never lose sight of the fact that the purchase agreement is the most important risk-limiting document in the process.

- Contingencies are your best friend at the beginning of the purchase transaction; use them well.

- Start the transaction with a thorough understanding of the market and the property values within it.

- Be candid with the seller. Let him or her know your parameters. This avoids wasting your time.

- The purchasing process involves the eliminating of as many risks as possible before committing your funds to the purchase. Use the free-look time to your best advantage.

The Closing—Pull the Trigger on Your Terms

In This Chapter

- ◆ Understand the paperwork
- ◆ What the seller provides
- ◆ Cash offsets at closing
- ◆ Paying the price

Before you start thinking that the closing is a simple transaction, let's look at it in detail. You should have a pretty good idea of what must transpire, but we need to cover the details so that you're ready for the experience.

You might think that you're buying a building, but in reality, you're buying a pile of paper about 2 feet high. The documents establish the value, and the building becomes secondary to the transaction. It only keeps the rain off your most important assets, your tenants. In this chapter we'll look at actually closing the deal. You need to be sure that all the homework is done to your satisfaction, and that all your contingencies are met before you close.

The Documents

If we break down the closing documents into three categories—your documents, the seller's documents, and third-party documents—you can see the rationale behind the exchange of money for real property.

Your Pile of Documents

Your pile is relatively small. It consists of the initial purchase agreement, a possible loan application or a loan assumption application, and any approvals you must grant in writing. Finally, you must sign the closing document, and in some states you must sign the deed, accepting its conveyance.

The Seller's Pile of Documents

The seller's documents are more involved, and they are, at the least, but not necessarily limited to, the following, shown in order of appearance:

Buzzwords

The **general warranty deed** is evidence of property ownership. The current owner, who is the "owner of record" in the county records, formally "deeds" the property to the buyer. When the deed is recorded, the buyer is then the owner of record.

- The leases
- The original loan documents
- Warranties and representations
- A complete accounting
- Copies of any contracts in force
- Any maintenance agreements
- Estoppel agreements
- The *general warranty deed*
- For the closing, a formal assignment of the leases and other contracts to remain in force

Third-Party Documents

The most common third-party documents originate from the title company, the lender, and the tenants. They are …

- The preliminary title commitment and the title insurance policy after closing.

- The loan documents, originated by the lender.

- Acknowledgment of assignment of leases from the tenants (not a common document, but one I'd recommend). It puts the tenant on record that there is a new landlord, and reaffirms the tenant's rental obligations to the new owner.

Seller's Chores

All of this documentation takes time and costs money, and the biggest problem of all is making sure that the submittals are complete. There is so much paper involved in the development and ownership process, that the parties have to make sure that it is all accounted for. Most leases have subsequent agreements that have to be approved, not the least of which is the parties' acceptance of the plans and specifications and the completed construction. These executed acknowledgments are, by reference, made a part of the lease along with the plans and specs. There may also be other agreements, made informally, through the exchange of letters that need to be disclosed to the buyer.

Estoppel Certificates

Every landlord's nightmare is the Estoppel certificate. It is a relatively simple document that becomes a formidable chore when it is required. Lenders and buyers will not consummate any transaction without them. The following is a typical example. In simple terms the Estoppel certificate states the following for the benefit of the buyer/lender:

- The lease is in force.

- The rent and terms are as follows: _____.

- The landlord is not in default.

- The lease expires on _____(date).

TENANT OFFSET AND ESTOPPEL CERTIFICATE

To:

RE: Lease dated _____, 20_____, by and between (Insert Landlord's Name) as "Landlord" and: _____ as Tenant, on Premises located in (Insert Premises Address)

Gentlemen:

The undersigned tenant (the "Tenant") certifies and represents unto the addressee hereof (hereinafter referred to as the "Addressee") its attorneys and representatives, with respect to the above-described lease, a true and correct copy of which is attached as Exhibit A hereto (the "Lease"), as follows:

1. All space and improvements covered by the Lease have been completed and furnished to the satisfaction of Tenant, all conditions required under the Lease have been met, and Tenant has accepted and taken possession of and presently occupies the Premises covered by the Lease.

2. The Lease is for the total term of _____ (_____) years, ___ (_____) months commencing ___, 20_____, has not been modified, altered or amended in any respect and contains the entire agreement between Landlord and Tenant, except as _____ (list amendments and modifications other than those, if any, attached to and forming a part of the attached Lease as well as any verbal agreements, or write "None").

3. As of the date hereof, the Minimum Rent under the Lease, payable in equal monthly installments during the term, is $_____, subject to the CPI Adjustment escalation and Percentage Rent, in accordance with the terms and provisions of the Lease.

4. No rent has been paid by Tenant in advance under the Lease except for $_____, which amount represents rent for the period _____, 20_____ and ending ___, 20_____ and Tenant has no charge or claim of offset under said Lease or otherwise, against rents or other amounts due or to become due thereunder. No "discounts," "free rent," or "discounted rent" have been agreed to or are in effect except for _____.

5. A Security Deposit of $_____ has been made and is currently being held by Landlord.

6. Tenant has no claim against Landlord for any deposit or prepaid rent except as provided in Paragraphs 4 and 5 above.

7. The Landlord has satisfied all commitments, arrangements or understandings made to induce Tenant to enter into the Lease, and Landlord is not in any respect in default in the performance of the terms and provisions of the Lease, nor is there now any fact or condition which, with notice or lapse of time or both, would become such a default.

8. Tenant is not in any respect in default under the terms and provisions of the Lease (nor is there now any fact or condition which, with notice, or lapse of time or both, would become such a default) and has not assigned, transferred or hypothecated its interest under the Lease, except as follows:

9. Except as expressly provided in the Lease or in any amendment or supplement to the Lease, Tenant:

   (i) does not have any right to renew or extend the term of the Lease,

   (ii) does not have any option or preferential right to purchase all or any part of the Premises or all or any part of the building or premises of which the Premises are a part, and

   (iii) does not have any right, title, or interest with respect to the Premises other than as Tenant under the Lease.

   There are no understandings, contracts, agreements, subleases, assignments, or commitments of any kind whatsoever with respect to the Lease of the Premises covered thereby except as expressly provided in the Lease or in any amendment or supplement to the Lease set forth in Paragraph 2 above, copies of which are attached hereto.

10. The Lease is in full force and effect and Tenant has no defenses, setoffs, or counterclaims against Landlord arising out of the Lease or in any way relating thereto or arising out of any other transaction between Tenant and Landlord.

11. The Tenant has not received any notice, directly or indirectly, of a prior assignment, hypothecation, or pledge by Landlord of the rents of the Lease to a person or entity.

12. The current address to which all notices to Tenant as required under the Lease should be sent is: _____.

13. Addressee's rights hereunder shall inure to its successors and assigns.

continues

continued

14. With respect to the Merchant's Promotional Association and/or the Promotional Service, if any, Tenant has no claims, liens, or offsets with regard to any amounts due or to become due thereunder except for _____.

If the Addressee is a purchaser or prospective purchaser of the Premises and/or the Building, Tenant shall also include the following:

15. Tenant acknowledges that Addressee is acquiring ownership of the building in which the Premises are located. Tenant agrees that upon Addressee acquiring ownership, Tenant will attorn and does attorn and agrees to recognize and does recognize Addressee as Landlord on the condition that Addressee agrees to recognize the Lease referred to in this document as long as Tenant is not in default thereunder; provided, however, that Addressee shall have no liability or responsibility under or pursuant to the terms of the Lease for any cause of action or matter not disclosed herein or that accrues after Addressee ceases to own a fee interest in the property covered by the Lease.

16. The Tenant agrees to execute such documents as Addressee may request for the purpose of subordinating the Lease to any mortgage or deed of trust to be placed upon the property by Addressee from time to time and any Estoppel certificates requested by Addressee from time to time in connection with the sale or encumbrance of the Premises.

17. Tenant makes this certificate with the understanding that the Addressee is contemplating acquiring the Premises and that if Addressee acquires the Premises, it will do so in material reliance on this certificate and Tenant agrees that the certifications and representations made herein shall survive such acquisition.

Executed on this   XXXXXXXXXXXXXX

Tenant: _____

By: _____ , Title _____

This document must be executed whenever there is a sale, or whenever there is a new loan. In fact, most loan documents provide that the lender may request that it be executed whenever the lender deems it necessary.

Warranties and Assignments

By comparison to the Estoppel certificate, the assignment of leases and warranties is a simple chore, and almost any language will satisfy the parties as long as it is simple and unequivocal. If the assignments of the documents are accepted or acknowledged by the third parties in question, then the assignments are considered to be perfected.

Tenants' and Utility Deposits

All lease deposits and utility deposits must be assigned to the buyer, and in the case of the utility deposits, adjustment in the purchase must be made. The cash on deposit with utility companies is the property of the seller, not part of the purchase price.

Your Chores

Your job is relatively straightforward. You originate the purchase agreement, then you approve all the paper piled in front of you, and, finally, you pay. Sounds simple, doesn't it? The long-term viability of the investment will depend 100 percent on two factors: the effectiveness of your evaluation of the documents, and your ability to manage and improve the property.

Evaluation

We have covered the evaluation process in detail, and you have seen the spreadsheet, wherein you can analyze the leases at a glance, but it is the projection of the data, your assumptions, and your game plan that will play a pivotal role in the future. You must determine whether to keep or rotate tenants, how much to raise the rents, and how to insert your lease into the equation. You will have to balance the difficulty of changing the lease with existing tenants against the cost of bringing in new tenants. You will have to evaluate the necessity of downsizing tenant size against the reality of periods of vacancy to implement that strategy.

These decisions are all trade-offs. You will be trading periodic cash flow for a stronger, more diverse, and more valuable income stream down

The Straight Skinny

The true entrepreneur will tend to go it alone, or find an investor to put up all the money, earning his or her equity through sweat and astute management. In essence the entrepreneur is using his or her time as leverage.

the line. In essence, it will be a trade of cash flow for capital gain—a difficult, but not too unpleasant, chore.

Ownership Structure and Capital

One of the largest decisions in the process will involve the money and the ownership. Are you going to go it alone? Will you bring in partners, and why? Most of us defer to the practical when making this decision. If you have sufficient capital—and all of the requisite skills—then you will most likely decide to go it alone. If, however, you're like the rest of us, you never have enough of either. The most likely scenario is that you will recruit some people with cash to invest who also possess skills that complement your own. If you recruit people with both, you can save money managing the enterprise, but most important of all, two heads are generally better than one.

The Money

The largest part of the equation is always the money. Without many exceptions, the purchase price must be paid in cash, retiring the old loans. The exceptions to this rule tend to be very new buildings where the developer has just closed some assumable financing. The reality we face is that most new loans will be limited to 75 percent of the purchase price, necessitating cash equity for the remaining 25 percent. Couple this with the necessity of also having reserves, and you have a substantial equity requirement. You may, of course, put the cash up yourself, or you may become innovative and see what the other possibilities might be.

Equity

Equity may be raised in a number of ways. The governing body for this process is the Securities and Exchange Commission (the SEC). It sets the rules governing the raising of capital through solicitation. Most of the process is exempt from these regulations by keeping the process well within its rules for what is known as "Private Placement." These rules state that if you solicit no more than 35 people with whom you have a pre-existing relationship, and, if you form an investor group with 10 or fewer of these people, then you are exempt from the formal disclosure laws that the SEC requires for public solicitation. The individuals must meet certain net worth criteria and must qualify as sophisticated investors. You cannot include "widows and orphans." These regulations are designed to protect the unsophisticated segment of the public that is not equipped to evaluate a complicated, long-term investment.

Another viable option in raising the equity is to find one investor who will put up all the money required and allow you to earn a share of the incremental increase in value realized through management and subsequent sale. Most investors of this type will make a deal wherein their equity is paid a preferred, minimum rate of return from day one and a percentage of any increase in cash flow as the property increases in value. Upon sale, the investor recaptures his or her equity prior to the agreed-upon split of the profits.

You might notice that I said split of the profits, rather than capital gain. Profit is defined as the increase in sales price over the original purchase price, whereas capital gain is defined as profit, plus the recapture of any depreciation taken during the period of ownership. This approach can be taken with any rental property where the manager earns his or her equity through leasing and management.

Loans

The balance of the purchase price may be in the form of a loan. The viability of the loan is determined by the amount, the term, the interest rate, and the debt service constant, or the amortization rate. Obviously, the amount of the loan must be sufficient to meet your needs, but what about the rest?

The interest rate of the loan is the interest charged annually to borrow the money. Interest paid, plus points paid, is commonly referred to as the cost of funds. Most loans are simple interest loans that calculate interest monthly based on the unpaid balance of the loan. The payment is determined by the amortization schedule or the debt service constant. This is defined as a constant percentage multiplied by the principal amount, sufficient to yield a payment that includes the required interest annually and which provides for the complete retirement of the principal balance over the life of the loan. The resulting constant is expressed as a percentage known as a loan constant. These constants are contained in tables or calculated as needed. From the loan constant tables I have used for years, the constant required to pay a loan at an 8 percent interest rate over a 30-year term is 8.81 percent. Used as a constant, the annual payment is then calculated by multiplying the principal amount of the loan by the constant .0881.

For example, a million-dollar loan would yield an annual mortgage payment of $1,000,000 \times 0.0881 = \$88,100$. This is then translated into monthly mortgage payments by dividing by 12, yielding monthly payments of $7,341.67.

The final factor in any loan is the term of the loan. A typical loan today would entail a 25-year amortization rate and a 10-year term. This means that the payments are based on an amortization rate of 25 years, but the principal balance is due at the end of 10 years.

This balloon payment is set up for several reasons. Lenders have learned over the years that income property can deteriorate under poor management, as well as improve under good management. The early due date does not necessarily mean that the lender wants the loan paid off; rather, the early due date provides the lender with the opportunity to re-examine the security to ascertain its continued viability at the 10-year mark. If the loan looks good, the lender will most likely offer to extend the term with or without changes in the interest rate and amortization schedule. This also provides the borrower with the opportunity to increase the loan dollars, recapturing cash equity in the event the borrower has been successful in substantially increasing the NIBDS (net income before debt service). This could provide the capital to further improve the existing property or to take on another property while keeping the existing one.

Reserves

The final part of the investment equation lies in the proper reserves, or emergency cash. How much is enough? How is it determined? The answer is that every investor must make his or her own determination. I can share with you my philosophy, but you must make your own determination.

I evaluate the following factors when constructing a reserve:

- The cash flow

- The relative size of the tenants

- The tenants' financial condition and business

- The lease expiration dates

- My take on Murphy's Law

If the cash flow is at 100 percent of GPI (gross potential income), I will always set aside the imputed 5 percent vacancy factor as a cash flow reserve. I will let it accumulate at least until such time as I have built up a six-month mortgage payment balance. This reserve will see me through the period of releasing, if it happens.

 Better Believe It!

Finding additional capital during a crisis is always expensive. Plan ahead and beat the odds.

The size of the tenants will determine whether I will need to replace large tenants with smaller ones. I will, at least, tie the large tenants into a long-term lease. At renewal time, I want them to extend beyond my projected sale date, or I will replace them. The cash flow fund will see me through this period of reduced cash flow.

The next consideration is the tenants' financial condition and the state of their business. If some of the tenants look flaky, I will set aside a month or two of rent, represented by the flakes, to allow me time to replace them. I will also set aside sufficient funds for recapitalizing the required tenant spaces.

The next significant factor is the expiration dates of the leases. I would generally provide for rent and recapitalization of any leases expiring within 24 months of the purchase date. Finally, there is Murphy's Law. Pick your own number. You will most likely need it.

Add these factors together and you will find that it's a big number. More than likely, you will not need it, but if you do, you will be glad to have it.

The Least You Need to Know

- To make sense of the paperwork, create a list for all the players.

- Get your end of the work done on time, and check on everyone else's progress. Be proactive.

- Be sure that you understand all the documents, and they say what you want them to say. Do not lose the advantage by not paying attention to the details.

- Always maintain control of the deal by controlling the paperwork and the money.

- Use the free look to set up and fine-tune your business plan. Find and establish your reserves.

- Check everything twice, then close.

Part 4

Ownership and Financing

Ownership and financing covers the gamut from choosing to recruit some partners, or not, selecting the most advantageous legal form of ownership for your venture, to drafting the documents. You may want to go it alone, or you might want some company and some other people's money to spread your risk. This part will tell you how to evaluate your situation while describing the pros and cons of partnership and other forms of ownership.

If you take on partners, you will need to decide who does what and what it is worth.

You will also need money. Discover the various forms of financing available, as well as the ins and outs of using your own and other people's money. See how to borrow and raise the required equity and the relative benefits of each.

Chapter 13

Go Solo or Take on Partners—Your Choice

In This Chapter

◆ The realities of partnerships

◆ Find your weaknesses and get help

◆ How to locate good help

◆ What help is worth to you

◆ How to get what you want out of the deal

When you need partners, and when you should avoid them, is the topic of this chapter. It's an involved topic. Some of the needs are apparent, such as the need for more cash and the need to add to the management talent pool. Other needs are personal and subjective. Sometimes the decision to take on partners is based, simply, upon the feeling that you will be more comfortable sharing the risk. The old adage that there is strength in numbers can be comforting for the first-time investor.

Pros and Cons

On the positive side, there is, indeed, strength in numbers, as well as potentially more cash and a greater talent pool. This can serve two purposes: to create a greater comfort level, and to save money in managing the investment. If, for instance, you have an investor, a broker, a manager, an architect, and a builder for partners, you will have all the bases covered. If everyone contributes his or her skills gratis, then the cost of management and improvements becomes much less than that of your competitors. Everyone benefits when the time comes for resale, as the partners' basis in the property is less, by the dollars saved through the partners' work contributions.

Problems can occur when people making these contributions believe that their contribution is worth more than that of another partner. Inevitably, someone always does more work than the others. How do you balance this disparity between contributions? What happens when there is a dispute over what to do and how much to spend? Should the majority rule, or the majority-in-interest? Whose contribution is worth what percentage of the ownership? How do you break the deadlock, or agree to disagree? Who makes the final decision? This possibility of deadlock is the ugly part of a partnership, and it has deterred many from having equal partners or partners at all.

When you have partners, you must find answers to these questions. My experience has shown me that partnerships need a responsible party. Since I play the role of the entrepreneur in my projects, I have always formed partnerships in which I was designated as the managing partner. My operating procedure has always been to provide the other partners with a detailed, monthly status report, and to poll the other partners before making final decisions regarding major issues. This practice has served me well for many projects. You, too, must find a comfortable role when you decide to take on partners.

The Lone Ranger Approach

If you elect to go it alone, you will have none of these problems and none of the comforts. There will be no one to listen to except your paid advisers. Your only counsel will be your best judgment regarding the opinions you pay for. If this sounds too lonely and harsh, you will most likely opt for some form of partnership arrangement as shown below.

Partnership Arrangements

The two most popular forms of ownership for real estate investments are the partnership and the limited liability company (LLC).

The Partnership

Partnerships come in two varieties: general and limited. All partnerships have a general partner. This partner must assume the management of the partnership, making the decisions and accepting, personally, all the liabilities assumed by the partnership itself. In a general partnership, all the partners are general partners, having the same rights and liabilities. The majority partner, or the majority-in-interest, generally manages these partnerships. Usually, there is no compensation for performing this role.

In a limited partnership, there are two classes of partners: the general partner, and one or more limited partners. The general partner's role in a limited partnership is the same as it is in the general partnership, plus, he has the added burden of a stricter *fiduciary* responsibility to the limited partners. The limited partners contribute only money or property and take no role in the day-to-day management of the partnership. Their role is totally passive, and their interests subject to the actions of the general partner. The limited partners, therefore, have no liability beyond the potential loss of their capital contribution. Their only permitted activity is monitoring the performance of the general partner, and stepping in to protect their interests if they feel their interests are in jeopardy.

Limited partners have the right to remove the general partner and assume the management of the partnership in this instance, but, in so doing, they may jeopardize their limited partner status. Their limited liability is directly tied to their passive role in the partnership. If they must act to preserve the asset, or to replace a general partner who is mismanaging, they may keep their immunity if they replace the general partner or dispose of the asset. Indefinite management by the limited partners will cause them to be treated as general partners.

Buzzwords

Fiduciary is an enforceable, legal obligation undertaken by an agent or partner to another person or entity. In practical terms, it means that you are totally responsible for your partner's investment. You must safeguard your partner's interests. It does not, however, imply any guarantees beyond due diligence and prudent and reasonable action on your part.

The LLC

The new alternative to taking ownership of real property, similar to that of a partnership, is to form a Limited Liability Company (LLC). This form of ownership came into being in the late 1990s, and is, by far, the best form of ownership available for real estate investment for the average potential owner. The limited liability company is a combination of corporation and partnership. The corporation's biggest appeal is the same as the limited partnership role. The owners, stockholders, or limited partners have a limit to their liability. They can lose only their investment. The partnership's major appeal, unlike the corporation, is that there is only one level of taxation. Both income and tax consequences flow through to the partners, and are taxed in the individual's return. The limited liability company combines the limited liability of the corporation with the tax benefits of the partnership. The owners are referred to as "members," and they may be active or passive in the management without affecting their limited liability status. LLCs can be managed by the members, or by a designated managing member, or by a manager hired for the purpose.

What You Need in a Partner

The choice boils down to what you need to manage your chosen investment, and where to find it. There are no guidelines for this, but I believe that you should consider partners for some skills and hire the rest. *My test when looking for a partner is to only consider, as a partner, someone whose interests are inseparable from my own. I hire the rest.*

Cash Availability

First, and foremost, you will need cash, and you will need enough cash to both purchase the property, and set up a strategic reserve. In addition, you will need a financial statement and credit history sufficient to stand alone in a lender's evaluation. Even if you have enough cash and your credit is good, you might fall short in the track record department. Most lenders require the borrower to have a background in development and/or investing on the other side of the note. Skills sufficient to prosper in a business environment, and the ability to save money, do not, necessarily, translate into entrepreneurial management skills.

Skills

Skills come under the list of items to consider when looking for partners. Chances are that if you have come to the point where you can consider investing your savings in a piece of investment property, you have proven to yourself, at least, that you are a good manager. You're not likely to need a partner who can do the overall management of the project, nor do you need one to help formulate the plan of action.

What you are likely to need, besides the money, are the skills of a property manager, an architect, a broker, and a contractor. If the property is a small one, if there are few tenants, if the building is in relatively good repair, and if the tenants are responsible, then you will most likely assume the role of property manager yourself. If, however, there are many tenants, some turnover, and if the leases are gross leases, you might well need a property manager.

Better Believe It!

There is more to money than just having the cash. Cash alone will not ensure profit. You must have a plan and the tools necessary to implement it. Hired guns without a vested interest in a property will not always do the necessary, especially after hours.

Unless you are a broker, an architect, or a contractor, you will need to consider acquiring these skills through a partnership. The difference between the property manager and the other required skills lies in the fact that the property manager's talents call for a day-to-day, ongoing involvement, while the other disciplines are only needed from time to time.

Where to Find the Partner(s) You Need

Once you have an understanding of your needs, then you need to explore how to fill them. One does not put an ad in *The Wall Street Journal* for partners. It would do you no good anyway, and it could get you into trouble with the SEC. There are, therefore, two problems to solve. First, you need an investor/partner, and second, you need to hire some brains. Let's deal with the brains first.

Consultants

Consultants are readily available, expensive, and not necessarily any good. How do you weed out the winners from the losers? The answer is that you talk to all of them, not only about their special area of interest, but also about other consultants you might need. Get their input and their reasons for recommending the people they do.

Often, consultants pass their customers around to other consultants within their clique. This is a network of consultants in the same industry who are accustomed to working together. The network operates much like a doctor recommending a colleague for a specialty. You do not necessarily get the right ones to pick from.

Great sources for recommendations are the lenders, but even there, they have favorites. Always ask your potential consultants for a list of customers, good and bad, and interview them, attempting to ferret out the pros and cons. Talk to the local

Better Business Bureau. Check their credit history and call Dun and Bradstreet. You will not get the whole picture from any one source of information, but an image will emerge. Ask about their competition. What they say, good and bad, can be illuminating. A reputable professional will rarely slam his or her competitors. They thrive on mutual respect and fair competition. Often, they will say, "If you decide not to hire us, at least go and see so and so." When you have made your checklists, you will find that obvious choices will rise to the top of the list, seemingly by themselves.

Partners and LLCs

The thornier problem is that of seeking out and acquiring an investor/partner. You will need someone who can complement your cash, your skills, and your track record. You want someone who shares the same goals and who is of like mind about how to accomplish them. Your management philosophies should be similar, and your abilities to access risk and plan ahead should be complementary. You will need someone who can add to your credibility and to your game plan. The alternative is to find someone with an established plan that you can assimilate yourself into. Either way, you must determine that, as a team, you will be stronger than you would be as individuals. The big question in any partnership is who does what and how decisions are to be made. Spell it out clearly in the partnership documentation.

What a Partner Is Worth

When you form a partnership or LLC, the first order of business is to determine who contributes what, and what it is worth. This is not necessarily an easy task with obvious answers. If you are dealing with an investment that is going to be built, you are assuming the role of the developer and the skills needed for the task are budgetary. There is no real need to incorporate these people in the partnership or LLC, unless you need to limit your up-front risk when creating the deal. Often, professionals who will be hired to do specific tasks will spec (speculate) their time at the front end of a transaction to help you pull the deal together and remove the contingencies. Their compensation for this arrangement is sometimes a sweetened contract, and sometimes a piece of the action. How much you give depends on your level of need. If, however, you are just buying a property, there is no reason to sweeten the deal for your consultants, because there is little or no up-front risk to your pocketbook. Most of the work to be done in removing the contingencies involves your decision-making process, and the largest expense will be your attorney's fees.

Working on Spec

If you are operating on a limited amount of capital and must ask your consultants to spec their time, I recommend that you consider a 10 percent interest in your operation as an inducement. Remember, the stake will be that of a partnership interest or a membership interest and the individuals involved will be subject to the lender's evaluation along with you and your financial partner. You must choose consultants with a good professional record and sound financial statements.

The consultants that you will most likely need are the leasing broker, the architect, and the general contractor. Assuming that you make a deal with all three, you now have 70 percent ownership left. Each consultant now has a 10 percent stake in the project. The consultants contributed their time and effort at the front end for no immediate compensation. In exchange for this, they have received a partnership interest and, later, when the project is funded, their full fees. The four of you now own the deal together, and when you go shopping for a financial partner, you are *all* shopping for a financial partner.

The Partner's Money

The final and most sought-after ingredient in any deal is the money. What is it worth to you? When will it be paid? Will the contribution be a finite one, or will funding be an ongoing obligation? All these aspects of the deal are subject to negotiation, and the reality is that you will have to pay as much as it takes to secure your equity financing.

If you are involved in a development project, the most effective time for you to solicit a financial partner is when the deal is ready to go. If you have secured all the required approvals and permits, if you have sufficiently preleased the project to satisfy a lender, and if you have received a construction loan commitment, then you are ready to cut a good deal with a financial partner.

The traditional deal is that the entity providing 100 percent of the required money gets a one-half interest in the project. Specific terms such as the timing on the pay in, preferred cash flow, priority return on cash invested, and additional funding are all terms that will need to be negotiated. If you are providing part of the funds for this venture, then your funds should be included in the money's half of the ownership.

If you are purchasing a property, the value of the money is not as clear-cut, and you are most likely to have some of your own cash involved. How the ownership will be allocated depends on the roles of the individuals involved. If you are the entrepreneur, and if you have ferreted out a spectacular deal with considerable upside potential, then you are in a position to take a piece of this deal for that work. If you are going to manage the project and take on all the chores, you are entitled to a return for that endeavor. If your investor/partner is going to take a totally passive role, then a 50/50 split is not unreasonable. The cash flow will have to pay some preferred return to the capital, then, there can be a split thereafter. When the project is sold, the capital will be returned first before the profit is split. There might even be a minimum capital gain to the investor against his or her share of the profit. The possible combination of elements in the arrangement is limited only by your imagination.

Selling the Deal to the Lender

Once you have found your dream deal, you will have to structure it, arrange the financing, and get it closed. Whether it is a development deal or a purchase, you must be able to sell the project to everyone involved. Finding a good deal, while not an easy task, is only the beginning. All the work will be for nothing if you fail to close the transaction. Your research and your analysis must now be synthesized into a package that properly represents your proposed investment. What do you need? How should you present it? The answers are the same for the people you are trying to reach as they were for you. You were, after all, the first person that needed to be convinced that this is a good deal. What led you to this conclusion?

Packaging

The answers to these questions become the package. There are no two packages alike, as there are no two deals alike. Most presentations, not intended for public funding, include, as a minimum, the following items:

For a development project:

- ◆ A written summary of the plan of action
- ◆ A detailed market analysis
- ◆ A survey and title report
- ◆ Plans and specifications
- ◆ A rendering
- ◆ A guaranteed construction cost breakdown

◆ The general construction contract and a resumé and financial statement for the contractor

◆ The leases

◆ A summary of the financing secured or in progress, together with a copy of the appraisal

◆ Financial projections known as the "pro forma," which include both cost breakdown and income and expense projections, in detail, with supporting data

◆ Financial statements for the existing principals and a resumé of past business dealings

◆ A summary of the proposed business deal

For a purchase transaction:

◆ A written summary of the plan of action

◆ A detailed market analysis, with photos of the immediate competitors

◆ A detailed summary of the leases

◆ "As-built" plans and tenant improvement plans

◆ Photos of the site and the buildings

◆ A summary of the financing secured or in progress, together with a copy of the appraisal

◆ Financial projections known as the "pro forma," which include both cost, strategic reserves and projected recapitalization breakdown, and income and expense projections in detail, with supporting data

◆ Financial statements for the existing principals and a resumé of past business dealings

◆ A summary of the proposed business deal

You can see that the list is similar for both types of transactions. By examining the components of the presentation, you will have a better feel for the package itself.

The package should be no more than 20 pages with supporting detail contained in separate reports. It should be simple and direct in a format that is readily understandable and intuitively arranged. If the proposed investor needs more data on the market, he or she can refer to the detailed marketing report attached. The income and expense projections should be shown over the anticipated life of the investment, with the corresponding expenditure schedule tied directly into the anticipated actions shown in the income projections.

The plan of action, often referred to as the executive summary, should clearly reflect your plan of action. It should address your specific plans for improving the value of the asset, as well as point out potential pitfalls along the way, with details as to how to plan for these contingencies. It should be easily tied into your budget projection. Both should be cross-referenced.

Your financial statements should be done on a cost basis with adequate footnotes showing current market value with an explanation of how the values were arrived at. Your resumé should give specific accomplishments with personal references from business associates and past partners.

Legal Requirements

Beyond the obvious need to be truthful in your presentation, remember that this presentation should not be broadcast to the general public. If your presentation is based on certain assumptions, state them clearly in a disclaimer section. Point out the obvious and subtle pitfalls.

The Least You Need to Know

- You must decide. Are you the Lone Ranger, or do you want partners?

- Partners are good and bad; look at the pros and cons, and act accordingly.

- Partners are everywhere; be selective, take only those who are a definite asset in money or skills, preferably both.

- Cut your best deal with them up front; you will not get another chance to improve your deal.

- A well-thought-out investment package makes it easier to attract the help you decide you need.

Chapter 14

Partners and Consultants— Working With Others

In This Chapter

◆ Your role as the entrepreneur

◆ How and when to use hired guns

◆ Should you take on employees?

◆ What about the tenants?

For this chapter, assume that you will be the motivating force in a transaction, and that you will be the one in charge of locating, selecting, and managing the investment. In essence, construct a transaction around you in your head, as if it were an actual project. This will personalize the exercise and start you thinking in the direction of practical solutions.

In any development or investment project, there are two essential skills required to create and enhance a successful income project. They are the skills of the entrepreneur and those of the manager, or bean counter.

These skills are not necessarily compatible, but often you will be required to serve both functions. Let's look at both to ascertain what their ingredients are so that you can see where you can fit into the picture. The characteristics of each personality type are evidenced by what they do and how they go about it. If you are fortunate, you might be someone who possesses enough of each type to really shine in this business. As you read this section, be honest with yourself when comparing yourself against the profiles outlined. If you approach the exercise honestly, you will have a better chance of pulling together a successful team when the time comes for your first deal.

The Entrepreneur

What does an entrepreneur really do, and how does she do it? This is not an easy question. I have been making a living as a full-time entrepreneur for over 25 years, and I'm not sure whether I am typical or not.

The Straight Skinny

Entrepreneurs see things other people do not. What they see is opportunity. They see it, because they are always looking for it. Persistence and hard work are 90 percent of entrepreneurship. The rest is vision and a little luck. By placing your judgment ahead of others, you will find that you are taking the road less traveled and doing something original.

Entrepreneurs look for opportunity. They are naturally curious and restless, generally unsatisfied with the status quo. In another era, they would most likely be explorers and immigrants. They populated the Wild West and expanded the country. They wanted more out of life and were willing to work hard and take risks to get it. Entrepreneurs generally do not shrink from hard work, and they seldom, if ever, give up on something once they have set it in motion.

You might think back on the need for research and fact-finding, and feel that this sounds more like bean counting than entrepreneurship. Not so! Research and fact-finding go hand in hand with curiosity and seeking. By unearthing the facts, something most people are too lazy to do, an entrepreneur will uncover patterns that are not apparent in the marketplace. Most people assume certain things, taking the opinions of others as truth. The entrepreneur wants to find out the real facts for him or herself. If this describes you, then you are most likely emotionally qualified for this endeavor.

An entrepreneur also needs common sense. Realism and pragmatism are the cornerstone of the entrepreneur's role. Vision, insight, and desire amount to nothing if the goal is neither realistic nor practical. You must be able to judge whether something makes sense, and understand how it will work. Entrepreneurship thrives on the KISS principle (Keep It Simple, Stupid).

The Bean Counter

Who, then, is the bean counter? People for years have poked fun at the bean counter, describing him or her as being excessively anal-retentive. Some of this is true. The reality of the bean counters is that they do a great job with what they are given. Most people charged with this responsibility shine when given a game plan to follow. One of their principal delights is finding holes in the plan and making improvements in it. Sound a bit like an entrepreneur? Maybe, but the entrepreneur is the one who created the game plan for the bean counter to follow.

The talented bean counter is innovative in his or her own right. The constant search for improvement is, most often, coupled with a fervent dedication to detail. They make great accountants and stewards of complex mechanisms.

To be effective in the income property-management business, they must also have the skills of the diplomat. They will be dealing with tenants who think that their payment of rent entitles them to more than just a place to do business. The inspired bean counters must point out that they are entitled to what is in the lease and no more. They must do this with diplomacy and tact. By finessing the situation, the effective manager will get the tenants to see that they are part of a community that needs to work together to ensure that everyone gets what they need and are entitled to, not necessarily what they want.

Both the entrepreneur and the bean counter should be in a position of ownership when dealing with income property. Rarely are these talents housed in one body, and in the practical world of investment real estate, you will see many two-person partnerships. Together, two talented individuals can make a formidable team. These two talents are complementary and incredibly synergistic.

Consultants

You need to regard consultants as hired guns. They should be experts in their field, hired, when needed, to perform specific tasks. When you contract with a consultant, you are purchasing knowledge and experience.

Better Believe It!

Do yourself a favor and verify the consultant's expertise. Talk to his or her clients. Look at his or her work. See firsthand how the consultant does the job.

You'll need to judge the effectiveness of the consultant's work. You have a right to get your money's worth. More important, you must evaluate the probability of that person's work being compatible with your game plan. You know where you're headed, and, therefore, you are in the best position to evaluate the consultant's effectiveness in helping you get where you want to go.

Managers

Managers are apprentice bean counters. Property management needs people who are in the field, overseeing maintenance and talking to tenants on-site. Most good real estate bean counter types made their start in the field. The hands-on experience is necessary to properly set up and administer a true management program. There is a lot more to property management than just collecting the rents. The proper care and feeding of tenants is an art form.

Remember, you are not dealing with a finite commodity. New rental space comes on the market every year, and all the new buildings need tenants. Your tenants are fair game for the brokers charged with filling the newer buildings. Remember also, that's how you got your tenants in the first place. Some were most likely new businesses, but most came out of someone else's buildings. Your manager's duty is to keep your tenants from moving to someone else's buildings.

Tenants move for a variety of reasons, not the least of which are …

- They need to expand, and their landlord cannot accommodate them.
- They feel that the building's location no longer meets their needs.
- They feel that they are not getting prompt service.
- They feel that the building is not properly maintained.
- They are mad at the landlord.

It does not matter why they move, and despite all your and your manager's expertise, some will always move. The trick is to anticipate their needs and accommodate them as much as possible. Figure out what they want and give it to them, and you will keep your tenants. When a manager becomes effective at this, he or she is well on the way to becoming a first-class bean counter.

Accounting and Legal

Both accounting and legal advice are needed functions in any transaction. The accounting is a day-to-day function with monthly reports, whereas the legal function is required sporadically. The key to the accounting functions lies not in the bookkeeping, but in the setup and presentation of data. The bookkeeping function is performed for the banks and the IRS. The owners require spreadsheets and other data so that they can see at a glance what they need to know.

The legal function tends to be front-end loaded. Most of the work is performed before and immediately after the purchase. In a development deal, most of the legal work occurs before the close of escrow. After that, unless there is a crisis, the legal function is confined to the odd lease or loan closing.

Both of these functions should be hired rather than made partners. While their contribution is necessary, they are relatively routine, and require little or no innovation.

Brokers

Brokers are not only necessary, they are vital in all real estate transactions. They are involved in all three crucial aspects of the investment, whether purchased or built:

The Straight Skinny

Making a broker one of your partners can provide a powerful incentive to the individual to perform beyond the call of duty. You should seriously consider it.

◆ They are involved in the purchase of the land or the income property.

◆ They are involved in leasing the property.

◆ They will be involved in the sale of the asset.

There is no way to be involved in real property as an investment without the services of one or more brokers. Of course, you can be your own broker, but even if you have the experience, chances are that you will be involved with other brokers as well. The practice of cooperation started in the residential industry is slowly filtering through the commercial industry. More and more transactions involve two or more brokers who cooperate by bringing buyer and seller together. In the not-too-distant past, commercial brokers seldom exposed their listings to other brokers. Today, most owners insist that commercial brokers cooperate with all other brokers to afford their properties greater exposure in the market. This is essential, and it is good business for the brokers as well.

Architects and Engineers

Most of the work of architects and engineers occurs at the beginning of a development project. Sometimes an investor will purchase a property for renovation, and the process becomes similar to that of a building project, with these two consultants involved at the beginning. Most common of all, however, is the instance in which an investor purchases a building full of tenants. The architect, sometimes aided by an engineer, is involved only sporadically when tenants are replaced. Rarely have I seen either of these two consultants involved in the ownership of an investment property unless they have been brought into the deal by the original developer.

Their services at the front end are a valuable contribution to the development effort, and often I have asked the architect to spec some early plans to keep my front-end costs down. In exchange for this favor, I have offered a piece of the action and the full fee when the project proceeds. If money is tight, I recommend that you consider this plan.

Hiring Employees

When dealing with this array of consultants, from market research through property managers, you will be tempted to add up the fees to be paid and conclude that you might be better off hiring these people as employees.

This is a big step and has some long-range implications. The largest consideration is cost. If you hire these people by the job, your exposure is limited to payment as needed. However, if you hire them permanently, you are taking on serious, continuous overhead. The only reason to justify this group as employees would be if you were embarking on a full-time program of acquisition and ownership of multiple properties. This could require the services of the consultants involved on a full-time basis.

Better Believe It!

If someone is empowered to act, or perceived to be in a position to act, he or she may find him or herself in a position where there is no way out of making a decision. If the consultant cannot act for you, the problem is rendered moot, and the pressure is off.

I would still be inclined to hire them as consultants, however, because I believe that the experienced professional who is not available for hire will do a better job. If, however, you are a generalist who wants to hire and train your own staff, then you might be correct in hiring them as employees.

Authority and Responsibility

One of the major considerations, beyond the cost of employees versus consultants, lies in their authority to act. When representing you with third parties, consultants are almost exclusively hired in an advisory capacity, whereas employees are construed to be the "owner's representatives," and, therefore, are perceived by third parties to "speak for the owner." If this is what you want, fine, but one of the most useful functions of a consultant is that of a buffer between you and any third party. The consultant's inability (or apparent inability) to commit you buys you time to consider all your options.

You will find that this will become one of your most useful tools in negotiation. Besides finding property and tenants, the most valuable service provided by a broker is to provide this buffer, leaving you free to think about the negotiations. The only time I like to be face to face with the other party is during lease negotiations. Most owners, however, prefer the "arm's length" approach.

Handling the Cash

Another aspect of the functions served by both consultants and employees is that of collecting and disbursing money. Collecting the income is why you made the investment in the first place. It is also where you can be most vulnerable to fraud. There is no problem having either the consultant or the employee collect the money as long as you follow three simple rules:

- Never allow them to accept cash. Make sure your tenants know that cash payments will not be credited as rent.

- All funds are to be deposited in an account controlled only by the owner.

- Handle all disbursements personally. Sign all the checks yourself, or have one of your partners sign the checks. Do not delegate check-signing authority to an employee or to a consultant.

Follow these three simple rules, and you will never get hurt. There are obviously circumstances in which these rules will be cumbersome, or become impossible to implement. The first instance is emergencies. Set up a special account for the use of your property manager with a deposit sufficient to pay for small emergencies. Seldom, if ever, would an emergency exceed a few thousand dollars. Most will fall into the $100 to $500 category. When the receipts are presented to you, replenish the fund. Your exposure is then limited to the original deposit.

The second instance in which this may become impossible occurs when the size of your investments and the sheer volume of the rents collected require a formal accounting department. When this happens, you will need to set up one group to do the accounting and issue the checks, and a second group to check the results and sign the checks. At this point, you may find that you will have to start paying close attention to your monthly reports, cross-checking them against your bank statements. This is a happy problem to have indeed.

The Family Alternative

You might have surmised that there will be many responsibilities, and a lot of work to go around. A great alternative for motivated family members is to attempt to do this as a family company, sharing the chores as much as possible, and hiring expertise when you need it. The big advantage to this approach is that you can let your kids into the picture and provide for a seamless transition generation to generation. You should also find a greater level of trust in dealing within a family framework.

Tenants

While all this is going on, what are your tenants up to, and what should you be looking for as far as their performance is concerned?

The two most important aspects of the tenants' role are the conduct of their business, in general and in your building, and the timely payment of your rent. You must, in a general way, keep an eye on your tenants to determine that they are prospering. This is crucial with retail tenants, and one of the important clauses in a retail lease is the quarterly reporting on gross sales. There may be little you can do to help, but if you can spot a downtrend early, you will be in a better position to replace a tenant who is going broke.

Their conduct in the building, their treatment of their fellow tenants, their adherence to the rules and regulations, their respect for the parking rules, and their business hours are all areas that need to be monitored by the property manager. You should instruct the property manager to inform you prior to taking any action so that you may provide some guidance in the matter, as you might be privy to information that is not available to the manager.

Their Business

There are things that you can do to help your tenants. Why should you bother? The answer is simple. A prosperous tenant can pay the rent, and a bankrupt one is a complication you do not need. If, for example, you have a small tenant that sells goods similar to those sold by one of the anchor tenants in your shopping center, you might consider intervening on behalf of the little guy. You can request that the larger store not emphasize this particular part of its business. If this fails, you might allow the smaller store to diversify, changing its line so that it does not directly compete with the major tenant. Today, with stores like Wal-Mart, Best Buy, and Home Depot, the small stores are scrambling to stay out of their way.

Paying Rent

Prompt payment of rent is crucial to your cash flow. You will, most likely, have a mortgage to pay, and if the rent, taxes, and common-area expenses (CAM charges) are not received on time, you will find that you can be in a cash-flow bind.

Better Believe It!

The threat of financial penalties for late rent payment is not enough. You must enforce penalties the first time, and every time.

The major problem in income-property management is late rental payments. The solution to this lies in the lease document. There must be a series of steps built into the lease that make late payment of rent very unpleasant and costly to your tenants.

Major tenants always object to this, as their credit is deemed to be superior. My response to this is that these rules are not a problem to anyone intending to pay their rent on time. If they do not intend to do so, I have second thoughts about allowing them into my building in the first place. The only reasoning I have ever heard is "It is our corporate policy." My response is always, "My policy is not to do business with people who will not commit to paying their rent on time." Stand firm on this point, or you will live to regret it!

The tools you need are, at the very least:

◆ A clear definition of the rent and how it is calculated

◆ A specific rent due date, together with a clearly defined place (address) where the rent must be received by the landlord ("in the mail" on the designated date is not deemed "received")

- A specific date on which the rent is late

- A specific financial penalty when the rent is late

- Clearly defined remedies for nonpayment, over 30 days, specifically the right to declare the tenant in default

- A default remedy that must include the right to accelerate the rent and evict the tenant within the shortest possible time allowed by the statutes of the state having jurisdiction

You must be able to evict the bad apples as fast as possible.

Do not be intimidated by large companies. They are subject to the same law as any other tenant. Make them pay the penalty, and your rent will start to arrive on time. The deliberate, slow payment of rent is a cash management tool used by many companies. They can only get away with it if you let them do so.

This is one of the most common management problems that you will encounter in the ownership of income property. You must develop effective tools for keeping this problem under control, as the consequences of failure can be dramatically damaging to your investment program.

The Least You Need to Know

- Entrepreneurship is hard work. Consider taking on partners to help with the work or the money.

- If you are going to manage your investment, set your game plan early. Select your posture and stick with it.

- Use the skills of others sparingly and economically.

- Take very good care of your tenants; they are your bread and butter.

- Enforce the lease every time. Be consistent.

- Collect all rents on time, every time.

Chapter 15

Conventional Financing

In This Chapter

- Obtain money for development projects
- Construction money and bridge loans
- Finding permanent financing
- Specialized financing
- Rolling over your loan
- Financing to sell

Major financial institutions, under terms and conditions common to all in the industry, provide conventional financing. New, unconventional forms of financing, if they become popular, find their way into the mainstream of the financing industry and become conventional. Financing for development projects differs only slightly from that available to finished projects. Development deals require temporary financing during the period of construction and lease up (the period during which you achieve a 95 percent leased building). This financing is considered interim, and varies from one to three years, depending on the size of the project. Unless you sell the property, you will also need a permanent, or take-out, loan to pay off the interim loan.

In some instances, existing projects could qualify for this type of financing. It can be useful when there is a major renovation contemplated and the project is considered to be under redevelopment. These forms of financing are covered in the following sections.

Development Projects

Traditional project financing falls into two major categories: equity (discussed in Chapter 16) and conventional mortgage. The resulting loans are either *interim* (or *gap*), and *permanent* (or *take-out*).

Buzzwords

The **interim** loan is temporary or construction financing (usually short-term, one- to three-year loans designed to fill the gap from the start of construction to the start of the tenant occupancy period, otherwise known as the operating period). A **gap** loan is the loan that covers the gap between equity and permanent financing, usually a land loan or a seller carry-back loan. A **take-out** loan is a **permanent** loan designed to pay off the interim or construction loan.

Historically, interim loans have varied from 75 percent to 105 percent of cost, and were customarily "converted" to permanent loans with a "take-out" commitment from a long-term lender. The market in the late 1990s uniformly limited the size (dollar value) of these loans to 75 percent of verifiable total cost. Since 2000, I have seen a resurgence of strictly spec deals where the preleasing has been minimal at best. Financing for these deals requires a deep pocket and good credit.

Most traditional *loan packages* start out with the procurement of a permanent loan commitment. This process takes the form of an application, and if successful, a commitment letter. The lender issues the commitment letter with certain stipulations attached when the loan application is approved. This becomes a *bankable* commitment, if the borrower can borrow a like amount of construction money from a short-term lender. The three parties (the borrower, the take-out lender, and the interim lender) then execute a *tri-party agreement*, also known as a buy/sell agreement, wherein the take-out lender agrees to take out or buy the interim loan from the lender.

This occurs upon the successful completion by the borrower of the construction and occupancy of the preleased tenants, and the satisfaction of all other stipulations contained in the commitment letter.

These stipulations are typically as follows:

- The satisfactory completion of the construction

- Occupancy by the required number of tenants

- Approval by the lender's attorney of all the leases, financial statements, continuing guarantees, and other documents involved in the project

Buzzwords

Bankable is a loan commitment that can be borrowed against and is easily financed. A **loan package** is a collection of documents that constitutes a complete loan application: the loan request, collateral description and appraisal, financial statements and projections, and sample documentation. A **tri-party agreement** is a contract, a buy-sell agreement, between the construction and permanent lenders and the borrower.

Interim Loans

Most construction financing covers the period from the start of construction to the achievement of the leasing requirement required by the permanent lender's commitment document. The typical period for this phase of the project is two to three years, but it may vary widely depending on the scope of the project.

Permanent (Take-Out) Loans

Buzzwords

Institutional financing refers to financing by an established institution, usually a bank, a savings bank, a life insurance company, REIT, or a trust.

Permanent (take-out) loans are made for terms ranging from 3 to 30 years, with additional conditions unique to the financial institution granting the loan. The most conventional approach is currently a 75 percent of value or cost, whichever is less, interim loan, partnered with a permanent loan of no more than 75 to 80 percent of projected value at completion. This is known as *institutional* or conventional mortgage financing. It is the prevalent loan package used in the commercial development industry. The primary lenders are life insurance companies, pension funds, real estate investment trusts (REITs), and local or regional banks. Refer to the "Long-Term Loans" section later in this chapter.

Short-Term Loans

The most common lenders in the short-term loan market are commercial banks. In the 1980s, they were joined, briefly, by the savings and loans (S&Ls) who, customarily, loaned construction dollars to the home building industry. After the deregulation of the S&L industry, these institutions decided to explore the commercial lending field. Since they had absolutely no experience in this business, the results were disastrous. Their lack of experience, compounded by frequent fraud on both sides of the notes, resulted in the great real estate recession of 1988 to 1991.

This collapse was due, primarily, to severe excess inventory placed on the market with little or no demonstrable demand. After the Resolution Trust Corporation (the RTC) demolished the S&L industry during the early 1990s and disposed of the failed assets, the short-term lending field returned to the commercial banking industry. Due to the magnitude of the disaster, however, many of the banks decided to terminate their involvement in the construction loan business. As a result, the field has been left to the true specialists. The bulk of these lenders restrict their loans to 75 percent of verifiable cost, requiring the borrower to substantiate paid in cash for the balance of the cost of the project.

Interim Loans and Gap Financing

What do these interim loans look like? They are fairly straightforward, and most loans share these common characteristics:

- The term varies from 12 to 36 months.
- The interest rate is generally 1 to 1.5 percent higher than the permanent loan market.
- They cost one point (1 percent) up front as a commitment fee.
- They require the personal guarantee of the borrower(s).
- They require a minimum preleasing to *break even*.

Large companies with very solid, liquid net worth can secure bank loans that vary the occupancy rule, but most of us have to meet this test, or borrow less than the usual 75 percent.

Roll-Over Loans—a.k.a. The Miniperm

Roll-over loans are a variation of the short-term construction loan. In most cases the bank will allow the initial loan, which is an interest-only loan, to be *rolled over* into an amortizing loan for a three- to five-year period. Developers like this feature, as the added cost, normally one to two *points*, provides a good hedge against the necessity of having to secure onerous, permanent financing. The roll-over loan gives the developer a breather, allowing the market to return to normal. The developer then shops for an advantageous loan for the longer term.

Buzzwords

Break even is defined as the level of occupancy at which the sum of the net rents is sufficient to pay the monthly mortgage payment. **Rolled over** is the ability to convert an interim loan to a permanent loan. **Points** are fees charged at the time a loan is committed. One point equals one percent. A **take-out loan** is a permanent loan designed to pay off the interim loan.

Prime Rate vs. Long-Term

From the latter part of 2002 to the present, we have seen long-term interest rates that are the lowest in 40 years. While there is no quantifiable connection between prime rate and long-term mortgage rates, it seems that long-term rates inevitably follow the short-term rates. The use of short-term loans and roll-over loans gives you, the borrower, the time and flexibility to shop for the best long-term financing. Look at the trends and give it your best shot.

Long-Term Loans

Long-term loans are, by definition, loans with terms of 10 years or more. They can be *take-out loans*, refinances, or new loans, and they are included in the general category of permanent loans. Historically, these loans were made for a period of 30 years and were designed to be completely self-amortizing over the term of the loan. This worked quite well until the late 1960s and 1970s, when the real estate development industry changed and expanded dramatically. At that time, borrowers and investors became smaller and more nimble, treating their real estate portfolios as interim investments. In the past, developers were large, well-established companies that built and held large blocks of properties.

This increase in demand and the resulting problems associated with new and inexperienced developers led the lending industry into new waters. They started changing terms and increasing interest rates. This proliferation of deals also pointed out to the lenders the possibility of increased revenues through the charging of points. The new diversity of deals, and the rapid spread of commercial, suburban development led to a veritable smorgasbord of loan types, terms, and rates. The great recession of the late 1980s further tightened the lender's resolve, and now the industry as a whole is intensely conservative.

Commitments

Long-term loans start out as loan commitments. If they are required as take-out loans for a construction lender, then they are usually contracted in a tri-party document. This commitment is issued under very specific terms and conditions, and if the conditions are met, the tri-party agreement allows the interim lender to cause the loan to fund independently of the borrower's actions, if necessary. The tri-party or buy/sell agreement is the interim lender's protection to ensure that the loan will be retired without default. The borrower is, in effect, locked into this permanent loan by both lenders. Should the borrower find another loan more to his or her advantage, then he or she would have to purchase a release from the take-out lender to fund the new loan. This situation has given rise to the now very popular roll-over loan (see the earlier section, "Roll-Over Loans—a.k.a. The Miniperm").

What to Expect

A permanent loan is composed of a "note" (the loan document), and a "deed of trust" or "mortgage" (the security document). In the eastern United States, the mortgage is recorded as a lien against the deed of the property when it is funded, and in the western United States, the deed of trust is recorded against the title at the close of escrow.

Whatever the form of security used, the note is likely to be uniform coast to coast. The note is the document that outlines the business points of the loan, while the security document spells out the lender's rights in the event of default.

Notes generally contain the following at a minimum:

- Names and addresses of the borrower(s) and guarantor(s), if any

- The name and address of the real property in question, with the legal description attached as an exhibit

- The amount of the loan

- The term of the loan

- The interest rate and amortization schedule

- The number and the amount of the payments

- The due date of the payments, late dates, and penalties

- The due date of the loan

- The signatures of the borrower(s) and guarantor(s)

The deed of trust and the mortgage will elaborate on the above terms, adding conditions to the loan. Common conditions include, but are not limited to, the following:

- Changes in the tenancy, with the lender sometimes having the right of review and approval of the new tenant and the new lease

- Elaborate statements of borrower's default and remedies available to the lender

- Provisions for insurance and other requirements

- Provisions allowing or prohibiting assignment and transferability

- Provisions requiring the borrower to assign all leases to the lender

- Provisions allowing or prohibiting secondary financing

- Lock-ins and other yield maintenance considerations

- Added conditions, such as reporting of rentals achieved annually

You will find that this document, whether it is a mortgage or a deed of trust, will be a daunting and non-negotiable document drawn totally in favor of the lender. I recommend that you close your eyes and sign it when the time comes. You'll avoid ulcers and live longer!

Better Believe It!

There are no bad loans when you really need one. Your job is to pick the best of the lot!

Lock-Ins

The newest wrinkle to come into the permanent loan field is the concept of the lock-in and yield maintenance clauses. This has come about due to the lenders' sales of "bundled" loans in the secondary financing market. Traditional permanent lenders have taken to making permanent loans as a means of short-term fees. They bundle them in large increments and sell them to long-term investors at a discount.

In an effort to guarantee the yields, the lenders have created the lock-in and yield maintenance clauses. The lock-in provision precludes any form of prepayment for a fixed period, usually five to nine years. The yield maintenance clause allows prepayment in years 6 through 8, or in the case of the 10-year loan, years 8 and 9, with the payment of a fee equivalent to the interest the lender would have received if the loan went to maturity. Generally, years 9 and 10 permit payoff to facilitate refinancing. This way the buyer of the bundled loans will not have to deal with foreclosure and resale considerations.

In this example, the lender makes a commitment fee, all expenses associated with the loan, a discount fee upon sale, and a servicing fee (for collecting and forwarding mortgage payments to the buyer). The net result to the borrower is a more expensive, less flexible loan package. There are still lenders, known as portfolio lenders, who make and keep their loans, and if you can find one interested in your deal, I'd recommend them over the "merchant" lender any time.

Other Financing

Other types of loans include, but are not limited to, the following:

- Land loans
- Seller carry-back loans
- Land-development loans
- Gap financing
- Equity financing
- Unsubordinated financing
- Syndication
- Improvement bonds
- Participating loans
- All-inclusive deeds of trust (wrap loans)
- In some cases, SBA loans

Land loans, seller carry-back loans, and land-development loans cover the period between the land acquisition and the start of building construction. These loans can vary all over the lot and become more expensive as the buyer's down payment on the land decreases. Routine land development loans made by local private lenders, commercial banks, or REITs are the norm in the tract housing industry, and generally, like seller carry-back financing, carry a participation in the profit on the finished lots. These loans are "retired," or paid off, when the building construction loans are funded or upon sale of the finished lots to a homebuilder.

Gap Financing, Equity, and Joint Ventures

Most conventional financing is intended to bridge the gap between the owner's cash invested or equity, and the total cost of the project. Traditionally, if the borrower owns the land free and clear, he or she is considered to have enough equity to justify financing the rest of the costs. Today, that holds true for residential loans, but in the commercial world, this rule no longer necessarily applies.

The modern lender wants to see verifiable evidence of cash investment in a project, not imputed equity acquired through the land's appreciation since purchase or option. A lender wants to see 25 percent or more cash invested before committing to any loan today, while in the past, if someone bought a property for $10,000 and it was worth $50,000 at the time of the loan application, the lender reasoned that the borrower really had the full $50,000 equity in the land. Today's lender looks only at the actual cash invested. The exception to this would be land purchased for future development and held for several years.

How does a developer fill the gap between his or her actual cash invested and the lender's required level of equity? Gap or equity financing. Most construction and permanent loans preclude secondary financing before or after their loans are recorded. Therefore, equity financing fills this gap. This money, raised specifically for the project, is not backed by a lien on the property. It is evidenced by a joint ownership of the land through legal entities such as a joint venture agreement, a corporation, a partnership, a limited liability company, or in some cases, a participating, seller carry-back land loan (a "subordinated land loan). This loan, when agreed to by the construction lender, is lien-wise subordinated to the construction loan. It will command a premium and generally a hefty participation in the profits, as it generally provides the lion's share of the required equity in the project.

Rarest of all of these arrangements is the pure *joint venture*—a legal entity, not a partnership, corporation, or limited liability company, but evidenced only by a contract

between the parties, known as a "joint venture agreement." This document does not necessarily provide for joint ownership of the land being developed. It is a contract stipulating all the business points agreed to between the parties. Each party assumes only the specific liabilities and obligations contracted for, and may or may not share in the land ownership. This arrangement is most common among very large companies who are able to command credit independent of their joint venture partner or the land being developed. Most of these transactions that I have seen are internally financed or financed by other means independent of the land itself. The most common joint ventures occur when one party develops the land and the infrastructure, while the other develops the buildings.

Equity Participations

Equity financing or participation runs the gamut, from one investor providing the required cash, to public syndication. Several common types are as follows:

- Limited partnership

- Private placement

- Land subordination with or without participation

- Land leases

- Public syndication

Limited partnerships, private placements, and other partnership arrangements will be covered in Chapter 16.

Land Subordinations

Land subordination is a type of seller carry-back financing wherein the seller, who is the lender in this case, agrees that his note covering the land will become a subordinate lien to new construction financing. This is, in essence, a joint venture, as the seller's equity is being used to fill the gap in the cash investment required by the construction lender.

Most often this accommodation is seen in the housing industry. The developer pays the seller not only the interest due on the note, but also a profit participation as the lots are sold. This allows the developer greater leverage on his or her money and sweetens the sales price for the seller. In a good deal, both parties benefit. In a deal gone bad, the seller may be forced to step in to cure any defaults on the construction loan to preserve the equity provided by the land loan. This further puts the original seller in the position of having to complete the development to retrieve the original sales price of the land. Failing this assumption of responsibility, the seller runs the very real risk of having his or her sales dollars foreclosed by the construction lender. This happens frequently during a down cycle in the economy, as sellers seldom have the added capital and/or expertise to finish the project.

Land Leases

Similarly, land leases of commercial property involve much the same process. The main difference is that these land leases come in subordinated and nonsubordinated varieties. The subordinated land lease works much the same as the subordinated land loan, except it is used primarily for projects intended for long-term ownership. The lessor (seller/land owner) participates in the profits of the venture as a "kicker" over and above the lease payment. In essence, he or she "participates" both in increases in rent over the base year period of the lease, and the appreciation of the project's value at the time of sale.

The rarest occurrence of this type of loan is the unsubordinated land lease. There are some around, but they are rare; when the landowner will not subordinate to financing, it makes the financing much more difficult, if not impossible to obtain. It places a lender in the position of having to make land lease payments in the event of a loan default, or risk the loan being wiped out through foreclosure of the underlying land lease.

For the landowner/seller, this is the best possible situation: long-term guaranteed income, backed by the lender and eventual ownership of the entire project at the time of the lease expiration. Most often, land leases are for a period of 99 years, but there are a few as short as 30 years. Generally, the shorter the lease, the harder the financing is to obtain. If it is financed at all, it is usually during a boom period, or if the borrower and/or tenants are extremely creditworthy.

Participating Loans

Participation loans are conventional loans that are sweetened to provide lenders with an increased yield on their loan dollars. Reasons for this type of loan are as diverse as the lenders who make them. Often, the lender has a long-standing relationship with the borrower, and in exchange for preferential terms on project loans, the developer/ investor allows the lender to participate in the upside of the projects.

Sometimes the credit involved in the project may be less than the lender's standard for making this type of loan, and the lender requires a sweetener to compensate for the perceived increase in risk. Sometimes the borrower, in exchange for a long-term commitment (say 30 years) will allow a participation to boost the lender's yield on the transaction in years 11 to 30. Suffice it to say that for a loan of this type to be palatable, both parties have to see some tangible benefits.

SBA Loans

Small Business Administration (SBA) loans are bank financing that are either backed or guaranteed, in part, by the federal government. These are business operating loans or loans for buildings using this government program. The rationale behind the program is that it promotes competition, aids in the diversity of business ownership (benefiting minority ownership), and helps to create jobs in the private sector. These loans are not commonly used for real estate investment, except to coincidentally house a company's business.

Loan Renewals

The shorter terms, 10 instead of 30 years, have resulted in higher fees, and some other benefits to the lenders. These loans are more trouble-free. The 10-year due date allows lenders to reexamine the security to monitor its progress, and reevaluate the loan. The increased expense and early due date are offset, somewhat, for the borrower, by the fact that the opportunity to secure new financing raises the possibility of lower rates and increased dollars.

Most property, over a 10-year time frame, will have appreciated considerably. The rents should have risen by an average of 35 percent or more. Increased operating expenses seldom offset this increased cash flow, as the expense increases are passed on to the tenants annually. The resulting dramatic increase in the NIBDS (net income before debt service), capped at the same cap rate as the original loan, would indicate to a new lender that the project is worthy of a greater loan amount. It is possible that all of the borrower's equity could be retrieved through this increased financing.

New Cash

This potential windfall of new financing at a greater amount, generating tax-free cash, can be put to good use. A borrower can retrieve up to the entire amount of his or her cash invested without any tax consequences. This cash may then be used to purchase or build another investment property without the necessity of selling the first investment. It is unlikely that you will always be able to retrieve all of your capital, but the newly freed-up cash will always be useful. Refinancing is always a viable alternative to selling or merely rolling over the loan, and it should be thoroughly explored before taking on other options.

The Exit Strategy

This brings us to another good use for this refinancing. Most buyers who are purchasing a property want to maximize their equity dollars. This is accomplished through making the investment property support the largest possible loan. If you have recently refinanced your investment with the right of assignment, then you have done part of the buyer's job for him. The new financing is already in place. This could permit you to maximize your price by the amount of the possible savings.

Selling Considerations

There are as many reasons to sell as there are to hang on to a property. They all relate to where you are in your game plan. To sell means paying the taxes on your gain. To sell and exchange means starting over with new investment property. To retain the property and refinance provides a means to expand your portfolio without having to suffer any tax consequences. Expansion means more diversity, and by extrapolation, more safety for your growing investment. It also means more work and more attention.

Existing Loans

Your existing permanent loan, if it is one of the old ones, may permit wraparound or secondary financing. A wrap loan is a secondary loan, which assumes the existing loan as a foundation and advances new funds at a new rate. The new lender collects the newly increased payment, based on the combined dollars of the primary and secondary loan amounts, and then disburses to the old lender. The advantage to the new lender is the leverage provided by the existing, lower-rate loan. If the existing loan is at a higher rate, you will not be able to secure a wraparound loan. You will then secure a conventional second at an independent interest rate.

Commitments

Exit strategies should be examined and planned for at the time of purchase. We all know that situations change, but having a plan is a great way to start. If you elect to sell rather than finance your cash out, then you could arrange the refinancing as a commitment on behalf of a buyer, making it available to a prospective buyer as part of the selling package. This could prove to be a very attractive feature, and possibly become a motivating factor in your buyer's decision-making process. The fact that a commitment exists is proof positive of the value of the project in a lender's eyes. All the buyer would have to do is qualify for the loan already committed.

The Least You Need to Know

- There are many different kinds of financing available. You should consider them all before choosing.

- Most likely you will settle for the conventional approach, but if your game plan calls for a more ambitious approach, there are loans that can accommodate your needs. Look for them.

- Financing should be committed with your long-range game plan in mind. Do not be shortsighted.

- Think before refinancing; fit the new money into your game plan.

- Develop an elegant exit strategy, but always consider holding on and refinancing.

16

Equity Financing

In This Chapter

+ Crafting partnerships

+ How to raise equity money

+ Syndication and the SEC

+ Corporations and stock

+ REITs and other mutual funds

When acquiring an income property, especially if you're developing one, you'll need cash for the equity part of the investment. If you regard the cash as any other commodity necessary to create the project, you will find it easier to deal with. Real estate investments are no different than any other investment, with one exception: The security is both tangible and lienable. You can raise the needed equity capital in many different ways. When building the investment, you will find that there is a market for the investment portion of the development team.

The same holds true for purchasing investment property. There are many people who need to and want to invest in real estate who do not have the time and the skills to manage the investment. They must therefore trust their funds to an experienced investor/manager. This is how the REITs came into being. An experienced professional property manager performs the management, while investors supply the cash. Individual investors also raise cash for both developments and investment purchases.

In this chapter, you are introduced to funding sources, public and private. Unless you have a good supply of equity available to you, this chapter will show you where to get it, and what it is worth to you.

Partnership Parameters

As you will remember, there are several types of partnerships. The general partnership is used when two or more active individuals want to work on an investment together. This partnership works well for that purpose. Most pure investors do not want to actively participate in the day-to-day management chores. In this instance, they will opt for the limited partnership role.

Better Believe It!

When negotiating a deal, do not get locked into your thinking. Stay flexible. Explore all possibilities. Do not reject a new idea until you have had a chance to study the concept.

When two or more active partners team up, they generally divide the ownership along one of several lines. The simplest is to prorate the ownership according to their relative cash contributions. The next method is to agree as to their roles in the deal and to assign values to the cash and the management roles. This allows for a disproportionate cash input, as well as a disproportionate management responsibility. There are as many variations on this theme as there are real estate investments.

General Partnerships

The appeal of the general partnership is that either partner may act on behalf of the partnership. This type of arrangement is common when the partnership is formed for a lengthy period, and when the partners intend to accumulate more than one property—it lends itself nicely to an operating company whose intent is to build a substantial portfolio. One partner can do acquisitions and financing, and one can concentrate on management. These arrangements are generally long-lasting and quite successful. Another thing to think about is that without a partner, you might find it hard to take a vacation.

Limited Partnerships

Limited partnerships provide protection for passive investors who wish to risk only their money. They are usually busy people with large incomes who require diversity and tax shelter in their investment portfolio. By making private investments with experienced real estate management people, these investors can realize better yields than if they simply purchased shares in some publicly traded REIT. Most REIT returns are in the single digits, with depreciation sweetening the return. Privately invested funds can earn up to twice the return in development projects, and over time, at least 50 percent more in individual investment deals. The return and the payout differ, based on the type of transaction and the skill of the manager.

No matter the arrangement, how do you go about raising the money if you are strapped for cash? There are two basic methods: private and public.

Better Believe It!

Soliciting money from the public is regulated by the Securities and Exchange Commission (the SEC). Its rules must also be followed when raising money from private sources.

Private Placement Equity Financing

The solicitation of funds from private parties is referred to as private placement.

Private placement is considered proper when funds are solicited from no more than 35 individuals with whom you have a verifiable, pre-existing relationship. The resulting partnership must contain no more than 10 of the solicited investors. The investors must also meet the minimum net worth requirements, as well as qualifying as sophisticated investors. There is a complete prohibition against having "widows and orphans" as investors. With these rules as a given, you are free to raise the required equity.

I strongly suggest that when you are going to be involved with more than one investor, you require the investors to form their own partnership and have the resulting investor partnership become the investor partner in your deal. This gives you only one entity to deal with, and may remove you completely from SEC scrutiny. The best of all possible worlds occurs when investors band together before you have contact with them.

How It Works

The practical aspects of raising money from investors are centered on the deal itself. My background is in creating investment real estate through development. One of the best sales ploys to utilize when raising money is to compare the proposed deal to other investment vehicles. Remember the unique qualities that pertain to real estate alone— instant return on investment, appreciation and tax write-offs, and capital gain or exchange at the end of the deal. One hundred percent of my transactions have involved investor capital, and while each transaction has been different, they all share some common elements:

♦ Each investment involved a specific dollar amount paid into the transaction at the formation of the partnership.

♦ There was an annual, preferred return, based on a fixed percentage on paid-in equity. If the equity was repaid partially, then the return is based on the remaining investment. If the equity is repaid in full, there is no preferred return.

♦ The annual return was sometimes cumulative, but most often not.

♦ The annual rate of return was paid against one half of the annual cash flow.

♦ I usually insisted that there was no return on the investor's equity money during the construction period—the investor's opportunity cost. If there is a cost to the investor (dead money for a year), the investor is more likely to take the deal seriously.

♦ Upon sale or refinancing, the investor's capital was repaid first, before any distribution of profits.

The Straight Skinny

A developer who is qualified for many different skills may greatly enhance his or her entrepreneurial profits through the earning of fees.

While these parameters are generally common to most joint ventures, there are always more added business points to consider. Additional considerations generally involve fees to the manager for management, brokerage fees, and, in the case of a development project, development fees. Since fees can make up approximately 23 percent of a project's total cost, they must be carefully allocated, both by magnitude and by timing.

A Typical Deal

Since there is really no typical transaction, I will outline a deal similar to several that I have created in the past. It starts with locating a piece of property deemed by me to be suitable for development as an income property project.

For this example, let's say that I'm acquiring a 4-acre property for development as a suburban office development. At the beginning, I use my cash to option the property, design the project, and do the required civil engineering to separate the property into three lots. I then entitle the property for use as an office building, a bank, and a restaurant. During this process, I am leasing the office building and locating users and/or buyers for the bank and restaurant pads in front of the office building. When the project is entitled and sufficiently leased, I am ready to enter into an agreement with an equity investor.

My offer to an investor will involve my contributing the property at cost, in exchange for the proposed investor replacing my out-of-pocket costs to date, and agreeing to fund the balance of the equity required to build out the project.

At this point, I own one half of the deal with no cash invested, and the investor has acquired one half in a prime property ready for buildout at a wholesale price. In addition to contributing the property at cost, I have sometimes agreed that the investor may purchase my half of the investment in years three to five of operation at a predetermined cap rate (say 8 percent). This gives the investor the opportunity to purchase my half at a retail price. The combination of acquiring one half at a wholesale price and one half at a retail price still gives the investor a sound real estate investment at a bargain price.

During the operating period, the investor receives an 8 percent preferred rate of return on cash invested against one half of the cash flow.

During the first partial year of operation, the investor might receive all the cash flow and not realize the 8 percent rate of return. In subsequent operating years, the investor receives the first 8 percent, then I am paid the next equivalent amount. We then split the residual cash flow fifty-fifty. In my development deals, using a gross cash-on-cash return on total cost of 12 percent, the cash flow after debt service (the *distributable cash flow*) starts out at more than 18 percent in the first full year of operation. Thus, the investor gets his or her 8 percent, I get the next 8 percent, and we split the remaining 2 percent.

Buzzwords

Distributable cash flow, also known as the net spendable income, is what is left after deducting the mortgage payment from the NIBDS (net income before debt service).

Public Fund Raising Through Equity Syndication

Public fund raising is accomplished by syndication, or the sale of stocks and bonds. Raising funds privately is referred to as syndication if the investors are not acquainted with each other, but the term is primarily used for the raising of money from the general public.

How It Works

A disclosure statement must always accompany a public fund raising by any entity. The SEC mandates the components of this disclosure statement, and in general, must detail the financial projections, as well as potential pitfalls in the transaction. It should stress that the proposed investment involves specific risks of loss. The disclosure form will detail the potential risks, stressing the lack of liquidity inherent in real estate transactions. It will also require that the investor certify that he or she meets the net worth and sophistication criteria.

Bond issues are another way to raise public money and are generally used to create specific improvement districts. The bond vehicle is common in instances when a municipality wants to upgrade an area, or to condemn property for redevelopment. The bonds are assessed against the specific real estate parcels they benefit and are retired by the collection of extra taxes over the period of the bond issue.

Other bonds, issued for similar improvement districts, are tax increment bonds. These bonds are retired by the increase in taxes collected due to the appreciated value of the tax base of the property directly benefited by the bonds. This fund-raising allows cities and other municipalities to raise money for schools, parks, and other public interest projects. Tax increment financing also allows for the development of business parks and other commercial ventures. When the properties are sold and built on, the resulting increase in value allows the municipality to raise the taxes to retire the bonds. When the bonds are completely retired, the municipality benefits from the increased taxation in perpetuity.

Private Companies—Public Financing

Private companies may, with the support of the municipality, use tax increment financing or improvement districts to pay for infrastructure for large development projects. While this is a common way to finance large land development projects in the western United States, it is used primarily for commercial subdivisions where the city has a stake in the creation of additional employment for the community. Municipalities also use this to entice new companies to an area. Their ability to raise money is based on the financial rating of the community. The relative cost (interest) ascribed to the bonds is directly related to the municipality's credit and bond rating.

Common Stock vs. REIT Shares

The sale of common stock is the most common financing vehicle in this country. Large real estate companies reliably use the sale of stock to increase their capital base. Most publicly held real estate companies are primarily involved in the residential housing market. These companies, because of their size, are able to create whole new communities, sometimes in five or six different areas of the country at the same time. They are responsible for the bulk of new housing. Most of these companies are regional, but more and more are building nationally. They pay a predictable return on their equity and show a relatively stable financial progression.

Due to their size and regional diversity, these companies are somewhat immune to local economic problems. It takes a national economic slowdown to make a severe dent in their cash flow. They represent a reliable and conservative investment for the passive investor. Most of these large housing development companies, however, are in the cash-flow business, rather than the investment property business. They do not lend themselves to long-term capital gain. A typical example of this company is the Del Webb Company, recently purchased by Pulte Homes, known nationwide for its Sun City retirement communities.

The SEC and Regulation

The SEC regulates the solicitation and sale of all public investment instruments. Stocks and bonds in all their forms come under its jurisdiction, and real estate companies are treated no differently than other companies when soliciting public funds.

The Cost of Public Fund-Raising

The cost of raising funds from the public is significant. The disclosure statements must be prepared with solid, reliable third-party analysis of the financial projections and exhaustive legal documentation. The large accounting and legal firms that do this type of work are expensive. Due to this, the raising of capital through public solicitation is confined to large amounts of capital, generally in the hundreds of millions of dollars.

REITs

Real estate investments became a factor in the commercial real estate market in the 1970s, with the advent of the real estate investment trust. REITs offered the general public an opportunity to invest in commercial real estate property without the necessity of spending copious amounts of time in the process. Most REITs specialize in specific property types, relying on geographical diversity for conservatism. The most common REIT was formed to buy and hold multi-family dwellings. Large blocks of apartments are a consistent source of income, as young people enter the job market, and as older people are increasingly mobile.

Today, there are REITs that specialize in housing, office property, retail complexes, mortgages, and other real property mortgage investments. There are also mutual funds that purchase commercial mortgages bundled by financial institutions. These funds invest in residential mortgages and commercial loans.

REIT shareholders get an important tax benefit. Unlike a corporation, where the income, less the depreciation, is taxed before dividends are paid to the stockholders (only to be taxed again in the taxpayer's return), the REIT shareholder's dividend is passed directly to the shareholder, with the depreciation to be taxed only in the share-holder's tax return.

What Is It?

A REIT is a public partnership with a managing partner and a great number of investors. The income and tax consequences involved in owning shares in a REIT are the same as those in a partnership. The profits, losses, and tax shelter flow through the REIT to the owners. This makes the investment in REIT shares an attractive alternative to common stock ownership in a company without the real estate benefits.

Pros and Cons

The pros and cons of owning shares in real estate through public companies like REITs are that the rate of return centers around the nature of the investment and the size of the portfolio.

The return on investment is due to diversity and ownership of multiple projects. The managers are paid professionals, not entrepreneurs. In a REIT, the entrepreneurial function lies only in the formation and initial capitalization of the REIT itself.

Thereafter, the properties are purchased from developers or other investors and are managed to produce stable returns.

Due to the volume of properties and the size of the portfolios, the costs of management and the rates of return are fairly predictable and unspectacular. Compared to today's stock market, however, REITs have become a sought-after investment. The higher return on investment commonly associated with real estate investment is found most often in individual, entrepreneurial ownership rather than in publicly funded real estate companies or REITs.

The Least You Need to Know

♦ Smaller projects generally yield a higher rate of return than larger ones, and the number of buyers, when you're ready to sell, is infinitely greater.

♦ Do not take on public syndications lightly. They are expensive and heavily regulated. Make sure the size of the project can stand the added cost of raising the money.

♦ You are better off doing your own thing rather than buying a piece of someone else's deal if you want to learn how real estate investment really works.

♦ In your first venture, I recommend that you consider taking on one or more partners to share the risks and the work.

♦ Take baby steps to a more profitable future. It may sound simplistic, but you should learn to walk before you start to run.

Part 5

Documentation

You might think that investment in real estate involves only dirt, bricks and mortar, and people; the truth of it is that the important part of investing is not the building, but the documents that support the ownership and tenancy. In reality, you are going to buy a pile of paper, and the seller is going to throw the building in for good measure. Find out about the various documents that will determine the health and desirability of your investment. Learn how to tell the good from the bad and how to bargain for a good price at the beginning.

Finally, you will need to know how to improve what you buy. This part will help you set up your management program, define your goals, and deal with loan documents, leases, consulting agreements, management contracts, and the various forms of financial analysis.

Chapter 17

Types of Ownership and Associated Documentation

In This Chapter

◆ The classic corporation

◆ General and limited partnerships

◆ The LLC, the new way to own real estate

This chapter covers the various forms of ownership, the requirements of the paperwork as it relates to that ownership, and the relationships between the parties.

All forms of ownership (except individual ownership) are evidenced by a written agreement between the parties and a notice filed by the public recorder for the purpose of notifying the public of the relationship between the parties. The recordation of the relationship informs the public of the following facts:

◆ The names and addresses of the owners

◆ The name and address of the agent for service

◆ The names and addresses of the managers of the entity

◆ A statement of the duration of the entity

If a corporation does business out of state, most states require that that corporation register with the secretary of state as a "foreign" corporation.

Corporations

Corporations are composed of stockholders who own the company. The company is created by incorporators who gather together to form the company and once formed, to select the managing executives (corporate officers) and the board of directors. The incorporators can become the board of directors, as well as the officers of the newly formed corporation. Most often this is the case.

Corporations go through transitions from small, fledgling entities, to companies the size of General Motors. The typical new corporation is owned by a few people and has a specific purpose. Its capitalization will likely be donated by the original incorporators. The original board will authorize the issuance of stock, and the allocation of part of the authorized stock will be assigned to the original incorporators and investors in exchange for their capital or other equity contribution.

The Straight Skinny

Avoid corporate ownership of real estate investments, as it will lead to double taxation of profits. This always dilutes your return on investment.

There may be two classes of stock: common and preferred. Preferred stock is generally nonvoting stock issued to investors who may have a priority call on net earnings of the company. Sometimes this stock will have the right to be converted to common stock under specific circumstances.

Common stock is the voting stock, and these stockholders annually elect the board of directors and the corporate officers. The officers manage the day-to-day business of the corporation under the guidance of the board of directors. The board has the right to hire and fire the corporation's officers. While mandatory annual reports are made by the board of directors to the stockholders, they have little or no voice in the daily management of the company. Large stockholders sometimes have enough percentage of ownership to appoint board members to look out for their interests. The board members and the corporate officers have immunity from liability unless they commit fraud or negligence in the management of the corporation's business.

The initial statement of incorporation is filed with the state's corporation commission, listing …

- The name of the company, and the address of its principle place of business.
- The names and addresses of the incorporators.

- The date of incorporation.

- The names, titles, and addresses of the initial corporate officers.

- The names and addresses of the initial stockholders of record holding stock in excess of 20 percent ownership.

- The name and address of the agent for service.

Relationships between the stockholders and the board of directors and corporate officers are contained in a document called a Stockholders' Agreement. This document will be modified as the corporation grows and its dealings and management will become more structured and diverse. This will eventually be filed with the SEC when the company goes public, offering its shares for sale to the general public. This document can then be modified by the board of directors with the concurrence of its stockholders at the annual stockholders' meeting.

Buzzwords

A *joint and several guarantee* means that each guarantor assumes responsibility for all of the loans guaranteed.

Close Corporations

Corporations, like all legal entities, evolve from formation to grow or die as the case may be. As they grow, they issue more stock to attract more capital, and the ownership becomes more diluted. Few very large corporations are closely held. A corporation with 10 or fewer stockholders is referred to as a "close corporation." Frequently, when close corporations borrow money, the corporate officers and/or stockholders are required to *jointly and severally guarantee* the loans. The reason behind this is that with so few individuals involved, the officers do not have any watchdogs looking over their shoulders. This is not a hard and fast rule, but most banks seem to require this added protection.

Sub S Corporations

The "sub S" corporation is a hybrid corporation whose tax situation is treated like a partnership. Unlike a regular corporation whose net income is taxable before dividends are paid to the shareholders, the sub S corporation is treated as a partnership with the gains and losses taxed only in the stockholders' tax returns. Once quite popular, the sub S corporation has fallen out of favor since the advent of the limited liability company. In all other aspects, the sub S corporation is treated as any other corporation.

Public Corporations

Public corporations are widely capitalized entities, managed by a stockholder-elected board of directors and an appointed slate of corporate officers. The management slate is voted in or out annually at the stockholders' meeting. Most directors represent specific investor groups holding large blocks of stock. When directors and corporate officers act lawfully and responsibly, they are immune from liability to the shareholders and the public. They are, however, held personally liable for willful negligence and fraud. The only relationship that exists between the stockholders is the right to vote their stock shares. The stockholders' total liability is the purchase price of the shares. In the event of bankruptcy, there is no liability assumed by the shareholders. If, however, shareholders elect to wind up the affairs of a corporation, dissolve the company, and distribute the assets, they will then become liable for any unpaid liabilities of the corporation.

Partnerships

Until three years ago, partnerships were the dominant form of ownership of investment real estate. The reason for this was the absence of double taxation present in the corporate form of ownership and the flexibility of capitalization and management. With profit and loss taxable at the individual partner level, the depreciation aspects of real estate ownership became a prime motivation factor in choosing real estate as an investment. The tax reform act of 1986 changed the depreciation allowance and made real estate less viable as a tax-loss investment, but it left straight-line depreciation to shelter annual cash flow. The new schedule, based on a term of approximately 31 years, allows most projects to provide their investors with some cash-flow shelter. The depreciation is then added back to the profit on resale in a tax maneuver known as recapture. The taxes on income are, therefore, not avoided, but merely deferred.

The major tax benefit is that if you do not sell, or if you exchange one property for another, you can defer the tax consequences indefinitely.

When partnerships are formed, the states require that an document called the articles of organization be filed with the secretary of state.

In general it would include, at a minimum, the following:

- The names and addresses of the general partner(s)
- The date of formation and the expiration date
- The principal place of business

♦ The name and address of the agent for service

♦ A statement of purpose

♦ A termination date

Unlike corporations, which have no finite life, partnerships must have a definite termination date. The date may be extended by action of the partners and a filing of the extension.

Partnership relationships are governed by a document known as a partnership agreement, which sets forth the arrangement between the partners and is not a document intended for public record. It spells out the capital contributions, the profit and loss allocations, dissolution procedures, assignment rights, and management rights and responsibilities. This document may only be modified by agreement of all the partners.

General Partnerships

Partnerships are self-managed. By definition, the general partner is responsible for the day-to-day business of the partnership, and he or she assumes personal liability for all debts and obligations of the partnership. If there is more than one general partner, all the partners have the same joint and several liabilities. Management is distributed between them as agreed. In the event of a disagreement that cannot be resolved, the partnership can, and generally is, dissolved by the retirement of one or more general partners. To avoid the constant threat of dissolution when multiple partners are involved, most partnerships have a provision that allows the general partner to act with a vote of the majority-in-interest of the partnership. If, however, the last remaining general partner elects to exit the partnership, the partnership must be dissolved and the asset(s) disposed of. Where voluntary dissolution is concerned, the individual partners assume any lingering obligations of the partnership upon dissolution.

Limited Partnerships

Limited partnerships are managed the same way as general partnerships, with one important exception. Since the limited partners will not be assuming any liabilities, they are not required to be identified in the articles of organization. The exception to this rule would occur if the limited partner(s) acted to remove a general partner for cause, and assume the management of the partnership. The relationship between the partners in any partnership is called a fiduciary relationship, and it is a legal obligation imposed on the partners by the law enabling the formation of the partnership.

The fiduciary obligation obliges the general partner(s) to treat the other partner(s') interest above his or her own. It mandates honest dealing and timely reporting. This is especially true in the case of limited partners. When a general partner is dealing on behalf of passive, limited partners, the regulations are even more stringent.

Whenever you find yourself dealing on behalf of anyone else's investment, I recommend that you adhere to scrupulous routines that become second nature to you over time. In this I also include lenders' funds. Treat the lender as if it was an investor. After all, chances are that the lender has more money (generally 75 percent) in the deal than anyone else.

You should always do the following:

♦ Create a new partnership or LLC for every transaction regardless of common ownership.

♦ Open a separate checking account for each operating entity.

♦ *Never* mingle cash from one entity to another.

♦ Put all reports and notices in writing—every time!

♦ Respond in writing to all queries, however routine, from limited partners.

♦ Write and distribute a monthly status report (every month), including anything of interest.

♦ Deliberately highlight any bad news in the status report.

♦ Send a copy of the status report to your lenders.

♦ Distribute your partner(s') earnings regularly and on time.

♦ Pay yourself last, and if you are taking fees, such as leasing fees as part of your arrangement, report them monthly.

The Straight Skinny

Most people are lazy, and when confronted with your position will tend to pick up the phone to resolve an issue. Fine; resolve it. Put your version of the resolution in a memo and send it off. If the dispute should ever come to court, you will find that the one with the most thorough, methodical, and complete paper trail will prevail.

Why be so scrupulous? The answer is simple. If the project goes according to plan and everyone makes money, no one will ever read the paperwork. If, however, something goes wrong, you will never have a partner or lender who can say, "You never told us."

Another piece of advice is also a simple one. Whenever you are in negotiations or working on a dispute, put your position and responses in writing.

You will find that if the paperwork and the proper treatment of your partners becomes second nature to you, there will be few surprises that can disrupt the partnership. There will always be the outside influences like the Great Recession of 1989 to 1991, but these events are beyond your control. If you have the confidence and trust of your partners, you will somehow survive. Sometimes there is no solution, but if you follow the guidelines above, you can never be faulted for your treatment of your partners' interests.

The LLC

The limited liability company (LLC) is a recent arrival on the real estate investment scene, and it is gaining popularity in almost all forms of business. Since its advent, I have not considered forming a partnership for a new transaction. One hundred percent of my business and that of all of my contemporaries, of whom I am aware, are now conducted in the limited liability company format. Since its inception, almost all of the states, as of this writing, have adopted one form or another of the LLC.

Its popularity is not confined to real estate development or investment. It seems to have invaded all endeavors with the possible exception of the professional partnerships between attorneys and doctors, who seem to prefer the LLP version.

What Is It?

The limited liability company is a hybrid entity combining the best features of the corporation and the partnership. The LLC offers its owners, referred to as "members," the limitation of liability of the corporation and the tax benefit of a partnership. It is, in practical terms, a streamlined version of the sub S corporation. The variation in regulation and rules for formation will differ from state to state, but the essence is as outlined previously. Some states require two or more members to form an LLC, while some now require only one.

LLCs are either member-managed, or managed by an appointed manager. Member management comes in two forms: by consensus of a majority in interest, or by a designated managing member. The most common arrangement is for the members to designate a managing member. The members do not assume the liabilities of the LLC, as do the general partners in a partnership. All guarantees of loans and other related elements are voluntary. It is only when an LLC is voluntarily wound up that the members assume any residual obligation(s). This rule seems to be consistent for all artificially created legal entities.

The paperwork for the LLC, at a minimum, involves two documents: the articles of organization, and the operating agreement. The articles of organization require, at least, the following recitals for recordation with the state:

◆ The name and principle place of business of the LLC

◆ The date of formation and the expiration date

◆ The purpose of formation

◆ The names and addresses of all of the members

◆ The members' election as to how the LLC will be managed

◆ The name and address of the manager

◆ The name and address of the agent for service

Other requirements may vary from state to state.

The operating agreement is similar in scope to the stockholders' agreement and the partnership agreement. It must contain the following:

◆ Operating rules

◆ Rights and privileges of the members

◆ Capital contributions

◆ Profit and loss allocations

◆ Dissolution and assignment clauses

Upon death or resignation of the last member, the LLC will be dissolved and the assets disposed of. The LLC is also required to have a definite termination date (most partnerships and LLCs are set up for 10 or 20 years).

Benefits and Limitations

In as much as the LLC is a new entity, there is a lack of established case law. It is impossible, therefore, to know with any certainty how disputes and differences will affect the investment vehicle. In general, it seems to be working quite well. In my experience, the LLC feels like a partnership on a day-to-day basis. I have not yet run into an LLC that has employees like a corporation, but as far as I know, there is no reason why an LLC cannot have employees. The problems, if any, endemic in the LLC will evolve over the next 20 years or so, as disputes between members make their way into our court system. The areas of conflict that I can foresee will be in the areas of assignment, profits and losses, and management rights. There might also be some issues with member liability. These problems are similar to those encountered in partnerships.

The LLC is similar to a partnership in the area of assignment of interest and membership. A member may assign his or her rights of ownership, but not the membership rights. For an assignee or a successor in interest to become a member, all of the other members must approve in writing. This does not diminish the assignee's rights to income or profits and losses, it merely restricts the assignee's right of management input. There is no provision in the LLC for a member to have a role similar to that of a limited partner. There is, however, provision within the LLC structure, wherein a member may have a specific allocation of profit and loss that bears no relation to the member's capital contribution.

The Least You Need to Know

♦ Avoid corporate ownership of real estate investments, as it will lead to double taxation of profits. This always dilutes your return on investment.

♦ If possible, choose the LLC as an ownership vehicle. It combines the best characteristics of the corporation and the partnership.

♦ Treat your fellow stockholders, partners, or members as if your interests are inseparable. They are!

♦ Do your paperwork diligently. Disclose everything!

Chapter 18

The Loan Documents

In This Chapter

- ◆ Who generates the paper and why?
- ◆ What are you applying for, and how?
- ◆ What is a loan commitment, and what exactly is being committed?
- ◆ How to understand the promissory note
- ◆ What's the difference between the deed of trust and a mortgage?

Whenever you seek to borrow money for a real estate investment, you will have to understand the process and the documentation. Most commercial lenders are represented by mortgage bankers. The rest are approached through mortgage brokers. The distinction between a mortgage banker and a broker is significant. The mortgage banker represents a fixed stable of lenders, and the relationship is generally a longstanding one. A mortgage broker shops the loan application to many lenders on a deal-by-deal basis. I would always recommend that you start with a mortgage banker, because he will know whether its lenders are in the market at the moment and if they are interested in your type of transaction.

The mortgage broker simply sends your project's information to any lender remotely in the market at the time. The danger in this shotgun approach is that your project may suffer from overexposure. Another problem with dealing with mortgage brokers is cost. You may find that the broker's approach is to take your package to a mortgage banker, who then takes it to his or her lender. The result to you is two fees. To avoid this, you must be aware of the potential problem and retain control over where your package is sent. In addition, you should be very specific about the amount of fees you are willing to pay, and for what.

From Whom and for What?

The first thing that occurs in the loan process is the loan application. It is prepared by the mortgage banker or broker and executed by you, the borrower. The term for this is *originated*. You and the broker are originating the loan application. The most important part of the application process is to determine exactly what you are applying for. There are many types of loans out there and only a few will fit your needs. First of all, you need to understand the difference between potential loans for a development project and those for an existing project. In a development project, there will be two loans required: a construction loan (interim), and a permanent loan (take-out).

Buzzwords

The term **originated** means created by, or applied for by. **Bankable** is a loan commitment that can be readily borrowed against.

The construction loan will be a short-term loan, and will require payment in full within 12 to 36 months. The permanent loan will be for a period of 10 to 30 years. This loan will be a fully amortizing loan, whereas the construction loan will be an interest-only loan. For an existing project, you will be applying directly for the permanent loan.

Construction

Construction loans are most often applied for directly to the lender. Most of these lenders are banks which specialize in this type of financing. There will be one or two in your area, and you can locate them by calling around to them or asking your local mortgage broker. Sometimes, if you are going through a mortgage banker for your take-out loan, the mortgage banker will agree to arrange for the construction loan as well. This is a good plan, as it will ensure that the take-out loan is *bankable*. We'll talk more on that later. Construction lenders today are fairly cut-and-dried about their loan programs. They usually specialize in a specific type of product, and they require significant preleasing and hard cash in the deal.

The typical interim lender today requires break-even occupancy prior to funding; an experienced or well-heeled borrower; and a strong contractor. The loan is funded when the lender's occupancy requirement is met, disbursed monthly throughout the project's completion. The interest rate will be pegged at a specific rate, or float over the bank's prime rate. The bank will collect its interest monthly from the proceeds of the loan draw. Often, the lender will have a third-party inspector, engineer, or professional inspection service to certify the loan draw requests.

Permanent

The permanent loan is, however, a more complicated matter when you are dealing with a development property. This loan will come in the form of a "forward commitment" to be funded two years or more in the future. This time frame imposes conditions on the process that become very specific.

The Straight Skinny

You are asking the lender for a commitment to fund, and in exchange, the lender will impose specific conditions that you must meet before he will be obligated to fund.

Due to the fact that the funding date will be in the future, neither you, nor the lender, can be aware of conditions that may be present in the market at that time. The lender will be striving to make the conditions somewhat vague and open to interpretation.

You want the lender committed to fund, and the lender wants an out if the conditions in the market have been significantly changed by the date of funding. This puts the responsibility on you to make the specifics of the lender's conditions as clearly defined as possible, so they may be clearly met. If any of the conditions are ambiguous, you might find yourself two years down the road with no firm funding.

Better Believe It!

Make sure the language of the commitment letter is firm, specific, and enforceable, if the language of the commitment is too general and open to interpretation, the lender could walk away at the funding date. Economic conditions always change, as do the financial condition of lenders. Under adverse circumstances, lenders in a bind have been known to walk away.

The Application

The loan application is a very specific document, and it will have several, very detailed components. They are at a minimum:

- ◆ The application or loan request, with specific conditions
- ◆ The plans and specifications of the project

- Financial projections

- A leasing exhibit showing current and projected leases

- Financial statements of the borrower(s)

This application will, in general, contain the following clauses in the form of a letter, addressed specifically to the lender:

- A specific file number and project reference

- A deadline date for the application

- Name and legal identity of the borrower

- The specifics on the proposed security and proposed document (deed of trust, mortgage, and so on)

- An application data sheet, including information regarding principals of the borrowing entity, financial condition of the principals, management of the property, additional information on the property, existing debt on the property, and authorization for credit inquiries by the lender

- A statement regarding any loan guarantees offered, if any, or a statement regarding the borrower's desire for a nonrecourse loan

- The terms and conditions of the proposed loan, including the following: loan amount, interest rate, payment terms, impound accounts for taxes and insurance, annual financials, prepayment terms, yield maintenance clause (if any), assignment and transferability clauses, secondary financing provisions, and lender's rights to approval of leases, fees, and costs

- The proposed application fee

- The commitment fee

- Conditions precedent to closing, such as appraisal, environmental report, architect's and engineer's certification, seismic reports, and others

- Broker's role and fees

- Breakdown of costs and who pays for what

- Proposed closing conditions, such as lender's inspection, required leases, documentation list, appraisal, change in interest based on prime at the time, environmental documentation, architectural and engineering report requirement, tenant Estoppel certificates, miscellaneous provisions, and boilerplate clauses

♦ Receipt by lender

♦ Borrower's representations

♦ Additional requirements

♦ The date and the borrower's signature

♦ A legal description of the property

Who Signs?

Who signs this application? You do! As borrower, you will have to qualify for the financing, and your partnership or LLC will have to qualify as well. The rule of thumb used by all lenders that I have ever done business with is that everyone signs. The lender wants all the components of the borrowing entity on the line. Even when the contemplated loan is a nonrecourse loan, the lender wants all the borrowers on the application. The reason is simple. If there has been any material misrepresentation, the lender will have recourse against every one of the applicants. While the loan is nonrecourse, the lender may still recover in the event of fraud or misrepresentation.

Key Elements

The key elements in the application are the specifics of the funding requirement. Make sure that they are spelled out clearly, and that the certifications required from third parties like the architect and engineer are clearly defined and not open to interpretation.

The Commitment

The loan commitment will be issued as a rider to the loan application itself, listing the loan application and the supporting documents as a material part of the commitment document. The commitment will be in the form of a letter addressed to the proposed borrower, and will, most likely, include the following elements:

♦ Acceptance language

♦ Expiration date

♦ Fees required and date for payment

♦ Specific closing date

♦ Additional conditions, such as achievement of rental income not less than a specific amount, and lender's approval of all leases

- A deadline for the borrower to accept the commitment and pay the fee

- Signatures of the lender and borrower with date blocks

- A definition of the effective date of the commitment, usually the date of borrower's acceptance

Bankable or Not?

The big question is, "Is this commitment *bankable*?" By bankable we mean, "Can I borrow construction money against this take-out commitment?" Typical construction financing requires a take-out commitment before it will fund. The alternative is a convertible construction loan, which becomes its own take-out upon payment of additional fees and achievement of the required rental occupancy. There are many commitments issued by lenders that are not deemed to be bankable by interim lenders, and your task is to determine whether your proposed loan commitment is bankable. The easiest way to do this is to have the mortgage banker or broker secure a bank loan based on the take-out.

Better Believe It!

Make your payment of any fees to the mortgage banker or broker contingent on securing both loans on conditions acceptable to you.

Funding

Having secured your commitment for an interim or permanent loan, you will have to close the loan to make the deal viable. You will find that loan closing is a long and laborious process, absolutely essential to any transaction. The easiest way to accomplish a closing is to create a laundry list of requirements and due dates, approved by you, the lender, and the mortgage banker/broker. This will enable you to attack the requirements with diligence.

Better Believe It!

Start the Estoppel certificates immediately; they are the only real problem as tenants are notoriously slow to execute these documents. They treat the Estoppel certificate as a nuisance. They delight in using this as an opportunity to renegotiate their lease.

All the other documentation relies on people who will be paid for the chore. They will be on time so that they will be paid. The Estoppel certificates are always delayed by tenants with an ax to grind, or their attorneys who want to show off. If you start early and nag everyone daily, you will finish on time.

The Promissory Note

Any loan will be evidenced by a promissory note. The note is generally a straightforward document containing the following elements:

- Principal sum

- Date

- Maker and entity identification

- Address of the maker

- Holder's name and address

- Interest rate

- Term

- Payments

- Definition of late payments and charges

- Default interest rate

- The promise to pay

- Partial payment provision

- Acceleration and prepayment provisions

- The security description (deed of trust or mortgage) attached as an exhibit

- Boilerplate regarding attorney's fees, governing law, venue, and so on

- The signature of the maker and the date

There may be more on your note, but these basics will surely be in any note.

Priority

In any loan, there has to be a *priority*. Most real estate loans require that the lender is in what is referred to as "first position." This means that the lender's rights are subject only to the payment of real estate taxes as a priority claim. This enables the lender to step in and pay the taxes to protect the lender's position. If a loan is in second position or a "secondary" position, the lender must step in to cure (bring it current or pay it

Buzzwords

Simply, the term **priority** defines who gets paid first. The lender, in first position, has priority over all other loans and liens, and by foreclosure she can wipe out any secondary debt obligations.

off) any default on the underlying loan (or first loan) to secure the secondary loan investment.

Loans in second position must protect their positions by making payments to any loans with priority over their positions. It is possible to have a number of loans on a property: first, second, third, and so on. Their priority is defined by their date of recordation. The second and subsequent loans are referred to in the lending industry as being "junior" to the first loan.

Secured

Notes are "secured" by the recordation of the loan in a document known as a mortgage or a deed of trust. These documents are recorded as being liens against the property. The purpose of recording these liens is twofold. First, they establish the priority of the lien, and second, they put the public on notice that the lien exists. In this manner, a prospective lender can determine the potential priority of lien of any proposed financing. A typical condition of any loan commitment is the payment in full and discharge of any and all prior liens before, or simultaneous with, the recordation of the new loan.

The Deed of Trust or Mortgage

The names of these security documents vary from state to state. In general, the eastern states use the traditional form of document known as a mortgage. The western states use the new land title system, wherein the lien securing a note is known as the deed of trust. No matter how they are known, the effect is the same. Both documents are recorded as liens, and both documents serve the same function. In states that use the mortgage document, these documents are generally required to be drawn by an attorney. In title states, the documents can be drawn by the title companies that record them. Most lenders, however, insist on drafting the documents themselves. The documents tend to be lengthy, complicated, and non-negotiable.

The deed of trust document is relatively straightforward in its requirements, but may have many interesting extras. The basic mortgage or deed of trust will include at least the following elements:

- The documents, entitled "Deed of Trust" or "Mortgage"

- The account number

- The borrower's name and mailing address

- The beneficiary's name and mailing address

- The trustee's name and mailing address

- The date

- The property's description: location, town, county, and state, address, and legal description attached as an exhibit

- The amount of the note

- The recitals (legalese for the document's purpose)

- The terms and conditions, legal defense, attorney's fees, liens, payments, and so on

- Mutual agreements: damages, trespass, rights of assignment, partial reconveyance, personal guarantees, surrender and satisfaction, and reconveyance

- Additional security, if any

- Default provisions and remedies in default

- Recording authority

- Successors in interest

- Rights of assignment by the beneficiary

- The borrower's signature and the date

These security instruments are common to all real property borrowing and are generally standardized. There may, however, be special provisions that accompany the documents. One of the most common of these occurs when a borrower has more than one property offered as security for a loan. The deed of trust or mortgage is then recorded against all of the properties in question. This form of encumbrance is referred to as "cross collateralization." This ensures the lender that, when any of the properties so collateralized are sold, the proceeds will go to the lender first, before any payment is made to the borrower.

Another common form of special condition is the personal guarantee of the borrower. You will find that this condition commonly applies to loans secured by properties that are deemed to be of special use, or where the collateral is not deemed to be sufficient to secure the note in full. The maker of the note is then required to guarantee the shortfall by his or her promise to pay the difference. If the borrower is regarded as not having sufficient liquid net worth to satisfy the lender, there may be more guarantors required.

The fact is that the lender may set any conditions and requirements that the lender deems necessary to secure the lender's position. The borrower is free to accept or decline the loan and its accompanying terms.

That having been said, sometimes there is a compelling opportunity for profit that is apparent only to you. When this happens, you might be inclined to stretch this rule a little bit. Just make sure that you have done your homework, because when you deviate from this rule, you put more than your investment at risk. You will be risking the additional security, or your own net worth. The problem with guarantees is that the lender is not under any obligation to foreclose the security and collect the difference from you. The lender can opt to have you pay the note in full and leave you penniless and stuck with a piece of problem real estate. Be sure you spell out the lender's rights in the security agreement. Indemnify the lender only from the shortfall.

The Least You Need to Know

- Keep the loan application as broad as the lender will allow.

- Be specific with your terms and conditions so that when you qualify for funding, the conditions can be easily substantiated.

- Read and understand all documents before executing them. This is good advice for any document you encounter in life.

- Do not stretch for a deal; make it stand on its own. Beware the old adage, "Be careful what you ask for, you might get it."

- Be very wary of personal guarantees on permanent financing. Avoid them at all costs. Make the real estate stand on its own.

Chapter 19

Leases

In This Chapter

- ◆ Gross leases and operating expense
- ◆ Net leases are the best way to go
- ◆ Lease structure and enforceability

Leases are the most important factor in determining the value of a real estate property. The sum total of the lease income is what is capitalized to determine the value of a property. In this process of valuation, the building is assumed to be in good repair. There will be no added value for a better than average building, but there may be a downward adjustment of value if the building is deemed to be in poor repair.

The lease must contain the proper tools for enforcement of the collection of rent and the orderly management of the building. A poorly constructed lease may cause more problems than you can imagine. If the lease has no teeth to enforce the timely payment of rent, you might find yourself in a constant battle to collect the rent. If the default clause is inadequate, you may find that you are powerless to evict a tenant who defaults on his on her lease obligations. This chapter covers the evaluation and rationale of commercial leases.

The Importance of the Lease

The ability to properly manage a building and collect rents on time is no accident. Leases must be drafted to provide for all these tools. The tenant's role in this process is to neuter these tools as much as possible to provide him or herself with more flexibility and latitude. You cannot permit this. The only opportunity you will have to set yourself up to have a successful building is during the lease negotiation part of the process. This assumes that you have a good lease to start with.

I have seen buildings with leases prepared on forms obtained at the local stationery store, and I have seen leases that are so bullet-proof that no tenants will sign them. A good lease is somewhere in between. The lease contained in Appendix B is an example of a lease that works well. This lease is one I have used in many different situations for the past 20 years. The copy contained in this book is my latest version. This particular lease was designed to be used for retail, industrial, and office space, created from my basic office lease with added provisions for retail space. It is designed to be a universal lease. I have used it on two projects so far and have not found any obvious problems. *It is not offered for your use without the advice of your attorney.* The purpose of including it in this book is to provide a point of departure for you when you create your own lease. If you would like a working copy of this document it can be found, along with many other working document prototypes, on the document and spreadsheet CD-ROM offered on my website (www.riderland.com).

The primary effectiveness in any lease lies in the owner's familiarity with the lease in use. If you are not familiar with your own lease, you will be ineffective in administering it. The only way to go for someone who intends to invest money in income-producing real estate is to create, understand, and defend a lease for all properties. You will find that merely creating a good lease is not enough; you must defend it during the process of lease negotiations, preserving the essential tools you will need for proper administration of the building. Then, you must administer the lease firmly and uniformly throughout your tenure as property owner.

Gross and Net Leases

Leases fall into two general categories: gross and net. Very simply, a gross lease is any lease that requires the landlord to pay any part of operating expenses, such as insurance, taxes, or maintenance of the building. When the tenant pays all the expenses including taxes, maintenance, and insurance, you have a net, a.k.a. NNN, lease.

All multi-tenant buildings were at one time leased by gross leases. The net lease was reserved for single-tenant buildings. Over the years, through negotiation and local custom, the definitions have evolved. It has come to the point where the true net lease is defined as the NNN, or "triple net," lease. All other leases are some form of gross lease. Some parts of the country include taxes as part of the landlord's obligation in their version of the net lease. Other areas include taxes and insurance as part of the landlord's obligation. Further still, some leases include roof and exterior maintenance.

The Straight Skinny _____

Do not be persuaded that a net lease can contain any landlord obligation to pay for anything except the expenses allocated to vacant space.

For the purpose of your investment, the net lease is only the NNN lease. Do not be persuaded otherwise. All other forms of lease should be suspect and read carefully. Remember that any lease can be modified by negotiation.

Better Believe It! _____

When purchasing a property, you must check for modifications to the landlord's standard lease. Failure to do so will result in severe financial pain later.

The True Net Lease (NNN)

The true net lease (NNN) is, in my opinion, the best lease for both landlord and tenant. The landlord must produce enough money from a building to pay the mortgage and provide a good return on equity. This is accomplished by charging the tenants more than the building's cost of operation. Without profit, none of these buildings would ever be built. Tenants know this and understand. They want to pay as little as possible, and the landlord wants to preserve his or her projected profit.

The true net lease charges rent in two forms: the rent, and "additional rent." The additional rent is defined in my NNN lease as follows:

> All direct costs of operation and maintenance of the buildings, real property, and improvements of which the premises are a part, as determined by standard accounting practices, including without limitation the following costs by way of illustration: real property taxes and assessments, water and sewer charges, insurance premiums, utilities, security, window washing, trash removal, snow removal, costs incurred in the management of the building and property, if any, including

Better Believe It!

The trick in controlling the building's operating costs is to set the standards at the point where the building is properly maintained without frills. Let the tenants order and pay for the frills individually.

administrative overhead or property management fees not exceeding 10 percent of gross expenses; reserves for replacement of machinery and equipment, supplies, materials, equipment, and tools, costs of maintenance, upkeep, and replacement, when required, of all landscaping, parking, and common areas. ("Direct Expenses" shall not include depreciation on the building or equipment therein, loan payments, executive salaries, or real estate brokers' commissions.)

The Big Advantage

In 1987, I decided that the NNN lease was a better deal for both landlord and tenant and wanted to use it for my office buildings. The lender, the broker, and the leasing agent all told me that I could not sell the concept. They were easily proven wrong. The tenants loved the idea. All I did was point out that the rent they paid under a gross lease or a net lease would include all the costs of operation one way or another, and they acknowledged this without comment.

The big advantage and the best selling point of the NNN lease resides in the tenant's ability to directly control some of his own cost of operation; this effectively lowers his or her occupancy costs. In an NNN lease building, the tenant's power (the largest single controllable cost) is metered individually and, therefore, is controlled by the tenant. I simply pointed out that if I was paying the operating costs, I had to assume the worst case (the tenant leaving the lights on at night and running the air conditioning or heating all night and on the weekends). The conscientious tenant would have to pay the same rent as the sloppy tenant. In a net lease, each tenant paid only for the power he or she actually used.

The Straight Skinny

The two biggest problem areas in any lease are timely collection of the rent and the landlord's remedies in default. Other problem areas center on the tenant's conduct within the building and the relationships between individual tenants. There are more potential problems involved in property management, but these are the real standouts.

The concept was further fleshed out to set minimum standards for maintenance and janitorial, allowing the tenants to contract for more services directly with the janitor and other contractors. For instance, we would wash the building windows a minimum of four times a year and more often at the request of the tenants.

The net result of this change in the lease document has enabled me to operate my buildings at an average of $2.00 per SF per year cheaper than my competition. In addition, when the time comes to sell, the buildings bring a better price because the real net income can be absolutely and unequivocally defined.

Lease Structure

The lease is constructed in three parts: the main body, the general provisions, and the exhibits. The main body contains the business points of the lease deal, the general provisions contain the boilerplate, while the exhibits contain specific construction and sign details for each tenant, as well as sample documents related to the project as a whole. Each section will be examined in its entirety, except that the exhibit section has been left out of the book's appendix for brevity's sake. The complete lease and other documents are available in usable form on the CD-ROM available from www.riderland.com.

The Main Body

Article 1 is a summary, and it is intended for use by both tenant and landlord as a quick reference. It contains the following:

- The date of execution
- The landlord's name
- The tenant's name
- The tenant's trade name
- The name of the guarantor, if any
- The lease term and any options
- The minimum rent
- The calculation of the additional rent
- Percentage rent if any (retail leases only)
- The size of the premises
- The intended use of the premises
- Addresses for legal notices
- A list of exhibits

The Straight Skinny

I insist that you realize that this is not a perfect lease, nor is it necessarily adequate for your purpose. It works for me—that's all. The examination of the lease document is intended to make you think about the lease and how it operates so that you may, together with your attorney, construct a lease that will work for you.

Article 2 defines the tenant's premises, referencing the exhibits for clarification, as well as spelling out the intended use of the premises.

Article 3 contains the term of the lease, defining how it is calculated, and spelling out the definition of its "commencement date." It references the exhibit wherein the tenant accepts the premises and acknowledges the commencement date of the lease term and rent payment.

Article 4 deals with the tenant's possession of the premises and spells out who is responsible for what. In this case, it is a developer's lease, wherein the developer has 24 months to deliver the premises to the tenant.

Article 5 deals with the rent: the amount and when it is due, as well as any local taxes pertaining to rent payment. It also details the rent and security deposits collected when the lease was executed. It further spells out the tenant's right to the use of the parking lot. It delineates the rent escalations after the base year of the lease, referencing the exhibit where the calculation is spelled out.

Article 6 deals with the additional rent, showing how the tenant's portion is calculated and defining, by inclusion, what items are included in the additional rental calculation. It also shows how the landlord will account for these expenses and how the tenant can monitor the expense annually. It specifies reporting and adjustments. The important section here addresses the issue of late rental payment and the charges and penalties that the landlord may apply when rent is late. It is specific regarding the tenant's time to cure the late rent before the lease goes into formal default.

Article 7 deals with the tenant's right to assign or sublet the leased premises.

Article 8 obligates the tenant to provide the landlord with specific insurances covering the tenant's premises, including rent loss endorsement.

Article 9 spells out the landlord's obligation to provide and maintain utility services to the tenant's demised premises.

Article 10 deals with the tenant's right to hold over or occupy the premises after the lease expires. It spells out the term of this right and the rent the tenant must pay when holding over. It provides for written notice of the tenant's intentions.

Article 11 is a crucial section dealing with the landlord's rights if a tenant defaults on the lease obligations. It should clearly define what constitutes default and spell out all of the landlord's options. It should be very specific about notices and times to cure the default.

Article 12 deals with the many remedies available to the landlord in the event of default as defined in Article 11. Some of these provisions will be subject to the courts and their laws regarding eviction and bankruptcy proceedings.

Article 13 is the covenant to operate. This will appear in retail leases only and parts of it can be stricken when the lease is used for other applications. It also addresses trash and waste disposal, deliveries, and hours of operation. It may address the issue of competing stores within a certain radius of the site.

Article 14 spells out the (ADA) Americans with Disabilities Act and how it affects the project and the tenant's requirement for compliance with the act.

Article 15 spells out who the brokers are in connection with this lease and who shall pay the commission. It provides for mutual indemnity by landlord and tenant regarding undisclosed third parties to the transaction. It further spells out that this entire transaction is contained in this lease document, with no other representations made by the parties, and that this is a binding and enforceable contract. It states that the tenant has been informed to consult with an attorney.

The section is then signed, dated, and notarized by both tenant and landlord.

The General Provisions

This section contains the boilerplate that is dear to the hearts of all attorneys. It is required by the lenders and will not be the subject of much negotiation, except with very large, national tenants. Your ability to alter these provisions is directly related to the lender's attorney approval to do so. I strongly recommend that you try to leave this section intact.

Article G-1 deals with the use of the premises, and it is here that you may insert any exclusives that you have granted to your tenant. These exclusives should be as specific and narrowly defined as possible. They prohibit the tenant from taking any action that will materially affect the project's insurance rates.

Article G-2 spells out the tenant's obligation to comply with all laws. It requires the tenant to indemnify and hold the landlord harmless against the results of failing to do so.

Article G-3 delineates the tenant's rights to make alterations within the demised premises. It spells out procedures for the landlord's approval, and specifies who shall pay the costs. It requires the tenant to prevent liens on the premises. It further details when and how the work may be done so that none of the other tenants are disrupted.

The Straight Skinny

The Article G-5 clause should be as nasty as possible. You do not want liens!

Article G-4 recounts the landlord's rights to enter and make repairs in the event of the tenant's failure to do so.

Article G-5 deals with liens, who is responsible for payment, and how and when they must be removed.

Article G-6 is the hold-harmless clause. To be effective, this clause must be mutually obligating. It simply states that each landlord and tenant will hold the other harmless from actions resulting from their conduct or that of their employees and representatives.

Article G-7 deals with the waiver of rights to collect on insured losses so long as the required insurances are in force.

Article G-8 deals with the collection and payment of real estate taxes, and taxes on the tenant's specific improvements and personal property.

Article G-9 spells out the tenant's obligation to abide by the rules and regulations of the project as delineated in an exhibit entitled "Rules and Regulations."

Article G-10 is the hazardous materials clause. It is an ever-increasing area of concern by landlord and lender alike. This clause should be as detailed as possible to protect both landlord and tenant from careless or negligent actions of the other. It must mandate absolute compliance with laws and regulations regarding hazardous materials.

Article G-11 deals with the landlord's continuous right to enter the premises to inspect and protect the project and the tenant's premises. It should provide for any actions by the landlord to safeguard and preserve the premises.

Article G-12 provides for reconstruction of the building in the event of a fire or flood or other catastrophic damage. It should spell out who should do what and who will pay for it. It normally says who controls the insurance proceeds until the building is restored. In practical terms, the lender will control the proceeds.

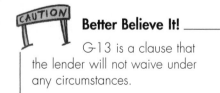

Better Believe It!

G-13 is a clause that the lender will not waive under any circumstances.

Article G-13 deals with the public's right of eminent domain and the potential results to a commercial project in the event of the public exercising its right of condemnation. It offers relief to lender, landlord, and tenant if business is sufficiently disrupted.

Article G-14 deals with the infamous Estoppel certificate referred to in Chapter 12. It will be an exhibit to the lease. This clause must compel the tenant to execute this document, whenever required, in a timely manner.

Article G-15 is a catchall clause that includes miscellaneous provisions such as the following:

- Riders, plats, and exhibits
- Waiver
- Notices
- Joint obligations
- Marginal headings
- Time is of the essence
- Successors and assigns
- Recordation
- Quiet possession
- Late charges (very important!)
- Prior agreements
- Inability to perform
- Attorney's fees
- Sale by landlord
- Subordination and attornment
- Use of the building name restrictions
- Severability
- Cumulative remedies
- Choice of law
- Signs and auctions
- Gender and number
- Consents

It is not necessary to dwell on this article. Your attorney will explain the items in general, and the lender will insist on this article anyway.

Article G-16 allows the landlord to expand the project and move parking and materials around as long as the tenant's ability to do business is maintained. It also contains strict guidelines for tenant parking and the landlord's ability to enforce the rules.

Article G-17 prevents discrimination as mandated by the government.

This section of the lease is then signed by the parties and dated.

The Exhibits

Each lease will require a different set of exhibits, but in general, they will include the following:

- The property description, which will include a legal description, a site plan, a floor plan, and a tenant layout

- The construction specs, plans, and costs delineating both landlord's and tenant's work, as well as the method of payment

- The cost of living adjustment or specific rent adjustment and how it is calculated

- Tenant's acknowledgement of commencement, which the tenant must sign to gain occupancy and which triggers the start of the lease term and the payment of rent

- Sign regulations, as detailed as possible to avoid disputes (this regulation is subject to the permits issued by the municipality)

- The Estoppel certificate

- The rules and regulations

- Special conditions spell out any specific, nonstandard agreement between landlord and tenant including exclusives, options, and additional rights granted as consideration for the lease

Finally, the exhibit section will be signed and dated. Modern leases generally require that all parties initial each page to acknowledge that each party to the lease has read and understood the entire lease.

All of the above will be the subject of negotiation, as was the main body of the lease. The exceptions are the rules, the commencement document, and the Estoppel certificate.

The Least You Need to Know

- The lease is your most important asset, much more important than the building. You must have a strong and fair lease to keep and enhance the value of your investment.

- Write a good lease; you will be living with it for a long time.

- Know your lease cold; that way you will minimize the management headaches.

- Defend the lease against all comers, always.

- Improve the lease constantly. There is no such thing as a perfect lease for all occasions.

Chapter 20

Consultant Agreements

In This Chapter

- ◆ Real estate brokers
- ◆ Architects and engineers
- ◆ Construction contracts
- ◆ Working with consultants

You will encounter a variety of consultants over the period of your involvement in real estate investment, and they require different contractual arrangements. You will find that there are some who do not work with contracts, such as attorneys and accountants. Research and feasibility people, such as surveyors, environmental consultants, and soils consultants, like to work from short, memo-type agreements written as loosely as possible. There are ways to work with these people that will be to your advantage when disputes arise. This chapter outlines the main stipulations and provisions you will want to watch for in your written agreements with these consultants.

On Consultant Agreements

Consultant agreements differ, depending upon which side of the contract you happen to be on. As a consultant, I want to draft a "best efforts" contract, but as an employer, I want to draft a "specific performance" agreement. The main difference between the two approaches is the ability to demand certain results. If the consultant is in an advisory position, or if the contract calls for a recommendation, the employer is in a better position when specific performance is required. A best-efforts contract is just that. Only the consultant's best efforts are called for, not a specific result. The enforceability of any contract regarding real property is tied to the criteria contained in the *Statute of Frauds*.

This may not seem like a big deal, but picture yourself asking a market analyst to find you an unsatisfied niche for your building. Or imagine yourself hiring a broker who says that she can fill your new building within a 12-month period. Would you like to be able to lean on the specific performance clause? It is not the possibility that you could force the consultant to guarantee the results; it is merely that you might be able to force him to add more people to the effort if the work is falling behind schedule. Another solution to nonperformance may entail reduced fees or increased scope of the work to ensure the success of the process. Most consultants specify their own scope of work, so it is your job to make them be as specific as possible. Build in deadlines and perhaps incentive/penalty clauses to enhance performance.

Buzzwords

The **Statute of Frauds** requires that all contracts regarding real property have to be of legal intent, in writing, executed by competent parties, and consideration must have passed.

Leasing Brokers

Leasing brokers always want to have you sign an exclusive leasing contract. They will tell you that they intend to invest considerable time and expense in representing you, and they want to be assured that someone else will not be cashing in on all their hard work.

This is true to a point; take it with a grain of salt. Have them spell out exactly what they propose to do for your project, how much it will cost, and when it will be complete. Ask them about their reporting procedures; put them into the contract, insisting on no less than a written, monthly report addressing all the issues that were included in their proposal. It should include, at a minimum, the personnel assigned to the job, the advertising for the month, the companies contacted, their relative level of interest, and the status of any negotiations.

If you can get the broker to commit to all of the above, then you should be assured of the brokerage firm performing for you. If you have pinned them down, and if you have performance clauses in the contract, then you have the right of cancellation if they do not perform. That is about all you can do to protect yourself. The best way to ensure a good performance is to find a broker who is enthusiastically recommended by other building owners.

Another consideration for the exclusivity issue is competing buildings. If you are giving the broker an exclusive, you can insist that the broker reciprocate by not handling buildings that will directly compete with your own. This is an important issue; do not back down on this point. The reason for this clause is that today, a large percentage of leasing brokers are tenant brokers that represent a certain tenant, or tenants exclusively in a certain area. This does not necessarily conflict with your building, but with respect for that tenant, they have a conflict of interest. If you ask the broker to list as part of the contract all the projects and tenants that he or she represents exclusively, this should clarify the issue. You might find that he or she may be reluctant to do so. Make up your own mind.

In addition to these considerations and any resulting clauses, the exclusive leasing contract should contain the following clauses, at a minimum:

- ◆ The recitals, the owner, the broker, the purpose of the contract, and the location and description of the project.

- ◆ The term of the agreement.

- ◆ The mutual rights of cancellation. Reference the performance clauses, if any. There should be strict guidelines relating to residual commission rights in the event of cancellation. It is not unreasonable to insist that all pending potential tenants be signed within 30 days of cancellation for the broker to have earned a commission.

Better Believe It!

The lease preparation is important, as all your profit and future value is tied up in this document. Do it well; take the time and spend the money to create a good lease.

- ◆ The detailed marketing plan, or a specific date for the broker's submittal of one—specifying that it must be approved by the owner. Spell out the reporting requirements and the details to be addressed in the reports.

- ◆ Personnel assigned to the project and their exclusivity.

- Services to be provided by the owner: tenant layouts, pricing, and so on. Commit to turnaround times agreed to by your architect. Specify any sales materials that you will provide, such as renderings and brochures.

- The publicity and press-release policy. You want to keep a tight rein on this one, as careless press releases can hurt your project.

- A clause that spells out the agent's reporting requirements, the frequency, and the detail required in the reports.

- The sign issue. Include the project sign and any "for lease" signs. Make sure that the agent complies with all laws regarding signs.

- Lease preparation. The typical agent wants a standard lease so that he or she can fill in the blanks. Develop your own project lease. Do not use their lease. Refer to Chapter 19 for the guidelines.

In short, have the broker bring you a letter of intent from the tenant and prepare the lease yourself. Meet face-to-face with the tenant if possible and do the following:

- Spell out the commission schedule, as well as when the commission is payable. In a development deal, it is customary to pay the first half at the start of construction, and the second half when the tenant occupies and starts paying rent. In an existing building, the first half will be paid upon execution of the lease.

- Insist that the agent cooperate with other brokerage companies, and look for proof that he or she is actively marketing your building to other brokerage firms.

- Specify the initial rental rate, and give yourself the right to raise the rate with 30 days' notice. Set down clear lease terms that you want to put into the lease. Set a minimum term lease that you will accept. I recommend no less than three years.

- Specify the dates by which leasing goals have to be met; reference the broker's marketing plan. Insist that these goals have to be met for the broker to retain the listing.

- Address the issue of commissions if the tenant renews the lease or exercises any options. This should not be a commission to the original broker. Renewals are due to your good management.

- Insert the boilerplate, including, but not limited to: notices, change of addresses, owner's representative, attorney's fees, governing law, successors and assigns, severability, and miscellaneous.

◆ Finally, sign and date the agreement, include as Exhibit A the legal description of the property, and as Exhibit B, the marketing plan when approved by you.

Architects and Engineers

These individuals are the most technical of any consultants you will hire. In view of this, you must research their backgrounds and verify their expertise. Get recommendations from people you trust—get references and check with them. Look into their financial standing and make sure that they will be able to back up any professional liability incurred during your project. Insist on "errors and omissions" insurance.

If you are developing a building, the architect and engineer will be on board as soon as you tie up the property. If you are acquiring an existing building, they should be hired to inspect the building during the free-look period. In either case, they are some of the first people to work on your investment. You should do your research and selection during the time you are completing your market analysis.

Better Believe It! _____

Try to get someone local, as code compliance, zoning regulations, and the like are administered by each individual municipality. The consultant's specialized local knowledge and reputation will save you both time and money in the end.

The average architect will want you to execute a preprinted AIA (American Institute of Architects) contract. I do not recommend this, but you will most likely have to use it as a place to start. My normal practice is to amend it by cross out and addendum. I have, over the years, developed a version of my own, which few architects will sign. You will, most likely, have to use the AIA document, incorporating your own modifications.

There are areas that you will need to amend, and they will include, at least, the following:

◆ The scope of work. This is usually an exhibit. Plan this carefully and be specific as to the work expected.

◆ Reproductions and other expenses. Include a basic list of the number of progress prints required, as well as a sufficient number of working drawing sets for permit submittal and for the general contract. Insist that he or she provide you

Better Believe It! _____

Any consultant that goes on to your building site or into your building must have the proper liability and workers' compensation insurance. If he or she does not, and something happens, you will pay for it!

with sepia (reproducible drawing) of each finished drawing, so that you can order your own sets when necessary. It is considerably cheaper.

The Straight Skinny _____

Make a list of the clauses in the previously mentioned contracts that are there for your protection, such as insurance, and so on, and create an addendum that can be added to any one-page agreement you have to enter into with consultants.

◆ Payment should be a flat fee, and extras or changes in scope should be agreed on in writing *before* the work is done, or do not pay for them.

◆ Insist on "errors and omission" insurance and liability insurance. This item is crucial, and it includes you as well, if you have employees. If you deal with consultants only, make sure you have the certificates on file before they enter the site to do work. Include it in all the contracts.

Attorneys and Accountants

These people customarily work on an hourly rate. There are ways to change that, and you need to explore them. Where attorneys are concerned, tasks that can be clearly defined, such as creating a lease document, or a reciprocal easement agreement, or any other definitive contract, can be pegged down to a flat fee. If he or she cannot, then you need another attorney. Other chores, such as negotiating leases with anchor tenants, will by the nature of the task be open-ended. You can, however, control these costs as well. Do your own negotiating, and use your attorney only for advice when you need clarification, or when you require some specific language drafted.

The Straight Skinny _____

Whenever possible, get a fixed price from a consultant, put it in writing, and allow no extra charges unless you approve the work in advance, in writing.

Accountants do a variety of chores. If you permit an accountant to study your operation, he or she should be in a position to quote you annual fees for a variety of chores, such as bookkeeping, monthly accounting reviews, and annual statements and tax preparation. Other chores can be accomplished on an open-ended arrangement.

Researchers

Research work involving the land and the market can also cause you some sleepless nights. These consultants work on informal letter-type agreements, and if they draft them, they tend to be very loose and prone to extras at a later date. The two rules that I always follow are ...

♦ Write the scope of work as broad as possible, and make sure that you tie the final payment to your satisfied review of the work.

♦ Make sure you include enough copies of the finished product (plans or reports) for your use. Add a few extra just in case. You will need them. Make sure that you can order more copies at a fixed price, stated in the original agreement.

Managers

Managers work from contracts, and they are always best-efforts agreements. They should contain some clauses that leave you clearly in control. At a minimum, they should contain the following:

♦ A mutual cancellation clause

♦ The statement that the manager collects the rents, and deposits them into your account

♦ The statement that the manager receives the bills, and approves them, forwarding them to you for payment

♦ A clause that you will never allow cash to be handled by a manager (tenants should be required to pay by check or money order)

♦ An emergency fund to be replenished when receipts are presented

♦ Requirements of detailed, monthly, written reports on rent collection, arrearages, bills and operating expense, and any maintenance or management issues that come up

While you will have to live with a best-efforts agreement, you can make it easier by including the above list; hold your manager to some well-defined standards of performance.

Contractors

Since there is so much money involved in the construction process, these contracts must be carefully drafted and administered. These documents can make or break a project. In general, the industry tries to use the AIA documents, but I strongly recommend against them. My reason is, as usual, they are drafted by architects and attorneys, and therefore, put the architect strongly in the driver's seat as the owner's representative. Even if you are a novice, you do not want to abdicate your owner's prerogatives to the architect. His or her expertise is supposed to be in building design, not real estate investment. Make your own decisions! The architect should oversee and report to you, and you should make the decision. This is true whether you are developing a property from scratch, or rebuilding tenant spaces in an existing structure.

General Contractors

Most people who invest in real estate use a general contractor to build anything. The "general" is the contractor with overall responsibility and financial accountability. He or she will give you a price, and you must make him or her build it as planned for that price. There are ways to accomplish this, whether using the traditional bid method, or the design-build method.

First of all, ask the general to state in the contract that he or she has reviewed the plans and specifications in detail, and that he or she did not find any design deficiencies. Further, have him or her acknowledge that he or she is an expert in the construction method contemplated in the plans, and is competent to review the plans and construct the building according to the plans and specs. Offer the contractor the opportunity to put any deficiencies in writing before the contract is executed, stating that this is the sole opportunity to change the scope of work and alter the price. Discrepancies discovered during the course of construction will be corrected at the expense of the contractor.

Once the stage is set, then the balance of the contract should contain, at a minimum, the following clauses:

- Name of the owner, contractor, and engineer or architect

- The location and description of the site, also shown in detail in Exhibit A

- A list of the contract documents and a detailed scope of work, as further detailed in Exhibit B

- The project schedule, including start and end dates, referencing a detailed schedule in Exhibit C, including incentive and penalty clauses

- The contract price, with a detailed cost breakdown shown in Exhibit D

- Progress payment procedures, including samples of the paperwork required by the lender, attached as Exhibit E

- When the final payment will be made, and under what conditions

- Performance and completion bonds, if any, required

- Who pays for temporary facilities such as power, storage, and security, and who is responsible for stored materials

- Insurance requirements for both owner and contractor (do not permit any work to start until all certificates of insurance are in your hand)

- Work rules requiring safety and drug laws (responsibility is on the general contractor to enforce them, including the expenses of delays due to shutdowns or delays due to noncompliance)

- Rights of assignment, owners' and contractors' responsibilities to each other

- Payment and lien procedures (no progress payment until all lien waivers for the previous payment are attached to the new invoice)

- Arbitration (it's faster and cheaper than litigation for all concerned)

- Termination of the contract for cause (contractor may terminate in the event of nonpayment of contracted work)

- The usual boilerplate clauses, signature, and date

You will find that an orderly, clearly enforceable construction contract will allow you to have a smoother running project.

Subcontractors

If you choose to use a general contractor as a construction manager instead of as a general contractor, you will have to sign contracts with all the subcontractors ("subs") and suppliers. This is a good way to go, as it gives you more control and reduces the contractor's fees. It is a lot more paperwork, but you will find that you can learn a great deal about the construction process if you go through this exercise at least once. I prefer it to the general contract.

The Least You Need to Know

◆ Remember the Statute of Frauds. To be enforceable, all contracts regarding real property have to be of legal intent, in writing, executed by competent parties, and consideration must have passed.

◆ Extend the discipline of proper contracts to all your consultant agreements wherever possible. Make all the agreements consistent, interlocking, and enforceable.

◆ Create the paperwork carefully, and administer it diligently.

◆ The job is never over until all the paperwork is complete!

Chapter 21

Management Documents

In This Chapter

- ◆ The property manager
- ◆ Supplier contracts and utilities
- ◆ The leasing agent
- ◆ Insurance—what you *must* have

Management documents are tools. If they are properly designed, you will have the right tool for the job. Like any other profession, the tools are only just that, tools. You must provide the expertise and skill to be successful.

In this chapter, we cover the management documents you need. We will cover the accounting documents in Chapter 22.

On Management Documents

Management documents start with the property management contract and the tenant leases. To that, as a base, you add contracts with various suppliers and contractors, such as utility companies, janitorial firms, maintenance companies, and other companies that will help you take care of your investment. The following is a list of services that you will need for most property types:

- Insurance

- Property management

- Leasing

- Janitorial

- Landscape maintenance

- Parking lot sweeping and snow removal

- General building maintenance

- Electric, gas, telephone, and water service

- HVAC maintenance and repair

- Window washing

- Security

- Legal and accounting

The Property Management Contract

The property management contract details need to be addressed. If you are going to manage your own property, you won't need this agreement, but if you hire a manager, or have partners in the investment, you will. If you have partners and you are going to be the one who manages the property, you will especially need an agreement. The following is a list of topics most often included in a basic management agreement:

- The duties of the agent

- Collection of the rent, covering invoicing and the physical handling of the receipts, including where and when they are to be deposited

- How to handle delinquency, notices, and so on

- Expenses: how they are incurred, how and when approved, and how they are to be paid

- Personnel, if any: the responsibilities and the authority to act, and restrictions

- Repairs and maintenance, casual and long-term arrangements

- Service contracts: who will negotiate and execute them, and how they will be administered

- Supplies: who purchases, inventories, and replaces them; where they are stored; and who has access to them

- Taxes and insurance: who is responsible for what, and how much insurance each party carries (co-insurance and "additional insured")

- Execution of leases: who can sign

- Leasing: who is responsible and who negotiates for the property owner

- Advertising: how much, how often, and how it is expensed

- Loan payments: who is responsible, and how they are to be accounted for

- Monthly reports: what is to be covered

- Books and records: all accounting, who does what

- Other miscellaneous duties

- Mutual "hold harmless" (mutual agreements to indemnify each other against acts by the parties or their agents)

- The owner's duties to the *manager* (agent)

- Compliance with laws

- Furnish documents to agent so that the agent may correctly represent the owner

- Expenses incurred

- Good Faith Acts (acts taken in good faith do not incur liabilities)

- Insurance: who carries what, coinsurance, and additional insured(s)

Buzzwords

A **manager** is the owner's agent with a clear, legal relationship that can bind the owner, with a legal and enforceable fiduciary obligation to the owner.

- Release of agent: covers acts of the agent in pursuit of his or her legal duties (must release agent from the effects of his or her responsible acts)

- Signage: what is allowed, who approves, and how to administer the sign program

- Compensation of the manager: how much and how it is paid

- Miscellaneous provisions (a catchall)

- Severability of clauses (an incorrect clause does not negate the agreement)

- Hazardous substances indemnity, by both parties (liability follows the polluter)

- Entire agreement

- Successors bound in the event of an assignment

- Independent contractor (clearly establishes that the manager is not an employee of the owner)

- Creditor or claims (how to deal with people claiming obligations)

- Legal proceedings (arbitration versus the courts in the event of a dispute; you must specify which governs)

- Equal employment compliance; federal EEO (equal employment opportunity) law

- Notices to whom and where sent

- The signature and date block

- Exhibits (what they are)

- The property legal description

- Miscellaneous charges (how to handle items not in the line item budget)

- Leasing commissions and renewals, if applicable; do you pay or not, if so when?

Managing the Property Manager

The property manager is an important ingredient in building management. He or she is the face of management, and he or she speaks for the owners. Managers handle money—lots of it—and they have a legally enforceable fiduciary obligation to both owner and tenant. Managers are held accountable monthly and annually. They prepare budgets and rental projections. Often, they are the ones who negotiate with new and old tenants when leases are executed and renewed. It is crucial that this management function in your investment be handled properly.

I highly recommend that you manage your first building. There are several reasons for this. First, you need to know how it is done so that you can properly manage the work of others at a later date when your portfolio becomes too large for you to handle alone. Second, you need an appreciation for the hands-on, day-to-day problems of a good property manager. This will help you differentiate between chores you will reserve for yourself and those you will delegate to the manager.

One of the best approaches to this agreement and all the others you will need is to include everything you need to include and nothing more. Say what needs to be said in a succinct and economical manner in plain English. The simpler the contract, the less chance there will be for misunderstandings. The simpler the agreement, the easier it will be to administer. Just keep in sight that you must build in the tools for enforceability.

> **CAUTION**
>
> **Better Believe It!**
>
> I highly recommend that you manage, at the very least, your first building. In addition, there are several duties that I believe should always be performed by an owner, and they are handling the money and negotiating the leases. These two items directly affect profitability of the investment and its long-term ability to compete in the marketplace.

Agreements with Subcontractors

Contracts with subcontractors, such as janitorial, can be handled in two ways. You can allow the manager to treat them as subcontractors, or you can contract directly with them, while having the manager administer the agreements. I recommend that you contract for these services directly, with the manager's help and oversight. These contracts will have to be year-to-year and mutually severable with short notice. It is important that you be able to get rid of a contractor who is not performing adequately. Generally, one written warning is sufficient. When you have to warn one of inadequate performance, you should start immediately looking for a replacement, and have the new company standing by.

These agreements should address, at the very least, the following issues as briefly and as specifically as possible:

- ◆ The parties to the contract
- ◆ The scope of the work (with an exhibit if it is lengthy or complicated)
- ◆ The compensation and method of payment
- ◆ Notice provisions and severance arrangements, keys, and so on
- ◆ Liability and workers' compensation insurance (absolutely mandatory before the contractor sets foot in the building!)

- Hours of operation, and nondisturbance of the tenants
- Miscellaneous clauses
- Sign and date
- Exhibits, if any

Utility and Service Contracts

Without these agreements, you will not have any services to your building. In many cases, especially if you purchase an existing building, you might be totally aware of these agreements. They are initially entered into by the original developer and the utility companies. They deal with the service to be provided, the date it is to be available, access to the building during and after hours, and any physical easements required to bring the utilities to the building. There will also be deposits required, initially. When you purchase the building, you should provide in the purchase agreement for copies of all the agreements and the deposit schedule. The seller will also want to retrieve his or her deposits at the time of closing. Check these agreements for any obligations you might have to assume at the time of purchase.

The Straight Skinny

You must always check the location of the utility easements, as well as any other easements that show up in the ALTA, or as-built, survey, because they might limit your ability to modify or expand your property in the future.

Do You Need Them and When?

These agreements are almost moot if you are purchasing a building, because most of the subject matter will have already been accomplished, such as the construction of the physical improvements. There may be, however, residual, hidden expenses that you have to assume. Most utilities are responsible for the maintenance of service up to the building meter. The owner is responsible for the maintenance of the service from the meter to the tenant. This might sound straightforward, but be sure where the meter is, and what the potential problems might be. If you are adding to a building, is the utility obligated to expand your service, or will you have to pay for the increase on the utility's side of the meter? These questions are not necessarily handled in a standard manner, and there may be exceptions.

If you are the original developer, these utility agreements are among the first items that need to be addressed when designing your project. You need to have the utility companies involved in the design process, and you need to have them committed to the construction of their work well in advance of your needing the service. You need to draw up the agreements and the easements and execute and record them. The utility companies need lead time to schedule the work, as they have many demands on their time. Plan ahead, and give them what they need, when they need it. You will find that you have little or no leverage over the utility companies, so you must have both your architect and your engineer on top of things if you want them to come out on time. If you do not get on top of this early, you might find yourself with a building full of tenants and no water, power, phones, or anything else.

What You Can Do to Enforce

When it comes to enforcing the utility service and extention agreements, you have little leverage. The best approach is to give them what they want on time. If this does not get the job done, you will have to resort to some behind-the-scenes arm-twisting. All utility companies, with a few exceptions, are monopolies, regulated by the public utility commission. You can approach them for help, and sometimes a word to the wise from one of the local politicians will help. Often, however, the situation is difficult. In areas of rapid growth and low unemployment, utility companies are stretched thin. Their physical and personnel resources are struggling to keep up with the growth and maintain the service to their existing customers. There is only so much they can do. Throw in a bad storm or a natural disaster like an earthquake, and schedules can unravel instantly.

Your best bet is to be proactive. Start early, plan well, and leave yourself a generous margin of time for their work to be completed. Pay your fees early and allow them to get a jump on the schedule. You will find them very cooperative when you take this approach.

The Leasing Agreement

We've been over an exclusive leasing agreement in detail, and it does not have to be repeated. However, in the case of the property manager, you will have to decide whether the property manager does the leasing or whether an independent broker does it. When a property is under development, you need to have a broker handle the leasing, but once the process is complete, you will have a choice. If the broker continues on, finding the occasional tenant when required, it allows the owner to maintain contact with the market, as well as an outside source of talent.

One distinct advantage is that if you maintain contact and a contract with the original leasing broker, he or she will be legally precluded from pirating your tenants for some new building project. Remember, the original broker knows all of the information regarding your initial tenants. Once the relationship is severed, unless you have a specific agreement to the contrary, there is nothing to stop the original broker from contacting your tenants around renewal time. An ethical broker will not do this, because word gets around, and his or her reputation cannot long survive the breach of trust. He or she can, however, do a considerable amount of damage in a short period of time.

As Part of the Management Contract

An alternative to this arrangement is to have the property management company do the leasing. This opens the question of paying for lease renewals. Most owners take the position that tenants will renew their leases if they are satisfied that they are getting good service in the building. Managers are paid to provide good service, and should not necessarily be rewarded when tenants decide to stay on.

In practical terms, I believe that the manager needs incentive to perform in an above-average manner. It is the "going the extra mile" that impresses tenants. Even if your manager does not do that, he or she may still be doing a good job. There is no practical way to contract with someone for going the extra mile, but the possibility of being rewarded when tenants choose to stay in the building is a great incentive. You do not have to pay your manager a full commission, as he or she has a captive audience and an advantage over another agent trying to steal the tenant. You can pay one third to one half of a commission for renewals, and most managers would be happy with the extra compensation.

As far as giving the manager the exclusive right to lease the building is concerned, this is another question. The manager must have a full-service brokerage house (one that offers sales and leasing as part of its services) affiliated with the management entity for you to consider this. Unless an agent is out in the marketplace, he or she is unlikely to have the contacts to keep up a steady stream of tenants. It is the day-to-day knowledge of the market and the constant contact with the potential tenants that keeps a building full.

Remain as Independent as Possible

How do you attempt to reconcile this dilemma? It depends on your goals. First, I believe that it is mandatory to maintain contact with the active leasing community, because you will, one day, want to expand your holdings or sell the building. You should ally yourself, whether you're building or buying, with a brokerage company that provides both leasing and investment services. This way, you will have a healthy, ongoing agency relationship that offers you a good resource and protection from raids from the company's employees. Your exclusive arrangement is with the company, and binds all its employees. In addition, you will have the most up-to-date information on market rents and trends in the rental industry. Your broker can keep you up-to-date on all movement in the marketplace. He or she will be in a position to advise you when the optimum time to sell occurs.

At the same time, you need a harmonious arrangement with your management company. The solution, as I see it, is simple. Give the broker an exclusive on new tenants, and give your manager a commission on renewals. Give your broker the right to resell the building when the time comes, as an incentive, and contingent with his or her keeping your building full and up to market rents. A good solution is one that all parties benefit from. The broker will be placated for not having renewal commissions by being able to earn the right to resell, and the manager will be happy with the commission on renewals. You will have ended up with the best of both.

Insurance

Insurance in any transaction is critical. There are two kinds of insurance that everyone must have when working on your property, including you. They are liability and workers' compensation insurance. There are other insurances necessary when dealing with specialized consultants, like errors and omission insurance and so on, but everyone needs liability and workers' comp to cover their potential liabilities.

Liability insurance insures you from injuries that happen to third parties. If someone trips and falls down your stairs, you're covered. Workers' compensation insurance, even if you do not have employees, covers you when anyone doing work on your building is hurt.

As an owner, you will need the following insurance to operate the building:

- ◆ If you are building, you will need course of construction, fire and extended coverage, workers' compensation, and liability umbrella insurance.

♦ As an owner operating a building, you will need fire and extended coverage, and rent replacement insurance with a workers' compensation rider. I also always recommend an umbrella override policy.

Rather than have everyone connected with the development or management of a building carry redundant coverage, you can buy and maintain the master policy, naming all the other entities as "additional insured(s)" to your policy. The other companies in question can then pass along the savings to you and lower your insurance costs.

If you are constructing the building, you will find that this option will save you thousands of dollars.

The Least You Need to Know

♦ Pick your building manager carefully. At least for the first deal, manage the building yourself. You cannot buy the experience you will gain. It will serve you well in the future.

♦ Write the management agreement carefully, succinctly delineating the responsibilities and obligations. Clarity is important in all agreements, but remember, the manager is your agent and can bind you legally.

♦ Keep a contract going with the original leasing broker. This way you can stay on top of the market at all times. This will ensure that your building stays competitive at all times.

♦ Keep the documents simple and unequivocal; they will be easier for everyone to use and follow. Keep them enforceable.

Chapter 22

The Numbers

In This Chapter

- ◆ Understand the various forms of accounting
- ◆ Make the numbers meaningful and useful to you
- ◆ There are different tools for different purposes

Whether developing, purchasing, or managing investment real estate, your second batch of tools is what is known in the business as "the numbers." Numbers include formal accounting reports, bookkeeping, and spreadsheets. Collectively, they can tell you at a glance what is going on with your investment. In this chapter we'll take a look at these tools.

As a developer, my only measure of a deal has been the cash-on-cash rate of return analysis. Most investors are horrified by this simplistic approach. They customarily want to see the internal rate of return, the after-tax yield, or a present worth analysis. My criteria, developed for my own use, tells me what I want to know: that is, whether I'm making money, and how much I am making as a percentage of the cash invested. Since I am accustomed to working with investors, I am concerned about achieving, at a minimum, the yields that I have represented to the investors as possible for that particular transaction.

In addition, since I only get paid after the investors do, I need to closely monitor the transaction to judge how my investment (in time) is paying off. A simple monthly look at the cash-on-cash rate of return tells me what I want to know.

Gathering and Presenting Data

There are two different types of data gathering and presentation systems: accounting and spreadsheets.

Accounting

Accounting is a uniform system based on double-entry bookkeeping. This means that any transaction has two sides (debits and credits) that need to be balanced on the books. For example, $1,000 of rental income would be entered into the ledger in two ways: on the one side, it is entered as rental income, and on the other side as cash in the bank. When $1,000 is entered on both sides of the ledger, the entry is "balanced." By keeping the ledgers in balance, the accountant can verify quickly that the transactions are properly entered. It is possible to mislabel a transaction on one side of the ledger, but this will show up during a trial balance. The accountant can then correct the error and "balance the books."

The results of this type of figure gathering and presenting are reports that are uniformly accepted as standard worldwide. This system can be used to generate reports, such as earnings statements, trial balances, financial statements, and month-to-month or year-to-year comparison reports. The data from these reports tell you what the overall picture is, and are necessary for the filing of income taxes and other required functions in the business world. These are good tools, but limited in what they can tell you about a particular investment.

Spreadsheets

The second system is known as spreadsheets, and these documents are designed to tell you what you need to know at a glance. They answer questions such as:

- ◆ What suite is Jones manufacturing in, and what is its rent?
- ◆ Who has not yet paid his or her rent this month?
- ◆ What will our income be at this time next year, or in five years?
- ◆ When is the next lease expiration going to occur, whose is it, and how much space will be available?

◆ How much could we raise the rent and still stay competitive in the market?

◆ Are our expenses going up or holding on a per-square-foot basis?

◆ How do our expenses compare to the competition, or to the market as an average?

◆ How do I determine the rent invoices for this month?

◆ When do our maintenance contracts expire?

In looking at these questions, you can see why spreadsheet information is valuable to a building manager. Imagine having to look in all the leases for the answers each time you have a question. Imagine having to go through the accounting reports to ferret out the data. These types of questions come up routinely every day in the management business.

If, as you process the data, you enter it into both systems at the same time, you will find that you are always up-to-date. The big trick is to enter the data in a timely fashion. If you accumulate the data and enter it periodically (monthly), then you will have to wait for the results until you are finished, and you will have a great deal of data to enter all at once. This will be frustrating, and can lead to mistakes. If, on the other hand, you enter the data as it arrives on your desk, you will always be current.

Spreadsheets are designed to be graphically and intrinsically informative. With basic accounting, if you enter the rent received from Jones, it goes into rental income and cash in the bank. The result, when you run a trial balance report, is that you can see the total rent received and your total bank balance. Informative, yes, but not totally so.

Look at the same transaction on a spreadsheet, and at a glance, you can see which tenants have paid and which have not. The same information is presented, but it answers a different set of questions.

To do your job properly, you need both types of information.

Accounting Documents

Sample accounting documents are shown here. They are the trial balance, the income statement, and the financial statement. These will be automatically generated by your computerized accounting system. Today's accounting packages, even for small business concerns, have increased capabilities. You should examine what is available and consult with your accountant. There are some that can export spreadsheets and save you having to generate them separately. No matter how you get the information, you will need it all to properly manage the project.

Typical company trial balance.

C & R Contractors LLC
Trial Balance (Cash Basis)   As At 12/31/98

	Debits	Credits
4053 TI Reimbursements	-	0.00
4055 Other Rental Income	-	0.00
4400 Interest & Finance Charge Income	-	325.08
4410 Miscellaneous Income	-	0.00
4500 Returns & Allowances	-	0.00
5010 Contracting Costs	226,279.22	-
5011 insurance & Bonds	2,585.00	-
5012 Other Contracting Costs	0.00	-
5050 Building Rent	2,667.94	-
5051 Taxes	0.00	-
5053 Insurance	-	590.00
5054 Utilities	0.00	-
5059 Management Fees	0.00	-
5500 General & Administrative Expenses	311.25	-
5510 Telephone	802.39	-
5530 Repairs & Maintenance	0.00	-
5540 Operating Supplies	160.06	-
5550 Guaranteed Pmts to Memebers - SLR	0.00	-
5551 Guaranteed Pmts to Memebers - BK	0.00	-
5610 Office Supplies & Postage	124.24	-
5620 Other Office Expense	73.60	-
5660 Bank Charges	44.85	-
5680 Office Salaries	0.00	-
5690 Payroll Taxes	0.00	-
5700 Insurance - General	-	637.72
5710 Insurance - Health	0.00	-
5750 Legal & Accounting	668.00	-
5771 Meals & Entertainment	0.00	-
5772 Mileage/Auto Allowance	0.00	-
5773 Travel	0.00	-
5780 Education & Training	0.00	-
5800 Dues & publications	0.00	-
5810 Permits & Fees	320.00	-
5850 Other Taxes & Licenses	0.00	-
5900 Depreciation expense	0.00	-
5920 Interest Expense	0.00	-
5950 Miscellaneous Expense	0.00	-
5970 Penalties & Fines	0.00	-
	446,883.34	446,883.34

Standard income statement.

C & R Contractors LLC
Income Statement (Cash Basis) 1/1/98 to 12/31/98

REVENUE

OPERATING REVENUE

Contracting Income		346,113.43
Rental Income		0.00
Total Rental Revenues		0.00
Interest & Finance Charge Income		325.08
Total Revenues		346,438.51

TOTAL REVENUE 346,438.51

EXPENSE

COSTS AND EXPENSES

Contracting Costs		226,279.22
Insurance & Bonds		2,585.00
Building Rent		2,667.94
Insurance	-590.00	
Total Common Area Costs		-590.00
General & Administrative expenses		311.25
Telephone		802.39
Operating Supplies		160.06
Office Supplies & Postage		124.24
Other Office expense		73.60
Bank Charges		44.85
Insurance - General		-637.72
Legal & Accounting		668.00
Permits & Fees		320.00
Total G & A Expense		232,808.83

TOTAL EXPENSE 232,808.83

NET INCOME 113,629.68

Company balance sheet.

```
C & R Contractors LLC
Balance Sheet (Cash Basis)   As At 12/31/98

ASSETS
          CURRENT ASSETS
                    Cash in Bank of America                1,193.99
          Total Current Assets                             1,193.99

          Construction in Progress
                    Total Land-Bldg                            0.00
                    Total Soft Costs                           0.00
                    Hard Costs                                 0.00
                    Total Hard Costs                           0.00
          Total Costs-Bldg A                                   0.00

          Building B
                    Total Land                                 0.00
                    Soft Costs                                 0.00
                    Total Soft Costs                           0.00
                    Hard Costs                                 0.00
                    Total Hard Costs                           0.00
          Total Building B                                     0.00

          Fixed Assets
                    Office Furniture & Equipment   2,077.97
                    Office Furn & equip - net                  2,077.97
                    Machinery & equipment          0.00
                    Accum Depr-Mach & Equip        0.00
                    Machinery & Eq-net                         0.00
          Total Fixed Assets                                   2,077.97

          Other Assets
                    Refundable Deposits                        2,186.00
                    Organization Expense                         192.00
                    Suspense                                    -203.37
          Total Other Assets                                   2,174.63

TOTAL ASSETS                                                   5,446.59

LIABILITIES
          CURRENT LIABILITIES
                    Payroll Taxes Payable                        0.00
                    Sales Tax Payable                         -8,661.57
          TOTAL CURRENT LIABILITIES                           -8,661.57

          LONG-TERM LIABILITIES
                    Notes Payable                                0.00
          TOTAL LONG-TERM LIABILITIES                            0.00

TOTAL LIABILITIES                                             -8,661.57

EQUITY

          MEMBERS' EQUITY
                    Member Capital                            69,013.74
                    Capital-Marvin Class                      15,000.00
                    Capital-Stuart Rider                      15,000.00
                    Distributions S.L.Rider                  -99,285.26
                    Distributions M.&.B.Class                -99,250.00
                    Current Earnings                         113,629.68
          Total Member Equity                                 14,108.16

TOTAL EQUITY                                                  14,108.16

LIABILITIES AND EQUITY                                         5,446.59
```

How to Create Spreadsheets

Any accounting process is standard, however, you must create your own spreadsheets, based on what you want to know. Let's start with basic tenant information.

To ascertain what you want to know about a tenant, start with a list of tenants in a column, arranged either alphabetically or by location in your building, or any other way that makes sense to you.

The next chore is to place categories of information you want to know horizontally, in line with the tenant in question. It will look something like the following table.

Tenant List	Suite Number	SF	Rent	Exec Date
Tenant One				
Tenant Two				
Tenant Three				

The Straight Skinny

Since you are only going to do this once, and you are going to use the results of this data-gathering monthly, get it right the first time. Check it, and then check it again, before finalizing the spreadsheet!

In this way you can see what is happening. A visual tool is evolving. Data that is buried in the lease document is being set up for instant reference without the need of further reference to the actual lease document. If you create the horizontal list in enough detail, you should never have to refer to the lease again. Obviously, in the event of default on a lease, you will want to refer to the legal questions addressed in certain clauses, but for management purposes, you will be prepared.

What You Always Need to Know

There are three types of information: basic information, monthly historical information, and projections. The spreadsheet shown on the previous page is an example of the basic information needed to create the other documents. From this start, all of your other information will be derived. What information do you need about each tenant? My list, evolved over a 25-year period, is relatively simple. It is created in the order in which I execute the leases, but you can choose your own order. It contains the following data in columns:

- Tenant name

- Contact person

- Street address

- Suite number

- City

- Zip code

- Suite number in my building

- Phone number

- Fax number

- E-mail address

- Number of square feet

- Date lease executed

- Expiration date of lease

- Rent escalation date

- Percent escalation

- Renewal options, if any

- Notes (rights of first refusal on contiguous space, and so on)

At the bottom of my columns, I have a row of totals that can be used to calculate percentages. In the following row, I express the results as percentages of the total. I also keep track of vacant spaces in the tenant column, by substituting the word "Vacant" for the previous tenant's name, so that I can know instantly what percent vacancy I am at any given moment.

Your next question might be: "Why have the address if they are in my building?" The answer is that the tenant may be a branch office for a larger company, and I need to know where to send the rent invoice and any legal notices.

Examples of Other Spreadsheets

From this spreadsheet, I can create all the other forms that I will need. In a modern building, you will need to keep track of rent and expenses. Before you create the rent sheet, you will need to create a master expense form as shown.

Monthly expense breakdown.

Expenses	Monthly	January
Actual Paid to date	Budget	$ 1,998.00
Real estate Taxes	$ 2,000.00	$ -
Maintenance/Repair/HVAC	$ 150.00	$ -
Insurance fire / liability	$ 551.58	$ 3,120.00
Elect	$ 300.00	$ 403.70
Water & Sewer	$ 200.00	$ -
Refuse	$ 51.00	$ 51.00
Janitorial	$ 1,300.00	$ 1,329.55
Windows / sweeping	$ 200.00	$ 210.00
Security	$ 360.00	$ -
Pest Control on demand	$ 75.00	$ -
Yard Maint & Common Area	$ 200.00	$ 200.00
Subtotal	$ 5,387.58	$ 5,314.25
Management Fee	$ 538.76	$ 531.43
Total Common Area	$ 5,926.34	$ 5,845.68
Average / month / SF	$ 0.36	$ 0.35

Tenant Pro Rata shares	% cam	1 st. Qtr.
Tenant # 1	8%	$ 461.81
Tenant # 2	16%	$ 931.22
Tenant # 3	12%	$ 720.19
Tenant # 4	4%	$ 224.83
Etc.	24%	$ 1,402.96
Vacant	36%	$ 2,104.44
Totals	100%	$ 5,845.45

Other spreadsheets can now be constructed from these two. The first one you will need is for income and expense monitoring. Using the tenant list from the tenant data sheet and some rental data we can extrapolate, we can come up with a sheet that can be used for rental invoicing and rent collections. It will look something like the following table.

Tenant	From Tenant Sheet		From Expense Sheet		Total Invoice	Month	
	# SF	Rent	% Occ.	% Expenses		Invoiced	Collected
Tenant # 1	800	$ 800.00	8%	$ 461.81	$ 1,261.81	$ 1,261.81	$ 1,261.81
Tenant # 2	1600	$ 1,600.00	16%	$ 931.22	$ 2,531.22	$ 2,531.22	$ 2,531.22
Tenant # 3	1200	$ 1,200.00	12%	$ 720.19	$ 1,920.19	$ 1,920.19	$ 1,920.19
Tenant # 4	400	$ 400.00	4%	$ 224.83	$ 624.83	$ 624.83	
Etc.	2400	$ 2,400.00	24%	$ 1,402.96	$ 3,802.96	$ 3,802.96	$ 3,802.96
Vacant	3600		36%				
Totals	10000	$ 6,400.00	100%	$ 3,741.01	$ 10,141.01	$ 10,141.01	$ 9,516.18

Rent invoicing and collection.

At a glance, you can see that 36 percent of the building is vacant, and this month you have invoiced $10,141.01 of rent, and only Tenant 4 has not yet paid the rent. This particular table can then be expanded to include the total year with quarterly summaries if needed. Extrapolating that, you can then start comparing year-to-year and month-to-month, if you choose.

Similarly, you can then create projections to show when leases will expire by editing the tenant information sheet and showing it over a period of time: monthly, quarterly, or annually. It will look something like the following spreadsheet.

Five-year income and expense projection　　　　　　　　　Leasable space 16,000 sf with rent escalation annual @ 5%

INCOME	NOTES	Year 1	Year 2	Operating Period Year 3	Year 4	Year 5
Gross Potential Income [GPI]	At 100 % Occupancy @ $14.00 / sf	$224,000.00	$235,200.00	$246,960.00	$259,308.00	$272,273.40
Vacancy Allowance @ 5 %	Per Lender's allowance	-$11,200.00	-$11,760.00	-$12,348.00	-$12,965.40	-$13,613.67
Effective Gross Income [EGI]	Projected EGI	$212,800.00	$223,440.00	$234,612.00	$246,342.60	$258,659.73
CAM EXPENSES	**All Leases are NNN**					
Real estate Taxes	Projected until first assessment	$24,000.00	$25,200.00	$26,460.00	$27,783.00	$29,172.15
Maintenance/Repair/HVAC	Budgeted	$1,800.00	$1,890.00	$1,984.50	$2,083.73	$2,187.91
Insurance fire / liability	Bid	$6,612.00	$6,942.60	$7,289.73	$7,654.22	$8,036.93
Elect	Estimated	$3,600.00	$3,780.00	$3,969.00	$4,167.45	$4,375.82
Water & Sewer	Estimated	$2,400.00	$2,520.00	$2,646.00	$2,778.30	$2,917.22
Refuse	Bid	$600.00	$630.00	$661.50	$694.58	$729.30
Janitorial	Bid	$15,600.00	$16,380.00	$17,199.00	$18,058.95	$18,961.90
Windows/sweeping	Bid	$2,400.00	$2,520.00	$2,646.00	$2,778.30	$2,917.22
Security	Bid	$4,320.00	$4,536.00	$4,762.80	$5,000.94	$5,250.99
Pest Control on demand	Estimated	$900.00	$945.00	$992.25	$1,041.86	$1,093.96
Yard & Common Area Maintenance	Bid	$2,400.00	$2,520.00	$2,646.00	$2,778.30	$2,917.22
Subtotal		$64,632.00	$67,863.60	$71,256.78	$74,819.62	$78,560.60
Management Fee @ 10% exp. Of CAM	Based upon actual expenses only	$6,463.20	$6,786.36	$7,125.68	$7,481.96	$7,856.06
Total Common Area [CAM]		$71,095.20	$74,649.96	$78,382.46	$82,301.58	$86,416.66
Tenent reimbursed CAM	Based on 95 % occupancy	$67,540.44	$70,917.46	$74,463.34	$78,186.50	$82,095.83
Net Landlords Expense	For Vacant Space	-$3,554.76	-$3,732.50	-$3,919.12	-$4,115.08	-$4,320.83
Net Income Before Debt service [NIBDS]	Before Debt service	$209,245.24	$219,707.50	$230,692.88	$242,227.52	$254,338.90
Less Mortgage	Based upon estimated loan					
	1.3 M @ 8 % 30 years	-$103,311.00	-$103,311.00	-$103,311.00	-$103,311.00	-$103,311.00
CASH FLOW	Return on Investor's Equity	$105,934.24	$116,396.50	$127,381.88	$138,916.52	$151,027.90

Five-year rent projection.

By studying the table, you will see that this is an income projection for a development project with several assumptions shown in the "notes" column. The income and expenses are escalated at 5 percent per year. This is acceptable when projecting a proposed cash flow. When you are dealing with actual leases, you will have to break down each year, by month, to show when the individual leases expire or escalate. This way, your projection will accurately reflect the executed leases. The year-end totals are then transferred to a master sheet for 5- and 10-year projections.

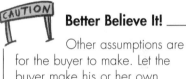

Better Believe It!

Other assumptions are for the buyer to make. Let the buyer make his or her own assumptions!

Making Projections: Spreadsheets as Sales Tools

These examples of spreadsheets are considered management tools. However, when you are preparing your project to sell, you must convert your game plan to projections that will show your project in its most favorable light. This is not an opportunity to gild the lily, but rather to make your best projection based on market data updated at the time of sale. If, for instance, you have been deliberately keeping your renewals below market to make sure that your vacancy was minimized, change the projections starting on the next renewal or expiration date to reflect the projected market rates at the time. This will accurately reflect where the project is headed if the buyer keeps the project at market value when renewals or new tenants are signed.

The Least You Need to Know

- ◆ Research and understand a good accounting system. There are many software packages available today; pick a simple one that may be expanded to multiple properties. Find one that has been in use for a while.

- ◆ Generate your own spreadsheets. If you do, then you will understand them thoroughly, and they will contain the information you want to see.

- ◆ Be accurate. Sloppy preparation will cause financial losses every time. It may also leave you open to liability for mismanagement.

- ◆ Remember, when creating these spreadsheets: "Garbage in leads to garbage out." Be accurate and check everything twice.

Part 6

Managing Your Investment

This part reveals the origination of a viable game plan, and concludes with preparing the property for sale when you are done with it. It deals with your management system, the tenants, the consultants, and managing the leases and improving them, as well as collecting the rent and managing your money.

It will walk you through setting up and administering reserves, and why you will need them. It shows how to truly have the tenants pay 100 percent of the expenses of operation. It will guide you through improving your leases for resale or refinancing, as well as how to work with your attorney to create the perfect lease.

It deals with accounting and spreadsheet creation, as well as cash flow management. It will show you (together with your accountant) how to create the necessary management tools and maximize their usefulness.

A typical property manager in action

23

Where to Start?

In This Chapter

- ◆ Should you manage your own property?
- ◆ What tools will you need?
- ◆ Project versus partnership costs
- ◆ Maximizing your investment

Now that you have made your decision to purchase a specific piece of real estate, who is going to manage it? The answer depends upon your circumstances and the size and complexity of your purchase. If you are starting out with a second home rental, or a small four plex of apartments, the time required for management is minimal. I would always recommend that you manage the property yourself. If, however, you and your partners have pooled your resources and purchased a 50,000 SF office building, then the management is going to entail some more work, and you will need to evaluate the time necessary, and the nature of the management chores. This chapter will help you do just that, as well as equip you with the tools you need to get started in either case.

Who Should Manage This Thing?

When you make your first purchase, you will be afflicted with buyer's remorse and self-doubt. This is natural, as you have just launched yourself into the great unknown. There is something about starting out into the unknown that takes all of us aback. The large decision to make a significant investment and the irretrievable act of purchasing a property can be heart-stopping, but only momentarily. You now have a second decision —who is going to manage it for you?

Owner-Managed Property

If you have a job that requires your attention 60 to 80 hours per week, it is not in the cards for you to manage the property on a day-to-day basis. But perhaps one of your partners can do it. Owner-managed property seems to run more smoothly, simply because owners spend the extra time and care more about the results. Employees have a different threshold of care than entrepreneurs.

CAUTION

Better Believe It! _____

Do not fear. Take a deep breath and think. Go back and review the process you went through to get to this point. Remember all you have learned about the market and your property in particular. This will start the blood flowing again to the brain.

If you are part of a group that made the purchase, you might consider splitting up the chores, appointing one member to be the "face" or the contact person with the tenants, and another to do the bookkeeping, invoicing, and rent collection. A third might be the handy type, who could become the one to oversee the maintenance and upkeep of the property, as well as supervision of the tenant improvement renovations required to keep the investment going. This is an ideal solution, as you will be learning the ins and outs of the business, hands on.

Third-Party Managers

If you are all 70-hours–per-week people, then you will have to turn to a third-party manager. How do you select the perfect candidate? You might start out by conferring with the broker who helped you buy the property, as well as talking to any of the other professionals that you encountered in the process. If you used an investment broker, you might ask her for a recommendation. Ask which properties he or she thinks are the best of their kind in your market area, and find out who manages them.

If you are going to hire a manager, I recommend that you start the selection process during the evaluation process. A manager should be involved in the inspection and selection decision early on. An experienced manager is in a position to point out some flaws and pitfalls in the investment property, as well as suggest some long-term management strategies for improving the property. A seasoned professional manager is a known quantity, and should be able to deliver almost as good a management effort as a motivated owner. You should consider all the incentives that can be made available to the manager as a sweetener. The more motivated you can make the manager, the better the results.

The Straight Skinny

Look around; the possibilities are everywhere. Sift through them and find someone who will fit into your plan.

It is not uncommon to have a manager participate in the increase in value of the property during his or her tenure. If the management company has a stake in the building, you will get better management. In any case, if you can find a good manager, you will get good management. Take your time, do the research, and find the right person. Even within a good company, there are outstanding performers. Often, they are looking to start their own businesses. You might get lucky and find someone who is ready to launch and is looking for his or her first property. If you sign up with a new company in the early days, you can take advantage of the hard work required to build a solid reputation. Do not underestimate the rewards of ambition.

Management Tools

Once you have selected the manager, it is up to you to provide some of the tools. By now, you have created one of your management tools—specifically, the tenant spreadsheet. At a glance you can see how many tenants you have and how soon leases will be renewing. You will have evaluated the leases and decided what changes must be made to improve the quality of the lease, as well as how much you can escalate the leases over the period of your planned ownership.

Take your lease spreadsheet and review it with the manager or better still, have him or her do a spreadsheet from the leases, and compare the two.

Leases

The leases are the main concern in the management plan. You must preserve them, improve their quality, and make the tenants happy. The first step is to have a game plan that your manager can support and that he or she thinks is "doable." The two primary areas of concern in the leases are the rent and the lease itself. You have been over the lease and have determined the ideal lease for you; now you and the manager must decide how to slowly convert the leases to your new ideal format. The rent is a function of the marketplace. You and your manager can look at the schedule of lease expirations and compare your rent levels with those projected in the marketplace. You can and must devise a strategy to improve the cash flow.

There are two ways to justify the rental increases. Normal cost-of-living increases are easy to justify, but if you want to make your building better than the average, you will need to justify better-than-average increases when the time comes. There are two ways to do that: increased tenant services and renovation.

Increased Tenant Services

If you are operating an existing office building, how can you improve services? You must ask yourself, "What do the tenants need?" There are many services that business owners require in the course of the day. They communicate with others, so can you work with the phone company to bring better and more flexible telephone service to the building? Can you bring in high-speed Internet and cable access? Can you arrange for better Fed Ex, UPS, or postal service? Can you find restaurants that will deliver food for lunches? What about starting a concierge service for your tenants? You might even find an existing concierge who will service the building. Can you arrange with a local dry cleaner to pick up and deliver? Can you arrange with a mobile car-washing service to take care of your tenants' cars by setting aside the worst location in the parking lot for the service? It will only take two spaces.

There are so many innovations that you can seek out and offer that you should be able to improve the level of service significantly. Most building owners think in terms of bricks and mortar. Use your brain to think globally and proactively. Think of what you would like to have for services and act on it. Most of these services will not cost you a dime. These businesses are always looking to expand and will jump at the chance to add a bunch of new customers all in the same place.

Renovation

The other side of the upgrade coin is the building itself. What can you do to take it up a notch? All buildings have limitations imposed by the design of the structure. Hopefully, you will have chosen one with good ceiling heights and ample parking.

The first thing you can do is beef up the landscaping. You can look at the air conditioning to see if it can be improved when you renovate the tenant spaces. Redecoration with a more modern look is always a good plan. The latest look is generally cosmetic in nature and can be done over time as you allocate a budget for these capital expenses. You might want to budget a lump sum and do it all at once when you take over to signal to the tenants that you are a with-it and proactive property owner, and that they are in for a treat under your tenure.

Accounting

Remember the numbers—they are your most important tools. They will tell you whether you are gaining or losing. If you have a professional manager, you will have to review the accounting documents carefully. The manager will have his or her own system, and you cannot expect the manager to change a system that works. Today, however, we have computers, and you can put them to good use. You should require the manager to submit reports both in written form and electronically. This will enable you to access the data directly, and manipulate it into the form you have chosen to keep track of the building's progress. Modern spreadsheet programs will enable you to set up a conversion process to input and export the new monthly data automatically.

Traditional Bookkeeping

You will use traditional accounting methods to handle the partnership's or LLC's books, and these will reflect income and taxable income, as well as provide data to establish your rate of return before and after taxes. You will find, however, that your manager will be providing you with data in spreadsheet form, because that is more useful for management than traditional accounting methods. Several modern accounting programs such as QuickBooks Pro and Peachtree are designed to export spreadsheets from the accounting data, but you are better off designing your own format, so that it is meaningful to you.

Spreadsheets

No matter what you are doing with spreadsheets, you are going to have to create one that reflects your long-term plan. It is against this spreadsheet that you will compare the actual results of your management plan. Remember, you and the manager are the management team, and you cannot abdicate the implementation of your plan to the manager. You must work together so you will be involved in the process. Any spreadsheet program today will allow you to plot numbers in a graph, so it is easy to compare the projected and actual, both numerically and visually. Sometimes a visual display will be more meaningful to you than just the numbers. You should negotiate your own leases unless the manager has a flair for the process, and your tenants should get acquainted with you even though your manager is running the day-to-day business of the building.

Integration

In the final form, your financial package will be an integration of both traditional accounting methods and spreadsheet analysis. You should seek out systems that allow you to cross the line between the two, so that you can minimize the amount of input-required research again. By the time this edition is published, there will be more software packages on the market, so it would be pointless to recommend one. Talk to your accountant and have him or her set you up with whatever you think you will need. It is a good investment to get it set up properly, as it makes the accountant's job easier to do, and therefore, is less costly to you.

Above and Below the Line

No, this does not refer to keeping two sets of books. This concept merely separates the building's operating expenses from those of the partnership or LLC. The "line" simply separates two classes of expense. Why is this important? Because when you sell, you will be selling the NIBDS for the building, not for the LLC. The building requires the expense of a manager, but the partnership or LLC requires the cost of an accountant to file the taxes. This tax preparation is not a building expense, and therefore, will be shown below the line (meaning after the NIBDS).

Operating Costs

You must clearly define operating costs. In an NNN-leased building, these costs are paid for by the tenants. If you cannot convince a tenant that a cost is directly related to the operation of the building, then it is not an operating cost. If it is not an operating cost, then it will become an ownership cost. Operating costs include, but are not limited to, the following types of expenses:

- ◆ Utilities
- ◆ Refuse collection
- ◆ Janitorial
- ◆ Maintenance and repair
- ◆ Window washing
- ◆ Parking lot sweeping

- ◆ Snow removal
- ◆ Landscape maintenance
- ◆ Taxes
- ◆ Insurance
- ◆ Management

Ownership Costs

There can be many costs that are paid (and perhaps deducted from the taxable income) by the cash flow of a partnership or LLC before distribution to the owners. The magnitude of these expenses is limited only by the agreement of the partners or the members. What expenses can there be? Would you believe an airplane? Obviously, this is not possible when you and your cohorts own a single 50,000 SF office building, but picture your group owning 20 properties scattered all over. Might it be reasonable to have a plane available for monthly inspections? It saves time, and is efficient for reaching smaller cities and towns. Extrapolating between the two extremes, you can imagine all sorts of other expenses. When you have multiple properties, you might start your own management company, or your own maintenance company. These can all be owned by the original partnership or LLC.

Why is a separate company for management a good idea? Having employees creates liabilities. In this world, the liabilities are increasing daily. Most liabilities are insured against, but the courts have shown that no one is invulnerable. If the people are employed by the property owner, then the investment itself is vulnerable to litigation. If, however, the people are employed by a separate corporation or LLC, the owners can lose only their initial startup capital. This theory assumes that there is no deliberate fraud or gross negligence on behalf of the corporate officers and shareholders.

Maximize the Saleability

The above- and below-the-line costs are geared solely to the time when you are ready to sell. You will sell the cash flow, not the ownership entity. It is, therefore, crucial that you keep ownership costs separate from the operating costs of the asset. Sloppy bookkeeping will come back to hurt you at a later date.

The way to do this is to keep ownership expenses out of the spreadsheets completely. These costs should be accounted for only in your accounting system. If you create a management company or a maintenance company, keep the ownership of these entities separate within your accounting system. They will be line items only with a note that they are wholly owned subsidiaries. When you sell the building, the buyer is entitled to examine the income and expense history, and if they are isolated, there will be no question of their legitimacy.

> **CAUTION**
>
> **Better Believe It!**
>
> One dollar on the bottom line capitalized at 9 percent is worth $11.11 at the time of sale.

Cash Flow—The Holy Grail in Every Deal

The final purpose of this exercise is to get your hands on the cash flow. The cash flow is what you have left after you have paid the mortgage. Its other term is "distributable funds," or the "net spendable cash."

This is the reason you have made the investment in the first place. Unlike owning stocks, income-producing real estate is designed to pay monthly returns on invested capital. It is most likely true that there is not as much potential upside in appreciation as there might be in the stock market, but there is little or no possibility of the dramatic downswing in value that exists in the stock market. It takes years of overbuilding to affect the value of real estate, and time and progress will mitigate or completely eliminate the effects of temporary overbuilding. It also takes years of a city's expansion to alter the desirability of any location. If you are alert to the market, and if you see vacancies cropping up or increasing throughout the market, you can react in a proactive manner to protect your investment.

The Documents

To sum things up, what are the management documents that you will need for managing the building? The obvious one is a contract between you and the manager. You should draft this, perhaps using the manager's document as a place to start. Build in whatever incentives you can afford. In addition, you will need to originate or inherit the following documents, at a minimum:

- The ownership document
- Construction contracts for tenant improvements

- Leasing agreement

- Consultant agreements, accountant, attorney, and so on

- Leases

- Utility agreements

- Maintenance contracts

If you are inheriting these documents, there should be nothing in your purchase agreement that obligates you to accept a document that you feel is inadequate. You can make it a condition of closing that a glaring inadequacy be corrected. It matters not whether the document is a consulting contract or a lease. If there is a fatal flaw, correct it before you accept assignment of it.

As part of the purchase, you will have to accept assignment of leases, so scrutinize them carefully. It might be impossible for the existing owner to negotiate a change in the lease to accommodate your concern, but it may be better to pass than accept a known problem without having a solution in hand. The other contracts, except for utility agreements, can be cancelled and renegotiated after the purchase. This is generally a good idea anyway, as it allows you to create your own contracts. If you create it, you will know and understand the agreement better. This will allow you to be more effective when administering the agreements.

The Least You Need to Know

- Make a good decision when you pick a manager. If you're going to do it, make sure you can do as good a job as your competitor.

- Good management tools and timely preparation will ensure that you can stay on top of the management on a monthly basis.

- Control the cash—it's why you're there. Without it there is no profit and no ROI.

- Get to know the tenants, as your profits depend on their continued and timely rental payments.

- Watch the cash flow monthly, and closely monitor the NIBDS.

- Never take your eyes off the market.

Create a Game Plan

In This Chapter

- ◆ Understand the acquisition process—it's the first step.
- ◆ Monitoring the deal's progress
- ◆ Always keep an eye on the market
- ◆ Realize that one man's bait is another man's dinner
- ◆ Constant vigilance increases profits and staves off disaster

During the research and selection period, you started preparing a game plan for your investment. This was finalized during the "free-look" period of the escrow ... right?

Do not take this lightly. If you make a game plan and stick to it, you might fail to achieve everything on your list, but you will accomplish much more than someone without a game plan. This chapter will help you formulate your plan.

The Acquisition Process

The first part of anyone's game plan should deal with the acquisition of the property. It should be incorporated into the purchase agreement and activated during the free-look period. This period is the best time to ask for something, as you are not yet committed to the purchase, and your money is not yet at risk. Once your earnest money deposit has become nonrefundable, you will have lost some leverage with regard to the negotiation process.

If you think about the seller's position, you will see that the seller must make certain representations to any buyer in order to close a sale. The most basic and minimum seller's representations are as follows:

Better Believe It!

Your primary goal is to acquire an investment that provides a reliable income stream at the lowest possible cost.

- The leases are real, in effect, and the tenants are paying rent.

- The building is in good repair.

- There are no latent defects in the building or in the title of the property.

The acquisition process starts with the examination of these representations, and if in your purchase agreement you have spelled out certain conditions that these representations have to meet, you can enforce them. What considerations should you build into your purchase document? The three major categories are the leases, the building, and the title and liens. Let's look at each item separately.

When the building was presented to you, you were given a financial projection (most likely a spreadsheet) showing the gross and net incomes of the building, as well as a breakdown of the total operating expenses. You need to read all the leases, create your own spreadsheet, and verify this income information. As far as the expenses are concerned, you can inventory the building, making lists of all expenses that you can see must be incurred to have the building operate smoothly and keep it in a good state of repair.

The second category is an area where you may incur hidden costs if you are not careful. If, as part of the conditions of purchase, you impose the condition that the building must be in good working order with all deferred maintenance corrected prior to the close of escrow, then you will eliminate the need for immediate cash outlay after the purchase is finalized.

The final representation and condition of purchase lies in the area of title and liens. This deals with the existing financing as well as the other potential liens. Your goal is to purchase the property lien-free, with the possible exception of the financing. Whether it is assumable or not will determine your approach. Most likely, the financing will be lower than you might like. Most buyers want to have 75 percent financing, so that they can maximize their purchase.

Minimize the Acquisition Price

Your cost of acquisition will entail not only the price, but all of the following items:

- The research costs
- The consultant costs relative to the purchase
- Attorney's fees
- The purchase price
- Any renovation budget you might have in your plan
- Deferred maintenance, if any
- Financing costs

Most of these costs are a given. You can minimize the research costs by doing all or most of the research yourself. Not only do you save money, but you also acquire a first-hand working knowledge of the marketplace. Attorney's fees are unavoidable, at least until you have acquired enough expertise to write your own purchase agreements. You will also need an attorney to create your new project lease. The purchase price is agreed upon if all the seller's representations are proven, so where can you save some money? About the only area is in the building's condition.

Make the Seller Pay Part of Your Plan's Projected Costs

Most sellers will be pleased to represent that their building is in good repair, and if they do not, you can always offer less. You can always agree that the price will be adjusted downward after you have had a chance to do a detailed inspection of the building. It is during the free-look period when you have the seller's permission to have your consultants on the premises that you can accomplish this detailed study.

The time to spend some money on consultants is during the free-look period. Get the best and have them take the building apart, looking for all possible defects.

You might be able to get these people to do their inspections in consideration of the maintenance contract for the building after you purchase it. Even if you have to pay for it, get a complete list of all areas of deficiency, and get firm prices for correcting the problems. Even a well-maintained building will have some deferred maintenance. If you can document it properly, you can have it corrected by the seller prior to the close of escrow. Most often, the seller will not want to spend the money unless he or she is certain you are going to close. Agree on the dollar amount and adjust the price downward. You can make the repairs after the closing. Your renovation plans might even preclude making some of the repairs, if you plan to replace some component. Either way, you will have made the seller pay for the repairs, lowering your total cost of acquisition. Remember this when it is your time to sell.

Continuous Reappraisal

During the period of your ownership, you will be working with your building to max-imize its potential. You will be able to measure your progress against the building's condition at the time of purchase. The components of increased value lie in several areas: the leases, the rents, and the building. Your evaluation of progress while you own the building can be described as a process of continuous reappraisal. You will need to look at your building periodically as if you were buying it all over again. Look at it with the same standard of care.

The building is a relatively simple matter. You have appraised it at the time of pur-chase and formulated a plan to improve it to a point where it will be competitive with other buildings in the market. This plan can be implemented in stages so that you can afford to pay for it.

While you are working on your building, you need to keep an eye on the market. You can do this by looking at competing buildings on a regular basis (a good idea) or you can have your broker give you a report on current rents and amenities. You can also keep in touch with your appraiser. Once you have paid for an appraisal, you become a customer, and the appraiser will be happy to keep you up-to-speed on changes in the market. He or she knows that you will be back again and will want to keep your busi-ness. Whenever you look at the market, look at it with a view of your game plan in mind. You must track the market to see if your game plan is remaining competitive.

Flexibility

Remember the advice I gave you earlier. Make a plan, work hard, and stay flexible. This is good advice for all endeavors, but it is crucial in real estate. The building keeps the rain off your tenants; the rest is service and attention to detail. Some of the suggestions I offered in Chapter 23 can be replaced by new trends in the market. Keep abreast of your tenants' changing needs and adapt to them.

How About Your Tenants?

The single most important factor in your building is your tenants. Their needs and what is available in the market will determine your building's place in the scheme of things. The most recent change in the market has been that of businesses' need to increase communication speed. Changes have occurred in the speed of communication, ordering time, and inventory control. More businesses are finding out that they can operate in a leaner manner by using the recent innovations in communication. They can lower their inventory levels and decrease the amount of space required, at the same time adding people and equipment to implement the new plan.

How to Cope with Your Competition

What does this mean to the average landlord? It means better telecommunication service to and throughout the building. It means better and more flexible access. This solution involves both you and the local phone company. It may even involve more than that. Some large buildings have become phone companies in themselves, installing major switches and reselling phone service to their tenants. Some developments are now linked to satellites for communication, with fiber-optic service throughout the development. I believe that in the future this will be the limiting factor in some areas of the real estate industry.

The Straight Skinny

You have heard the saying that one man's disaster is another man's opportunity. Make it work for you.

Disaster or Opportunity?

Major change in the technology available to industry today is a two-edged sword.

Imagine what tomorrow will bring. It does not matter what type of real estate investment you have, it will be affected by change. If you keep up with the trends in industry and watch for technological innovations, you will be able to see how it can relate to your business.

For a while, property owners across the country who held retail property were concerned that the surge in online retailing would have a dramatic effect on the retail industry. There have been some changes, and there will be more, but it seems that there will always be a need for stores with goods on the shelves. The industry is in the process of adapting to this change. Will it be traumatic? Probably. Will it cause some people problems? Certainly. Will the industry survive it? Absolutely!

Typical Problems—Strategic Thinking

Strategic shifts in any industry, whether due to technological innovation or to any other cause, will always be with us. The real effect of this change for building owners is a change in tenancy.

For the past 10 years or so, office buildings have been adapting to the gradual downsizing of tenant space as large tenants grow smaller and more geographically diversified. The trend in the industry has been for fewer central offices and increased peripheral offices and home offices. The general shift from the Industrial Age to the Information Age has resulted in more business startups, and therefore, more small tenants. This necessitates a change in building design.

For many years, buildings have been designed for tenants in excess of 10,000 SF (square feet), and that must change. If I were going to design an office building today, I would most likely design one for tenants who will average well under 2,500 SF apiece. Larger tenants can be in that building comfortably, but you must make sure that you can accommodate the proliferation of smaller tenants. This holds true for retail tenant buildings as well. Several store types are growing larger, and some are shrinking. The trick is to understand why, and to get ahead of the curve.

Local grocery stores are growing, adding more general merchandise space. Large discount merchandise stores are growing, adding food-retailing space. What seems to be happening is an attempt to become a "one-stop shop." This trend parallels the trend on the Internet retail sites. Will it continue? Will it prosper? This is your call, and the correct answer will spell success for some of you.

Solutions and Alternatives

How do you combat this constant change? I do not have a ready answer, except to say that there seems to be a pattern in all things that repeats itself. Before you buy or build a building, look at the new buildings under construction. How do they differ from their more established competitors? What are they offering that the older buildings do not? What is happening to location?

When the shift from downtown to suburbia occurred, the old concept of "location, location, location" changed dramatically. Instead of the Main Street location, people now need accessibility and visibility, oriented around the automobile. Once this flight to suburbia became the established norm, people and office space are moving back downtown, as cities fight back. Will this trend continue? I believe it will.

You might have also noticed that the regional malls have changed. Instead of pure retail centers, they now have a heavy emphasis on entertainment. This trend started in the late 1980s, and has continued unabated. Is this the future? I believe that the regional malls will evolve into the new downtown of the suburban sprawl. What I see is that these centers have become a hangout for various people at different times of the day. In the morning, you can see the senior citizens walking the perimeter. They are out of the weather and love the exercise. In the afternoons, the teenagers take over, as they cruise the malls to see and be seen. In the evenings, you get the late shoppers and the people going to dinner and a movie.

The place that I see relatively little change is in industrial products. The warehousing and distribution centers seem to get busier. The business parks are flourishing and becoming more heavily office-oriented. So, with all this information, where is the best place to invest? I think that you should stay slightly behind the front-runners. Don't try to be a trendsetter, and don't try to be the snazziest building on the block. Go for the value. Stick with well-located, relatively stable buildings. If you realize that it takes time for change to become apparent, and if you are on the lookout for the trends, then you are in a position to acquire and dispose of investments at fortuitous times.

Better Believe It!

Given this constant tug of war, where should you invest? It's not too hard. All these changes take time, and the first to innovate will always make a killing. Remember, however, the first to innovate may also lose his or her shirt!

Fine-Tuning Your Property

This brings us to the subject of optimizing your leases and maximizing your cash flow. The object of investing is to keep your building's bottom line increasing faster than the rate of inflation. When you find that it is only keeping pace with inflation, sell it and look for another opportunity. The alternative to selling it off is to keep it and add to your portfolio. There is nothing wrong with owning a building that keeps up with the market. If you are able to generate more capital, you can add to the portfolio, but if you need to sell to expand, so be it, sell, and exchange or just sell and reinvest.

The Value Documents

The biggest impact on value will be found in improving your lease documentation. You should constantly seek to improve your leases wherever possible. When a tenant decides to exercise an option in his or her existing lease, you will not likely have an opportunity to change the lease. However, when it comes to renewal time, you can offer a new lease with as many changes as the market will bear. When you rotate tenant space, the new tenant will have no problem with your new lease form, as he or she believes it to be the building standard. No matter what type of property you own, you will always want to convert all your leases to the pure NNN lease. This establishes, without a doubt, the clearest bottom line for any income property investment, and the fact of the matter is that a NNN lease gives the tenant the best ability to control his or her costs of occupancy.

You must identify the problem areas in the leases you have inherited, and at the very least, change these clauses, substituting your own at every possible opportunity. There are buildings that may not lend themselves to the NNN lease. The design may preclude separate meters for electricity and other utilities, but there are solutions for this as well. You can submeter the power consumption to prorate the power bills. You cannot become a reseller of power at a profit, but you can charge for actual usage at the going rate, plus the costs of submetering.

Cash Flow

Why bother to convert your cash flow to a more clearly defined NIBDS (net income before debt service)? The answer lies in the art of buying and selling. When you are buying a shovel, it is easy to ascertain the quality of the shovel. You can examine it, you can try it out, and you can easily determine its strengths and potential weaknesses. With income property you are dealing with concepts, documentation, and cash flow. All of these are subject to interpretation, and hence, valuation.

If you have a lease that is ambiguous about expenses of operations, but you are able to collect the expenses anyway, you might find a day when someone on the other end of that lease takes the time to read it more carefully, and contests your ability to collect so completely. If you have left anything out of the expense clause, or if you have added a service that is not included, you might not be able to collect for it. You might even add a service knowing that you cannot charge for it yet, just to keep your tenants happy. All these potential problems will come off your bottom line when a buyer is evaluating your leases. This happens when you sell, as well as when you buy. Every year buyers and sellers are getting more knowledgeable. That is why you are reading this book. There are sellers reading it, as well as buyers.

If you have fine-tuned your leases, your cash flow should follow suit. When you have clear, unambiguous leases, there can be no debate on the quality and consistency of your existing and projected cash flow. Couple this with a well-maintained and competitive building, and you will have an asset that will consistently perform for you, and which will command a great price when you decide to sell.

Why Bother with All This?

If your goal is to just have an investment, then there is little to think about when selecting a building. Any good one will do. When you decide to build a portfolio, as discussed in Chapter 31, you will have to consider diversity of product and geography. You never want to become your own competition. Select your properties with an eye to a position in your market so that if you want to acquire a similar property within the same market, there is ample room for two buildings you control. You can accomplish this by having the two buildings aimed at different segments of the market so that they do not compete. If that cannot be accomplished, then choose a different product entirely, such as one office building and one shopping center.

The Least You Need to Know

- ♦ You make money when you buy, maximize it through astute management, and collect the profits when you sell; so buy it right, every time.

- ♦ Stay on top of your investment monthly, if not weekly. Good communication with your tenants will pay off handsomely.

- ♦ Continually seek to improve your property, whenever you can, and in any way that's feasible.

- ♦ Monitor the industry and the market. Be alert to trends.

- ♦ Sell when you're ready, but be ready to sell at all times. Keep an eye out for good refinancing opportunities.

Chapter 25

The Care and Feeding of Tenants

In This Chapter

- ◆ With different buildings you have different types of tenant
- ◆ Office building tenants
- ◆ The right tenants can enhance your building's appeal

The type, size, and occupation of your tenants can have a demonstrable effect on your investment. It matters little whether you have purchased apartments, a retail building, an industrial building, or an office building, your tenants and their relationship with each other will affect the building in a positive or negative way. In this chapter, we will explore the difference between tenants, their business, their size, and their potential synergy.

Tenants and Investment Types

Imagine going to your doctor. Upon entering the building, you have to wade through a large crowd of office workers taking a smoke break at the front door. This is not a desirable scenario. The problem is twofold. First, the building designer did not provide smoking space away from the front entrance of the building. This results in people entering the building having to wade through a cloud of smoke. Second, you are experiencing incompatible office uses. You might have noticed that different buildings have different orientations. There is no Costco in a regional mall, and you will not find an orthopedic surgeon in a suburban office building surrounded by real estate companies. How then are tenants distributed? They are housed, ideally, in groups differentiated by industry, size, and public visibility.

First, tenants are separated by industry types:

- Residential
- Retail
- Industrial

- Office
- Recreation
- Special uses

You may find instances in which the uses are mingled, but in general, most developments tend to specialize in one type of tenant. You will find mingled uses in business parks and regional-mall developments, because these afford large concentrations of development spread over large areas.

Retail

Retail developments break down into the following general categories:

- Strip centers
- Neighborhood centers
- Community centers

- Power centers
- Regional malls

These different types of centers attract different types of tenants and come with their own set of economics. The strip center is usually a small development, under 30,000 SF, geared to highway traffic. Due to its size and general lack of credit tenants, the development is considered risky by most lenders. The combination of high-price land due to the very visible location, smaller land size, and the higher-than-average interest rate of the available loans, create higher rents. This attracts tenants who need the high degree of visibility and who do not necessarily have the greatest credit. The landlord is compensated for the increased risk by the higher rents, and the tenants, in exchange for the higher rents, get greater exposure to the buying public.

Neighborhood centers are built around the grocery store. They have evolved from the local supermarket and bank into complexes that take up to 150,000 SF on 15 to 16 acres. They contain all the convenience services needed by the surrounding residential community. These services include, but are not limited to: grocery stores, drug stores, banks, dry cleaners, sandwich shops, fast-food restaurants, and limited offices.

Community shopping centers are expanded neighborhood centers often containing the smaller "junior" department stores, as well as the standard neighborhood mix of tenants. These centers can reach 250,000 SF. They are not common, but can be found in the larger suburban cities.

The power center, also known as the discount center, is a recent arrival on the development scene. Started in the 1980s, this center sprung up around the growing discount retailer. Starting with the advent of Wal-Mart, Costco, Home Depot, and similar retailers, these centers soon grew to be a popular venue for America's shopping public. These centers have now grown to exceed 1,000,000 SF each. They tend to cluster in areas near regional centers or heavily traveled suburban arterials. They account for a significant part of America's retail sales. The late 1990s saw explosive growth in this type of development as retailers staked out territory in the growing communities. This has resulted in empty stores in certain cities as these retailers jockey for position in the market. The empty stores can be another opportunity. Look them up in *The Complete Idiot's Guide to Investing in Fixer-Uppers*.

Better Believe It!

The regional shopping center defines the "megabuck deal." It takes hundreds of millions of dollars and 10 or more years to create this type of development.

Finally, there is the regional shopping mall, the traditional new downtown of American retailing. As the population moved to the suburbs following the World War II residential-building boom, the regional mall became established as the downtown for these new communities. These centers house the traditional department stores and an ever-changing array of specialty retailers. These centers are also evolving into major centers for entertainment and leisure activity.

Industrial Tenants

Industrial tenants, by their very nature, segregate into manufacturing, warehouse, and distribution facilities. There seems to be little commingling of uses. In general, however, they all seem to mix well in an industrial park setting, as all uses are generally compatible. Industrial buildings that cater to smaller users tend to be grouped in similar industry types. Industrial buildings are one type of investment that lends itself well to the single-tenant, build-to-suit project.

Offices

In the office-building category, you will find that the product is even more diverse, separating tenants by occupation and size. Tenant size restricts where the tenant can find space to occupy. Very large tenants are relegated to the large, mid- and high-rise office buildings, and smaller tenants can only find a home in the smaller, suburban low-rise buildings.

Tenant Size

The tenant size you have targeted will dictate which type of project is built, and if you purchase a particular type of building, you might find yourself having to cull the tenants, and massage the leases to create a more compatible tenant mix. It is true that a large tenant may occupy a building designed for smaller tenants, but in so doing, this tenant becomes a blessing, as well as a liability.

If you have a building with this type of tenant, you must budget enough money to carry you through the transition period when this tenant is replaced. Sometimes this tenant will not want to move, because the location is such that it is vital to the tenant's business. When this occurs, you must raise the rents to a point where the extra rent compensates you for the eventual risk of loss of the tenant.

Often, this situation leads to the tenant purchasing the building so he or she can stay on. You can look at this potential problem as an opportunity as well. Most large tenants have negotiated concessions from the developer that are not available to the average tenant, but when their leases expire they are not necessarily in as favorable a position. It is very expensive to move, and the larger the tenant, the greater the expense.

Better Believe It!

If you have any tenant occupying more than 20 percent of a project, you will find that this one tenant represents 100 percent of your cash flow. Avoid this situation if at all possible! If not, formulate a game plan to alter the situation or turn it to your advantage.

If you can find a building for sale with this type of situation, in a great location, you can look at it as an opportunity to greatly increase the rental revenue. If this tenant wants to stay, he or she will most likely be willing to pay market-rate rents to do so. If there is no serious newer competition nearby, you are relatively assured that the tenant will stay put. Do not, however, push the rental increase too far. Make sure it is still a good deal for the tenant. Make sure you're aware of any rent-control laws in your area. Some cities do regulate rent in certain areas including the terms and amount of increases.

The trouble with large tenants in suburbia is that most developments cannot accommodate them unless they are under construction. Once a building is built and occupied, the remnant spaces tend to be too small and scattered for the larger tenants. If the tenant is well heeled and you are able to keep the building at market rate, chances are that the tenant will be interested in purchasing the project when you are done with it. By buying the building, the tenant can use the cash flow to lower his cost of occupancy.

Tenants' Occupation

Further differentiation occurs in the office building category based upon tenant occupation. Tenants tend to stratify into several well-known categories: medical, general, and back-office uses. Within these categories, there are also subcategories, such as real estate, government, and legal. Some buildings are deliberately built to attract specific tenants. If you built or bought a building near the courthouse, you might expect that you would attract lawyers as tenants. Similarly, if you have an office building near the hospital, you will find that medical uses are a natural fit. You can design a building to attract specific tenants by adding specific improvements that cater to these tenants. Buildings designed to attract attorneys now offer a built-in legal library and communication system. Medical buildings require extensive plumbing and cabinetry modifications, as well as specialty areas for x-ray and other testing facilities.

In suburban areas where there are no obvious specialty requirements, your building must be adapted to be usable by a variety of tenants. This can be accomplished by providing utility access throughout the building and custom designing the office suites for each tenant. In the future, any office building will require state-of-the-art communication facilities. Therefore, it is best to design them in at the development stage. If you are purchasing an existing building, you would be well advised to find out how to modify the building in the future as fiber-optic communication capability becomes the norm. This does not have to be done immediately, but you should plan for this modification in your planning and budgeting.

Government Tenants = High Density and Crowded Parking Lots

Government tenants can be a real problem for the rest of the building. For many years, government has been building its own buildings, but they never keep up with the growth of the bureaucracy. Both state and federal governmental agencies rent privately owned office space, and often you must bid for them as tenants. Their requirements are spelled out in the RFP (request for proposal), and your bid, if successful, will require you to meet the governments' specifications. These specifications require you to meet all federal and state standards for handicap access and some of the new energy requirements.

The main problem with government tenants is the number of employees. In most buildings, parking is required in the ratio of four cars per 1,000 SF of occupied space. Government tenants have a greater employee density, around one person for every 150 SF. This means that these tenants fill your parking lots. In an effort to forestall this problem, you must specify that the government employees must occupy specific parking and no more. This is quite common, and most government agencies offer incentives to their employees to car pool and use public transit. Forewarned is fore-armed. Do not ignore this if you are considering any form of government tenant.

How do you avoid this problem? You must monitor your prospective tenants carefully, specifying that if they have an inordinate number of employees, they must make off-site parking arrangements for the overflow. The types of tenants to be wary of, in addition to government tenants, are schools, telephone solicitation companies, and the so-called "back-office" operations.

Back-office operations are companies that have a large number of telephone operators, such as airline reservation offices and telemarketers. These companies must be handled differently than normal tenants. There are no rules about these uses. You just have to find your own solutions. Luckily, these tenants are not attracted to class A or even suburban office space. They like converted industrial space, or old shopping center properties. They require extra parking and a low level of tenant improvement, and these secondary locations work well for them.

The Number of Tenants

We've looked at tenant size and diversity, but what are the implications of size? If you have your cash flow tied up in one or two tenants, you are vulnerable to the tenant's plans. I recommend that you plan for replacing these larger tenants with smaller ones. This is a good strategy, especially if you are planning to own the building for a long time. If you are building a portfolio of property, and you want to keep them for the long pull, then this is a necessary strategy.

Set up some reserve capital and start prospecting for new tenants well in advance of the large tenants' lease expiration dates. If you have things arranged in advance, then your vacancy period will be confined to the time it takes you to remodel the tenant space. In very few cases will it exceed 60 days. Once you have accomplished this, you will have a better building from a cash flow and diversity point of view. You should look for this when purchasing a building. While it is not necessarily recognized, I believe that more and smaller tenants make for a more stable, and therefore, valuable property.

What if, when purchasing a property, you find that several of the tenants are too large for your comfort? How should it affect your offered price? Most buildings will be offered for sale with no detail on the tenancy, so it is not until your offer is accepted that you will have a chance to examine the leases and discover the details of the tenancy. When you encounter this problem, examine the tenant in great detail. What does the company do? Is it expanding or contracting? What is the company's financial standing? Could it be a likely candidate to purchase the building, or is it rent-sensitive? You must make your own determination. The key piece of information is the length of the lease. If the lease expires within five years of your proposed purchase, you need to discount that cash flow by whatever you believe it will cost you to replace the tenant. This is a task for your leasing agent and your contractor. The cost of replacement will be brokerage fees, tenant improvements, and lost rent. On the plus side, you will, most likely, improve the rental income on the space in question.

What are you shooting for? My take on an ideal tenancy for a suburban office building is a mix of tenants in all different professions, with few, if any, tenants occupying more than 5 percent of the building. Why do I want this? First, smaller tenants are easier to replace with little or no tenant improvement work, and second, they pay more rent than their larger cousins. The larger the tenant, the larger the bank account, and therefore, the more they feel they can demand when they are negotiating their leases. If you find yourself needing them as a tenant, you will find this quite true. If, however, you are in a position to pick and choose, you can still take large tenants, but give them less in the way of improvements, keeping the unused portion in a fund to replace this tenant when you can. This will enable you to live with the large tenant on your own terms.

Better Believe It!

Unless the market is in recession, remember that it's your building, and you call the shots. If you act in haste, you *will* repent at leisure. It is very annoying when all the old wives' tales are proven true.

Optimizing Tenancy and Synergy

Your goal as a building owner should be to have the best possible tenant mix and the most stable and reliable cash flow. The two components of this are a compatible tenant mix and restricting your tenant's size.

Compatible tenant mix is defined as tenants that have a synergistic relationship. If, for instance, you have a real estate broker in your building, then an escrow agent, a mortgage banker, and an insurance agent would be compatible uses. All of these tenants can be involved in the same transaction. It is the same if you have a family doctor and a dentist in the building. Adding an optometrist would be a natural thing to do.

You need not seek to make the entire building into one great synergistic cabal. Rather, you can separate compatible uses in different areas of the building. In a multistory building, you can separate the different categories by floor, and in a single-story building, you can separate them in different wings. There are many ways to accomplish this, and it is not a life-and-death situation. It only requires some thought when you are leasing the building. If you have a vacancy next to a medical use, have the broker look for a tenant who will be compatible. The negotiations will be easier.

What you want to avoid is too many tenants competing with each other. This will cause you to have premature vacancy, as one tenant drives the other out of business or out of your building. Do not get into the habit of granting exclusives in your building, as it will tie your hands, but use your judgment. A shopping center cannot survive having two grocery stores. Your office building can survive having two real estate brokers, but you are better off with one broker and one title company. If you achieve a synergistic tenant mix, you will find that your turnover will decrease, and your tenants will do better. When this happens, you will have become a destination, effectively bettering your location. Eventually, this will show up in better rents and a more stable cash flow.

Signs Are a Necessary Evil

One of the real problems in managing an office building is sign control. Tenants want to put signs everywhere. You need to create a comprehensive sign policy and stick to it.

Things to know about signs are:

> **Better Believe It!** _____
> You cannot make any exceptions to your sign policy. This will cause a full-scale tenant revolt, and if that happens, you will lose tenants. No exceptions!

- All door information signs should be standard. You can allow the company logos and other distinctive features in the names.

- Signs on the building must be built the same way, and all the signs are on your timer, so that they are all on, or all off. There are no exceptions.

- No signs in the windows. It is very tacky.

- It is best if all the building signs are the same color, but this is a hard one to enforce, as most companies have distinctive logo colors.

Strive for uniformity; the building will look more professional. Oddball or nonconforming signs are like a poke in the eye with a sharp stick.

The Least You Need to Know

- All your profits reside in your leases. Select them carefully, tend them with diligence, and preserve them against all challenges.

- Beware of government tenants. Their habits are not good, and they can hurt your real estate's value. They *will* flood the parking lot.

- Weed out the big tenants; they are a potential threat to your monthly cash flow.

- Constantly fine-tune your tenant mix to improve your occupancy and your bottom line. It's what you bought the building for.

Chapter 26

Reserves

In This Chapter

- ◆ The why and how much of reserves
- ◆ Costs can add up
- ◆ The seller's reserves
- ◆ Reserves and the sales price

Reserves are cash or cash equivalent accounts established for several reasons. You might need to refurbish your building when moving a new tenant, or you might want to upgrade your building, or you might need to replace the air-conditioning system. You might find yourself in a position where your largest tenant has decided to move, and your residual cash flow is no longer enough to make the mortgage payment. You will have to tide yourself over the vacant period and fund tenant improvements for the new tenants. For a variety of reasons, reserve accounts are mandatory for responsible managers. In this chapter, we'll explore the ins and outs of reserves.

Do You Really Need Reserves?

You need reserves for different reasons. If you own a building that uses gross leases, you should have a line item in your expense column that reads, "reserves for replacements." This line item is designed to repair and replace building components that wear out. The most common use of reserves, other than new tenant improvements, is for parking lot maintenance, HVAC repair and replacement, and painting.

A parking lot of standard construction is designed to be failure-free for no less than two years. It is usually guaranteed by the contractor for one year, two at a maximum. After 10 years, it is normal to see the wearing surface dry out and start to crack. In areas of the country with freeze/thaw cycles, it is common for the pavement to deteriorate completely, necessitating a repaving after 15 years or more. In the rest of the country, the paving will require resealing and restriping every 8 to 10 years. The average air-conditioning system will operate trouble-free for about 15 years. Then, it will require periodic repair. When the repairs get to be too expensive, you will have to replace the unit. Painting is an annual, ongoing maintenance requirement.

If your building is an NNN lease building, you will have to build this fund into your lease under the "additional rent" clause. It is a reasonable expense item that should be set at around 10 percent of your budget before management expenses. This fund should be kept separate and held against the day when you will need it.

Capital Requirements

There is also the instance in which you are purchasing an existing building, and you plan for some upgrading of the building to keep it competitive in the market. For this purpose, you will need funds that cannot be generated by the expense portion of the lease. These funds are capital improvement funds, which cannot be expensed against operations. The building improvements must be capitalized and depreciated along with the entire building. That is also the case with new tenant improvements. The money to recapitalize a tenant space must come from your cash flow. This fund should be established at the beginning of your ownership and should be set at a size to pay for the first lease when it is due for renewal. This fund should grow until you are satisfied that you have enough reserves so that you do not have to borrow for the purpose.

Where Do You Get Reserves?

Where do these funds come from? There are three major sources: your initial cash investment, lease deposits, and retained earnings. Your initial cash is just that, an additional cash investment set aside at the time of purchase. When you purchase the property, the seller will have to turn over the tenant lease deposits to you, as they are held by the owner as a guarantee of the tenant's performance. When an individual tenant vacates, and you have to return the deposit, it will be replaced by the next tenant's larger deposit.

Some states require that tenant security deposits be kept in a separate interest-bearing trust account. Some states, however, treat these deposits as a liability only and allow the funds to be commingled with your own. Retained earnings are funds that are part of your NIBDS (net income before debt service). These funds are not operating expenses, but capital improvements, and are, therefore, accounted for "under the line." These are cash-flow funds that you do not distribute, but retain in the owner's account. You will pay taxes on these funds along with the rest of your cash flow.

Better Believe It!

You should set up reserves for all three contingencies: replacements, vacancies, and tenant improvements. You will need them.

How Much Is Enough?

When you purchase a building, I recommend that you set aside up to 2 to 5 percent of the building's purchase price in a fund for reserves and replacements, as well as capital improvements. This fund can be replenished monthly from your normal cash flow. The amount must be large enough to accomplish the upgrades you have selected in your game plan, as well as enough to recapitalize the first lease premises to be renovated. Starting with the first month of operation, your cash-flow fund will add to this reserve. The object is not to be caught short if you lose a tenant, or if there is a large item that needs to be replaced in the normal course of business. You should be able to handle anything that comes your way.

Routine Cash Requirements

What can you expect? You can expect the following occurrences in the management of any form of income-producing real estate:

- Losing a tenant
- Mechanical breakdowns
- Occasional severe weather damage
- Late rents
- Tenant bankruptcy
- Parking lot repairs

- Roof leaks
- Refitting tenant space for a new tenant
- Constant painting
- Legal expenses
- Increased taxes

Disaster Funds

There is no such thing as enough money when a disaster occurs. This is what insurance is for. However, you will need to make the mortgage payment while the insurance company is sorting out the problem. When a disaster, such as a flood or a tornado, occurs, you will be able to collect, and in the meantime, keep your mortgage payments current!

Who Owns the Reserves?

Who owns the reserves? How are the funds treated? If your tenants are contributing to maintenance through a reasonable reserve for replacement fund in their monthly expense column, these funds belong to the building tenants and must be passed on to the new owners when you sell. This is important to know when you are buying, because the seller must also pass these funds along to you. If he or she does not, then any maintenance item that occurs before the fund is built up will be out of your pocket. This is not necessarily an enforceable item, either by you as the buyer or by any one buying from you. You must build it into the contract from the outset.

Better Believe It!

You must insist on a reasonable vacancy factor, as part of the valuation when you buy, and you should expect to accommodate a buyer with the same percentage when you sell. It is reasonable at both times. Make sure that they are the same when buying and selling.

There is another important item to build into your purchase contract, and that deals with any vacancy at the time of purchase. When you buy, even if the building is 100 percent full, you will be buying with an assumed vacancy factor of at least 5 percent. If the building is full, then this is not a problem. If, however, there is a vacancy, and you are paying for the income stream from this vacant space, you must have the seller credit your purchase price with sufficient money to improve that space for an incoming tenant. Without the tenant, there is no cash flow. Without the improvements, there is no tenant.

Tenant Lease and Security Deposits

Tenant lease deposits are always the property of the individual tenants, and, regardless of whether you keep them separate or not, you are only holding these funds against the time when the lease is terminated. If the tenant leaves the premises in the condition specified in the lease, you must return the funds to the tenant. These funds are replaced by the next tenant. The only time you need to worry about this is when you have commingled the funds, and you are losing tenants without replacing them. You will need to have cash available for this purpose.

Your Cash—Below the Line

Any funds set aside by you, either in cash at the outset or from your NIBDS below the line, are your funds. They need not be accountable to anyone else when you sell. You have paid taxes on these funds, and you own them outright. Your reserves are no one's business but your own. You'd be surprised at the number of building owners who do not have reserves. They pay for it in the end anyway. It is like any form of maintenance. You can pay for it a little at a time or in one lump sum when it comes up.

When You Sell

If you get into the habit of proper accounting for funds placed in a common account, then you should be in great shape when the time comes to sell. You will know what is what and your accounting system will have the correct totals. It will, however, be easier if you keep the funds in separate bank accounts.

You can open two or three additional bank accounts: one for the tenant lease deposits, one for the tenants' reserve account, and one for your own funds set up by a capital fund or funded from your cash flow after the NIBDS line. The accounting will still be the same in the general ledger, but you will know at a glance what is what, and to whom the funds belong. Commingling funds is not a good habit to get into.

State law permitting, the lease deposit account is a fund that you can use, so long as you know it will come off the purchase price when you sell. If you use it at all, use it to improve the building, not for the routine replacement of worn-out building components. Treat it as a fund that goes

Better Believe It!

It is always cost effective to be proactive rather than reactive. You will find, if you develop this trait, that it prevents all sorts of crises.

with the building, established by the tenants. It can be yours to use while you own the building, but you must replace it when you sell, sometimes, mandated by state law, with interest.

Forestall Problems

Having established a fund for replacements and routine maintenance, you should use it regularly. Remember the deferred maintenance you inherited. Do not let that happen to you. The reason for maintenance is not to have the building look good, although that is a by-product. It is to preserve and enhance your capital investment. This is the preeminent goal of everything you do. The details are only the means to get to the end. Do it properly and you will prosper.

Be Proactive

There are two types of people in the world. Those who wait for something to happen and then react to it, and those who see what can happen and act before it occurs. The latter personality is known as proactive.

The Least You Need to Know

- You *will* need reserves! Set them up in a realistic manner, based upon your spreadsheets.

- Add a reserve for replacement line to your tenant's monthly expense bill. If you run into objections, just explain that it is less of an impact in small bites than in one large monthly hit.

- Start out with as big a reserve fund as you can afford, and build it up monthly. It remains your money. Look at it as a savings account. If you don't need it, no harm done, but if you need it and don't have it, it could spell disaster.

- Use your reserves to keep the building in great shape. You never know when you might decide to sell.

Chapter 27

Maintenance, Accounting, and the Future Sale

In This Chapter

- ◆ Determining your building's condition
- ◆ Keep it up to par
- ◆ Bookkeeping
- ◆ How NIBDS equates to value

To maintain and enhance your property's value, you must keep your real estate investments up to snuff. It is not enough for you to know that the building is in good shape—you must have a paper trail to prove it. Starting with the reports you created when you purchased the building, create a file on building maintenance logs. This will be backed up by the expense ledgers. When it comes time to sell (for the payoff is the ultimate goal for any investment), or time to reinvest, you can use these documents together to convince either buyer or lender that your building is in great shape. This chapter shows you how to get to know your building, maintain it, and document your maintenance efforts.

The Building's Condition—When You Buy

When buying any building, you must determine its physical condition. This process is reversed when you prepare to sell the building. If you approach each situation the same way, you will profit at both ends. At the front end, you can uncover the real condition, and at the same time, gain a thorough understanding of the building and how it is put together. This is the process of inspection.

If you are not particularly experienced in building ownership, or if this is your first time investing, I recommend that you hire an experienced contractor, architect, and specialists to help you evaluate the building. Building inspection is now an established routine in the housing market, and it should be even more so in the investment real estate business.

Deferred Maintenance

Any defects, minor or major, are known as "deferred maintenance" items. The big trick is to distinguish between the routine maintenance items that are normally scheduled and those items that have been completely neglected or inadvertently overlooked. It will be your job to inherit the tenant's repair and maintenance fund and take over the routine maintenance chores. The rest of the items are the responsibility of the seller.

You would be surprised to know that less than 15 percent of buyers go through this exercise. Many do not want to hire the experts, and many rely on a cursory inspection. They all regret it later. Do not skip this step; it will cost you a lot of money during your ownership.

Make the Seller Pay for It

When you write your purchase agreement, carefully include a clause that states that the buyer (you) has the right to inspect the building for defects, and the seller agrees to repair before the close of escrow, or to adjust the price at the close of escrow, so that you may do the repairs. This will guarantee that you will be inheriting a building that is up to snuff from the beginning. Personally, I favor adjusting the price and doing my own repairs. This gives my contractor a chance to get better acquainted with the building.

When you are inspecting the building, what specifically do you look for? If there are elevators or escalators, you should talk directly to the company servicing the equipment, and if you are not satisfied, find another company to inspect the equipment. The same holds true for all the mechanical equipment, from HVAC to boilers, to exhaust systems, and so on. Personally, I would have them all inspected. Do not forget the fire safety systems. The law requires regular maintenance. Check the logs and talk to the company doing the maintenance. Definitely inspect the roof. A leaky roof can be costly, as water damages electronic equipment.

The rest of the items are not critical, just costly. They need to be checked anyway. At a minimum, look at the following:

- Inspect the ceiling. Broken tile and stains indicate roof leaks.

- Check the walls for cracks. They might indicate differential settlement in the foundations.

- Look at the floors. You can tell if there is a problem even if they are carpeted.

- Check the rest rooms for functioning fixtures, fans, and so on.

- Look at all the door hardware, including closers.

- Check all security equipment and door locks, exit signs, stairways, and so on.

- Walk the entire parking lot looking for cracks and pavement failures.

- Check all the curbs and parking lot lights.

- Inspect the landscaping and turn on and check the irrigation system.

- Check all the paint, noting locations in the common areas of the building that need immediate attention.

- Walk through the tenant spaces looking for inordinate wear. The tenants will want this modernized at renewal time.

- Make a list of all the items above and get a bid from your contractor to fix all but the wear and tear in the tenant space.

Problems such as hazardous waste pollution, mold, duct contamination, asbestos, etc. are problems to be avoided at all costs. If they exist, cancel the escrow and go find yourself another building.

The Straight Skinny

The inspection and repairs stage sounds like a lot of work. On the positive side, it is not brain surgery. Do it right and the seller pays. Do it wrong and you pay.

A Strategy for the Future

Having done all that, you should have a building that is in good condition when you take it over. Together with your maintenance people and your contractor, make a list of all the routine items that will be regularly checked during your tenure. Set up schedules and a budget for implementation.

Routine Maintenance

Your front line in the maintenance campaign is the janitorial staff. Their daily routine in the building should include chores that are in addition to the daily janitorial work. In addition to the clean-up, they should check the lights, replacing burned-out bulbs daily. They do not charge extra for this if you furnish the bulbs. They should do a weekly inspection of the premises and furnish you with a written report of its condition. Due to the nature of the janitorial business, you should make this as easy as possible for them. Create a checklist with items to be inspected weekly and monthly, with a column for comments. This makes the inspection process easier, and will ensure that it is done. Check it monthly yourself.

Janitorial services exist only in office buildings; therefore, for industrial buildings and shopping centers and any other buildings, you must have your manager do the inspections. Check up on the manager from time to time. The maintenance will have to be contracted out, and I recommend finding a company that specializes in building maintenance. They are generally jacks-of-all-trades, and can handle almost anything that does not require heavy equipment.

What Maintenance Is Needed?

Specific services to be included in routine maintenance depend on the type of building you have invested in.

If you purchased a single-tenant building with an NNN lease, the maintenance is 100 percent up to the tenant. You must still inspect the building routinely to be sure that the tenant is maintaining it properly. The lease should give you the right to give the tenant notice of any deficiencies, and if they remain uncorrected, allow you to do the maintenance and charge the tenant. The same holds true for all buildings.

The multi-tenant buildings are the easiest ones to ascertain, as you will be doing the maintenance anyway and are, therefore, in a position to be sure it is done. After your purchase inspection, you will have created a list of chores and a schedule. Stick to it, and you will avoid having to pay for these items when you sell the building.

Better Believe It!

Passing along to the tenants the increased costs of proper maintenance is the hard part, but you must be able to make this transition. Take it slowly. Do not lump all the increases into the first month or even the first quarter. If the increased maintenance program is going to be a significant increase in operating expense, phase it in over a year. You should budget for this expense when you buy the building.

How to Pay for It

Sounds expensive, doesn't it? It is, but it is cheaper than letting the building get run down. When that happens, the costs go up, and you run the real risk of losing your tenants. The lease gives them the right to expect a well-maintained building, and it also provides that they will pay for it. Whether it is a gross lease or an NNN lease, there should be provisions in the lease for maintenance and repairs, as well as reserves for replacement. If the previous landlord has been lax, you must persuade the tenants that the increase in this monthly expense item will be for the building's welfare. To help sell it, do something visible at the start. Add some amenity that will be a one-time cost to you, but will be a long-term benefit to the tenants.

Accounting

In Chapter 22, I discussed accounting systems. Here is where they are implemented. You will have two sets of accounting tools: the bookkeeping portion and your spreadsheets. The spreadsheets are your management tools, while the bookkeeping system allows you to report the overall progress of the investment and pay your taxes.

Billing and the Cash

Starting with the tenant information spreadsheet prepared when you purchased the building, adding the monthly expense and tenant allocation spreadsheet, you can construct your monthly tenant rental invoice. It is necessary to be specific, because no matter what form of lease you use, the tenant will have the right to inspect your operating costs annually.

Keep good expense records in a form that is easily understood. This is not a profit center. It is a pass-through expense item, so you need to be reimbursed by the tenants 100 percent. If your records are good and easy to understand, you will be able to recover. If, however, you cannot substantiate an expense, you will end up eating it. The monthly invoice should show the following breakdown:

- Rent

- Operating expense

- Special services ordered by the tenant

- The total rent

- Any rental tax required by the local government

- The total invoice

Again, your manager should collect the rents and deposit them into your bank account. From that account you will pay the bills.

Formats and Tools

In Chapter 22, I discussed the types of spreadsheets that I recommend, but you will have to take them apart and modify them so that you find them useful for your style of management. In general, you will need some basic information to base your management decisions on. The spreadsheet should answer the following questions:

- Who has paid their rent, and who has not?

- What are the expenses, and how are they escalating? (The rent should escalate at a rate greater than inflation, but the rate of increase in operating expenses should never exceed the rate of inflation.)

- When are leases going to expire, and how much space will be available?

- What is the market rate for new leases?

- What does the cash flow projection look like for 5 and 10 years? (Update it every time you have any specific change in rent or expenses.)

The Straight Skinny

Total familiarity with the books will enable you to monitor and spot-check anything at a glance. That is proactive management. Make sure you can access the accounting from your own computer.

Accounting Packages

Accounting packages are getting more elaborate every day, and I believe that you should seek out a package that will suit your specific needs. If you are operating only one property, you will most likely not require a very elaborate system. The problem with a simple system is that it is difficult to upgrade. If you are like most people who get into real estate investments, you will most likely expand your operation, and you will eventually have a full-time bookkeeper. When this happens, whatever system your bookkeeper starts with will be with you for a long time.

The bookkeeper is a creature of habit who loathes change. Start your bookkeeper off with the best accounting system that you can afford. Try to pick one that can generate the spreadsheets you need and be sure that the company writing the software has been around for a while. Get all the updates when they are issued and insist that your bookkeeper stay current on the system. You should know the system as well as your bookkeeper does, because you could lose that bookkeeper and have to hire a replacement. Someone on the ownership side should know and understand the system.

Integration

Your management skills will depend on how well you integrate the information from the spreadsheet system and the bookkeeping system. If both are properly done and accurately kept, you can use them to verify each other. The trick is not to post one from the other. When you receive a rent check from a tenant, post to the spreadsheet, and then repost it to the accounting system. This way, when you run the totals, they must agree. If they do not, you know you have an error. By doing this weekly or monthly, you are always in a position to know that everything is in balance. This is true integration.

Establish Real Value for Resale

Why are you going through all this work every month? The answer is simple: you will profit from it. A well-managed building will show a consistent monthly profit, which is why you got into this in the first place.

The payoff for this is twofold. First, you will have established a regular, ever-increasing cash flow that will pay a good return on your invested capital, and second, you will have created a capital gain upon sale. The increase in the monthly cash flow increases the annual NIBDS. This is what you sell when you sell.

Reinvest or Sell?

The ultimate goal for any investment is the payoff. This can be accomplished by either buying or refinancing. If you have purchased a good property and managed it well, you will face the decision to sell with a certain amount of trepidation. If you sell, you will pay a capital gain tax of 20 percent on your profit, and then you will have a rather large sum of money in your hand. What will you do with it? If you remember, you were facing this question when you bought the building in the first place.

If you do not sell the building, what is the future for your investment, and how can you add to it? The answer is to keep the property and refinance it. If you were clever at the time of purchase and selected a multi-tenant property, and you have subsequently improved the tenancy to the point where all your tenants have less than 5 percent of the occupied space, and the building's location is holding up well against the market's changes, then you should strongly consider holding on to the building. Unless you really need the money, there is no reason to sell a building you know and are happy with to buy someone else's building. Rather, refinance it, and buy another building. Build your empire.

A good multi-tenant building with an established track record of increasing rents and a great location is very financeable. If you have owned it for 10 years and your first loan is due to be retired, you stand a great chance of securing a bigger loan, based on your newly enhanced NIBDS. If you make the decision to keep it, go for a 30-year loan. You might have to agree that the lender will have the right to adjust the interest rate every 10 years, but try to lock in the loan. You can finance out some, if not all, of your initial capital investment using the proceeds to buy another building. This is how real estate empires are built.

What Do You Have for Sale?

You can still build your empire by selling. When you sell, you have two choices: sell and pay the tax, or sell and reinvest the money in a like investment. This "sell and reinvest" option is called the right to "exchange" one investment for another. The two properties must be of like kind. Consult your attorney on this one. There is latitude in the definition, established by legal precedent, so that you may exchange a shopping center for an office building, but you will need to have a good attorney experienced in exchanges to advise you on the procedures and the latitude of the exchange possibilities.

You may even exchange for more than one property. There are advantages in having more than one property, so long as you follow some simple guidelines. If you purchase multiple properties in the same market, make them different types of property. You do not want to become your own competitor. If you have become enamored of a particular type of property, acquire the same properties in different markets. This is geographical diversity. It might be nice to own the best of that type of property in several markets. You will have to do the same research and selection in each market, but the diversity is worth it. Some investors opt for a diverse property mix in one market. Whichever option you select, go through the acquisition process for each property exhaustively.

The Least You Need to Know

- Continuous, ongoing maintenance will make you money in the long run. Insist on it.

- Create your own tools to administer a good maintenance program. Monitor it frequently.

- Have reports and spreadsheets to document that program. See that everyone charged with the program both understands and uses the system.

- Decide early on whether you will want to sell or refinance. Sometimes you can and sometimes you cannot, but never let the possibilities be far from your mind.

- Once you are comfortable with the role of real estate investor, decide to expand either geographically or with diverse properties in the same market.

- At all times work your plan and stay flexible.

Part 7

How to Sell and Reinvest—or Not!

The final part of the investment game plan is to collect your profits. This does not come about haphazardly. You must systematically set it up, do the paperwork, and then prepare to cash out.

Your buyer is no idiot either, so remember your original purchase and eliminate all potential objections to your price and terms before they can be put forth by the buyer.

A systematic, organized approach, starting with an intelligent purchase, followed by astute and organized management, will pay off in a big way when you sell.

The best part is that you may choose to avoid the taxes by exchanging your successful investment for another opportunity to profit. This part shows how to do that, and some of the reasons why taking this approach can create a real estate empire for you.

What Do You Have to Sell?

In This Chapter

◆ Set your price and defend it

◆ Sales plans and selling tools

◆ Good paperwork should sell the building for you

◆ Sell the sizzle—throw in the steak

After all your hard work, you may decide to sell the property. If that happens, you will need to know how to maximize your profit. The key to doing this is to remember what you went through when you purchased the property. Your goal as a seller is the opposite of what it was as a buyer. The two objectives of a seller are to set the price and be able to justify it, and to present a building that is so clearly well-maintained that there is no room for deductions.

If you have ever sold a car, you know that a car that is clearly spit-shined and in good working order will sell for a lot more money than one that is indifferently presented. Real estate is no different. Part of any buyer's decision is logic, and part is emotional. If your property clearly looks like the current owner has pride of ownership and is organized, then the property will appeal to a wider range of buyers. It will appeal to someone who is not as organized because it will mean that they will not have play catch up to get up-to-speed immediately. This chapter shows you how to present your property and justify your asking price.

An important note: The sales package and documentation outlined in this chapter are for the buyer *only when the property is in escrow*. You do not turn it over to the buyer until the buyer is under contract (has executed a nondisclosure agreement). Your financial information is proprietary and should never be exposed to the brokerage community. In the wrong hands, it could be used by another broker to loot your building of tenants for a competitor's building.

Establish the Value

Establishing the value of the property is based on the numbers. If you have maintained an up-to-date spreadsheet on the operating costs since you took over, you can clearly establish the building's financial track record. With this in hand, you can then justify your forward projections.

Buildings are sold, not only on the basis of their current earnings, but also on their potential. An indifferently performing building will have a poor chance of justifying an ambitious projection. The current NIBDS (net income before debt service) will be used to calculate the price of the building, but projections and imminent lease escalations can be factored into the mix. If your building has a significant portion of the leases due to be automatically escalated within the next year, you can make a good case for averaging the projected NIBDS with the current NIBDS. In addition, you can affect the cap rate by showing your building as having made better than average gains under your ownership. When selling a successful building, you must share your game plan with the buyer, and if you have proven that it is effective, you will most likely be able to get your full asking price.

Over 75 percent of my project sales have been at prices that are 15 percent over the competition. This is strictly due to the potential built into the leases. The leases are what you're selling.

Remember How You Bought

If you retrace your footsteps to the time when you were looking at the building, you can remember how you dissected the leases. Refer to Chapter 9 and you will see what you went through. If you put your buyer's hat back on, you will know what your prospective buyer wants to know. You can answer questions before they are asked. If all the information you need is current (and as a good manager you will have all the current information), then you are in a position to shut down any objections to price before they are stated.

Set Yourself Up to Get Your Asking Price

As in any other enterprise, the proactive approach will be the most aggressive one. Pretend you are a mother protecting her young. If you take steps to avoid danger, they all will be well. The proactive position is to anticipate objections and have the answers as part of your initial presentation. There is no way to anticipate 100 percent of every potential buyer's questions or objections, because no one is omniscient. However, if you follow these guidelines, you can anticipate over 95 percent of the potential queries, and have the appropriate answers to bolster your price and terms.

How to Present the Building

If you eat out a lot, you know the major difference between two restaurants serving the same quality meal will be the presentation and the atmosphere. The same is true of your building. The presentation will make the difference between a full-price sale and a sale at a lesser price. Your sales package will be the presentation, and the condition of your building will provide the atmosphere.

The ideal sales package has three components, and I break them down as follows:

- Building's history
- The game plan as implemented
- Current situation and projections for the next five years

These three components will create a convincing case. This will require some work on your part, but remember that you have all the information readily available.

History

The building's history is composed of the condition it was in when you purchased it. You should have photos, your original tenant information spreadsheet, and your initial building condition reports. What does this show a prospective buyer? First of all, it shows him that you are a knowledgeable buyer in your own right. It puts him on notice that you know how to buy a building, and by implication, how to sell one. This, coupled with the next two components of the package, will prove it to the buyer.

Your Game Plan

The next component is your game plan. If you did it right, you have two versions: your initial one, and your current one. Show the buyer both plans. First, it bolsters your position, and second, it may be a big help to the buyer. The buyer may be a novice, who could greatly benefit from your input.

The Straight Skinny

Not all buyers are proactive ones. You might find one who wants to buy a great building, and then just sit around and clip coupons. Aggressive buyers will not want your building anyway. They, like you before, will be looking for a building that is sound, but has unrealized potential. If you have done your job right, your building will not qualify for that type of buyer. Your buyer will be a fatter cat who does not want to work too hard. This represents the bulk of the buyers out there today. They are too busy to spend the time to make the extra money.

Projections

To be irrefutable, your numbers should cover day one to five years in the future. You have these records, so use them. Since they represent fact and projections based upon solid leases, no one can tear them apart. If the buyer sees how the building has progressed under your ownership, he or she can see that it can be sustained by simply following your game plan. You have nothing to lose by sharing it with the buyer.

Support the Numbers

The best way for your package to work is to be self-supporting. The numbers are the key, and their support is the lease documents. Your package should contain the following numbers:

- The historical cash flow, year-by-year, or better still, quarter-by-quarter, or best yet, month-by-month

- An equally detailed expense history, broken down the same way

- Your initial tenant information spreadsheet

- Your current tenant information spreadsheet

- A side-by-side comparison of these two with a column showing the percentage increase in revenue

- A copy of your above-the-line income and operating cost history from inception to the present

History Above and Below the Line

If you have done the accounting properly, you will be in a position to share with the buyer the ledgers showing all your income and expense numbers above the line. *The LLC or partnership operating expenses are none of the buyer's business.* If you wrote off your Ferrari against the profits, it is not the buyer's business. All the information they are entitled to stops at the NIBDS figure and the details on the current financing.

Tax Returns

This brings up the question of tax returns. I believe that these are privileged information. I do not show them. I have no problem with a partner's auditor looking at the partnership books, but tax information is privileged information from all outsiders. When you do your accounting properly, all the relevant information is contained in the operating reports. There is no useful information for the buyer in the partnership or LLC operating expenses. The below-the-line costs do not pertain to the building. If you are operating multiple properties, these costs may be assessed against one property, but be for the benefit of all. They can, therefore, be misleading. The best course of action is to keep them to yourself; avoid confusing the buyer at all costs.

The Straight Skinny

What happens when there are problems with your building? Do you work around them? Cover them up? Absolutely not. You must disclose any potential major problems (ethically, and often, legally). What is the best way to get around them? Fix them in advance or be up front about the situation and lower the price accordingly.

How Good Is Your Building?

This is a fair question and again, if you have managed the building properly, you should be in a position to state that it is in excellent condition. The other side of the question is "How does it compare to the competition?" This, too, you should be in a position to answer. Your building will be in a certain class and should be readily competitive, if not above par, with all its direct competitors. Since you have kept abreast of the market through your broker and your appraiser, you should be able to present a detailed market comparison for the buyer.

Is the Building "State of the Art"?

There is no way that your building will stay directly competitive with the new buildings, but it can do the next best thing. Its services can stay competitive. The only real differences will then be reduced to the physical. The newest design innovations can be copied to a point, but you can never truly duplicate the appeal of a new building. You don't have to. Your building, by virtue of its age, will cost considerably less. If, however, your building is up to par in services and location, your rents should not be far behind those of the newer buildings. Location, services, and amenities can make up for a host of architectural innovations. The fact is that once a tenant is through the lobby, the tenant space and its amenities will make or break the building.

Your Building's Niche in the Market

As an example, compare a garden office building (one or two story) with a heavily landscaped campus and a very modern, state-of-the-art, mid-rise building with a five-story parking garage. They have completely different appeals, but there is no reason that they cannot have the same rents. They appeal to different types of tenants.

The point is that for an individual or a small investor, the garden office building is an easier building to keep competitive with the market. The size of the structure lends itself better to modernization, and its amenity, the landscaped common areas, are easier to upgrade and to maintain than seven stories of steel and concrete. Is it a better building? I cannot answer that question. For me, as a small investor, it is a better deal, but for a large REIT, the mid-rise building is a better deal. When you purchase and when you sell, you should know who you are competing with. These two buildings can stay competitive on rents and NIBDS, but in reality, they will never be competitors. They appeal to different clienteles.

The Straight Skinny

You made the money when you bought, you increased the profit through astute management, but you will only collect your profit when you sell.

The Buyer's Objectives

This brings us back to the buyer's objectives. They are the same as yours when you bought. The buyer wants the best building he or she can get for the lowest possible price. For you to get the best possible price, you need to market your building, not to an entrepreneur like yourself, but to a coupon-clipping larger investor that plays the percentages. This class of buyer will appreciate that you have created a superior building package, and will be willing to pay more for it, especially if the buyer is exchanging out of another property. Once a building is properly set up, it is easier to maintain. Ease of maintenance is what this type of buyer is looking for, no-hassle cash flow. His or her rate of return requirement is lower than yours, so your cap rate can be higher than normal in the market.

Set Up the Win

Part of your entrepreneurial profit is tied up in your proactive entrepreneurial approach to selling.

A large part of your ability to sell well is to set it up yourself. You must pick your target market, select the broker, and provide the selling package. Remember, the package outlined above is only for the buyer when the property is in escrow. This detailed financial profile of the building, together with a detailed graphics package, will become the buyer's total due diligence package to be furnished by you, the seller. The preparation of the sales package to be used by the brokers is dealt with in Chapter 29.

The Least You Need to Know

- You have all the information you need to sell the property. Your presentation and documentation should make it an easy job.

- Put it together intelligently to forestall objections. Again, take the proactive approach.

- Back up all the information with facts and leases. The buyer cannot refute or devalue the facts.

- Show it only to the buyer. The detailed building information is not for public dissemination. Make the buyer sign a nondisclosure agreement before presenting the facts.

Chapter 29

Your Sales Presentation

In This Chapter

- ◆ Should you sell your own building?
- ◆ Sales tools
- ◆ Disclosure
- ◆ Market price and your price

If you decide to sell the building, how should you go about it? Can you sell it yourself? Should you list it with a broker? There are many different answers to these questions. The answer that fits your situation will depend on how long you have been in the business and how well-known you are. This chapter answers these and other questions about how to actually put your property on the market.

Representation

If you are relatively new in the business, you should use an investment property broker. If you have been in the business for a while and are known to the community, you might be able to sell it yourself. If you do not have an established relationship with an investment broker, you can give an *open listing* to any broker.

It's a business decision. On the one hand, using a listing broker is expensive, but the property should sell faster. If you attempt to sell it anyway, you will, most likely, end up having to deal with the buyer's broker. The important thing to know is how much the brokerage transaction is worth.

Most brokers charge a fee that is a fixed percentage of the selling price. What is the impact of this? Let's take a look at a typical transaction. If you purchased a property for $4 million, with $1 million cash down, and you sell it for $5 million, you are looking at a potential profit of $1 million, or a 100 percent gain on your invested equity. If, however, you pay a 3 percent commission, you will pay the broker $150,000 for the sale of the building. This commission will reduce your profit to $850,000, or an 85 percent return on equity. This is a significant amount of money, and the size of the commission will color your decision.

There are ways to mitigate the impact of this type of transaction, and you must find one that makes you comfortable. Most owners feel that they have worked hard to establish the increased value of their buildings, and are understandably loathe to share a significant part of the upside with a broker.

If You Sell the Property

If you sell the property yourself, you will be faced with some work, but you can save one half of the potential commission. You can still reach the brokerage community by advertising that you will pay the buyer's broker a one half commission. This is fairly common, and a number of owners are successful with this approach. If you will be an infrequent investor, or a one-time investor, this is a good plan. If you fail to sell the building, you can always hire a broker later. This approach, at least, provides an opportunity to save money.

If you are in the real estate market to stay, and you intend to buy and sell properties for a long time, I recommend that you make an accommodation with an investment property broker.

Using a Broker to Sell The Building

If you're in this for the long haul, you will need to build a cadre of trusted consultants, and a good investment broker is a great place to start. If you are able to establish a long-term contractual relationship with such a broker, then you will benefit from that association. In exchange for the exclusive right to represent you in both buying and selling, the broker should be willing to make some concessions relating to the price of the service. What can be done? The possibilities are limited only by your imagination and your ability to negotiate. You can, for instance:

- Simplistically negotiate a lesser commission for your broker because he or she will make two commissions on the same property.

- Allow the broker to invest the commission at the time of purchase with you, and therefore, earn a substantial return on his or her investment when the property is sold. This is referred to as a carried commission. It is quite common in the land investment business, not as common in the income property business.

Some limitations on what you can do will depend on whether the broker is independent or affiliated with a larger brokerage house with which he or she must split the commission. Typically, brokerage houses permit a lower than market commission, but they seldom, if ever, permit a carried commission.

The potential of carried commissions is a prominent reason in a good broker's decision to become independent. This allows the broker to be entrepreneurial without leaving his or her chosen specialty. Many brokers have become wealthy through the practice of carrying commissions with carefully selected clients. In fact, it is not uncommon to find real estate–owning entities composed of a coalition of expertise in architecture, brokerage, construction, and financial management. This is a powerful combination.

You must decide which way to go. I believe that when you have completed the investment cycle with your first property, you will be in a better position to make this type of decision. At that time, when you are deciding to sell or refinance, you can examine all the possibilities.

Eyewash

No matter who sells the property, you will need a sales package to attract the buyer. Remember, the documentation referenced in Chapter 28 is not a sales tool until after you have a buyer under contract.

A traditional sales package to be distributed to the investment community will contain two elements: *eyewash* and numbers.

Buzzwords

Eyewash is a slang word for graphic art or photographs used as a sales tool. It can be either photographs or artists' renderings. The term eyewash is used to indicate window dressing. It's used to attract the buyer's attention; the numbers sell the deal.

Proposed office building, Prescott, Arizona.

Photos and Renderings

Whether you use renderings or photos depends on what you are selling. The type of graphic depends on whether you are selling an existing structure or one to be built or modified. An artist's rendering should look something like that shown here.

The Straight Skinny

Prepare the best package you can without disclosing any details pertaining to your tenant leases.

Photos of existing buildings or land are just that. However, it is very common to add two important graphic elements to the eyewash package. The first is an area map showing the location of the property in relation to the city and the highways. It could look something like the following figure.

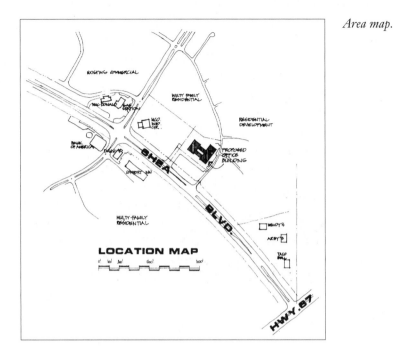

Area map.

The second, often-included graphic is an aerial photograph, either a vertical shot, one taken straight down, or an oblique one, taken at an angle. Both are shown in the following figures.

Vertical.

Oblique.

When dealing with a multi-tenant building or project, you need an overall site plan and floor plans. The site plan is shown below, and the floor plan follows.

Site plan.

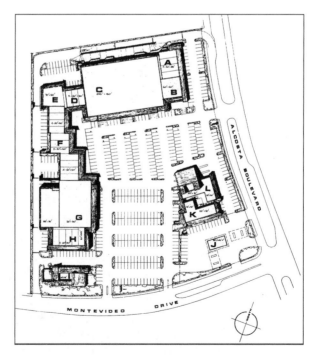

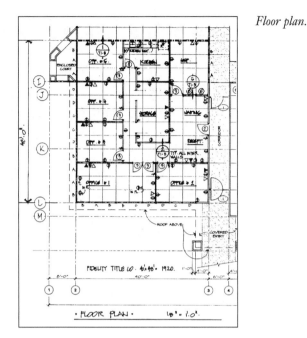

Floor plan.

Detailed Floor Plans

The detailed plans for the individual tenants will be included in the second part of the complete, due-diligence package presented to the buyer for evaluation after you and the buyer have executed the purchase and sale contract and the buyer has executed the nondisclosure agreement. This package will include the plans and specifications from which the building was originally constructed and up-to-date plans of the existing tenant improvements. The last drawing will be the as-built plans.

As-Built Plans

As-built plans include all specific changes from the original blueprints. The information contained is usually confined to the site plan and is generally presented in the form of an ALTA, title company certified, boundary survey. Typical items shown are, at the very least, the following:

- ◆ The building location in relation to the property boundaries and setbacks
- ◆ The location of any easements
- ◆ The specific location of all buried utilities
- ◆ The location of any additional structures such as trash enclosures or utility installations

The Numbers Portion of the Sales Package

The numbers portion of the sales package will be the important part for the buyer. There are many theories about what numbers to show the buyer. There is no reason to disclose any part of the accounting at this time. Any accounting presentation should be in the financial-disclosure package presented to the buyer after the contract signing.

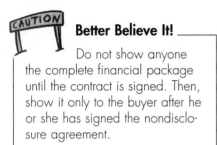

Better Believe It!

Do not show anyone the complete financial package until the contract is signed. Then, show it only to the buyer after he or she has signed the nondisclosure agreement.

Spreadsheets are the most useful financial selling tool. They are graphic in nature and can be, therefore, very effective in presenting the information you want to get across. What has worked best for me as part of the initial presentation is a five-year cash-flow spreadsheet. I show two prior years' history, the current year, and two years of projected income and expense.

The information contained should be a summary of your building's financial performance. The line items shown for each of the five years should include the following:

♦ The gross potential income (GPI)

♦ The actual vacancy

♦ The effective gross income (EGI)

♦ The total operating expenses

♦ Operating expenses recaptured from the tenants

♦ The net operating income

♦ Property management fees, if any

♦ The net income before debt service (NIBDS)

♦ The debt service

♦ The cash flow

♦ The percentage increase or decrease per year over the first year shown

Comparisons

Comparisons are a little risky. You can, with impunity, compare your building's performance against its base year (the year you purchased it), but you must be careful when comparing it to the market.

If you have some general market data supplied by a reliable third party, such as an appraiser or a reputable brokerage house, you can use it to compare your building's performance against the market's average.

The Competition

Finally, there is the competition. The information on other sales in your market should be furnished by an authoritative source other than yourself. Put yourself in the position of representing your own building only. Market comparisons are generally done by the buyer and the buyer's consultants during the due-diligence process. If your building is priced higher than comparable sales, and it should be, you will be in the position to prove its superior performance without denigrating the competition. Make no comment on other properties. Sell your building. Its performance should speak eloquently for its value.

The Least You Need to Know

- ◆ Prepare the best package you can without disclosing any details pertaining to your tenant leases.

- ◆ Create and use graphics effectively; they will generate interest in your property.

- ◆ Simplify your spreadsheet data so that it can be understood at a glance.

- ◆ Highlight your building's above-average performance, making it leap off the page at the buyer.

Chapter 30

The Price

In This Chapter

- ◆ Before you enter the market
- ◆ Check the competition
- ◆ Establish your price
- ◆ Potential financing as a sales tool

Most people do not wake up in the morning and decide to sell an investment. If, however, you have followed the previous chapters on management diligently, you could, in fact, wake up and decide to sell and be ready to do so. If you are like most people, and you have done a good job, in general, but have not necessarily done everything I recommended, then you will have to prepare your project for sale. Part of the preparation will be physical, while the rest of the process will be paperwork.

You can refer to the list shown in Chapter 29 for the paperwork recommendations and to the maintenance section as outlined in Chapter 27 for the maintenance recommendations. This chapter covers sizing up the competition.

Selling vs. Buying

Buying and selling are two sides of the same coin. You know what you went through when you purchased, and most likely, the owner at that time was a fairly typical investor who had not diligently prepared his or her building for sale as I have recommended. That is why you were able to acquire the property at a good price. You, on the other hand, have been more diligent and are prepared to sell in the most advantageous way. The process does not happen overnight.

Anticipation

When you start to consider selling, you must, at the same time, look into refinancing so that you will have all your options up-to-date. This will enable you to make a more informed decision, and it will tell you what options will be available to your prospective buyers. Upon learning what financing is available, you might decide to keep the building and refinance. You never know. You cannot consider an option that you are unaware of. Check it out.

Be Prepared

If you have assembled the paperwork, and if you have investigated the market, and if you know what the potential financing is, then you are ready to make the decision. What remains is to create your sales plan, as discussed in Chapters 28 and 29. This process is no different than your approach to buying. What you are doing is anticipating the buyer's moves. He or she will be doing the research and attempting to understand the market and your building's place in it. Your sales plan should address all the relevant questions that you would be asking.

Reconfirm Your Assessment of the Market's Current Condition

If you take a proactive stance in this process, you will repeat the steps you took when you purchased the building. It will be much faster and easier to do, because you have been an active participant in this market for a period of years. This exercise is a double-check and a last-minute fine-tuning of your perception of the market.

Remember that your results will not be for public consumption. The resulting data will be used by you during the negotiation process to refute any false claims about the market. The most important data will be the facts on your immediate market area and the segment of that market in which you compete directly.

Your Specific Market Segment

You will need to know everything there is to know about your competition. This is where your relationship with the brokerage community will become invaluable, and any information you can extract from your appraiser will bolster the data. You can even pose as a prospective tenant and "shop" the competition. This is done in almost every industry and is not unethical. It is time-consuming, but it will give you a first-hand look at your direct competitors.

You will need to find out where your building fits into the picture. Its relative position is not as important as its position relative to when you purchased it. If your segment of the market is the upper-middle rent range, then that defines your competitive niche. If you have transformed the building

The Straight Skinny

If you follow the general rule, "buy at the bottom and sell at the top," you will always come out a winner.

from a lower rental niche to the upper-middle segment, then you have elevated the building during your tenure, and you are now ready to cash in on your profits.

The SMSA

A quick check of the regional market is also in order. What do you look at? Mostly, you are looking for signs of economic well-being. If employment is up, if the average wage compares favorably with the national average, and if vacancies are down, then it is probably a good time to sell. The worst time to sell and the best time to buy are in times of recession.

Cap Rates

Once the decision has been made to sell and the market has been checked, you will be tasked with establishing your price. To do this with any conviction, you will have to construct your scenario. Your price will be above the market, so you must have sound reasons to justify the price. If you have done your job correctly, you can do this with ease. For years, I have achieved 15 to 20 percent over the market on building sales.

The first order of business is to establish a cap rate for the income stream. Refer to Chapter 9 for the establishment of your cap rate. To decide on what to capitalize, you need to do a little more work.

Look at the Competition

Before setting your price you must check the competition to see what prices other buildings have been fetching. It is especially helpful to know whether they are using gross or net leases. If the competing sales are still using gross leases, and if you have completely converted your building to NNN leases, you will be able to command a much better price when you sell. Make a spreadsheet for your research, then set it aside for the moment.

Investment Alternatives

The next area of investigation is to examine what the competition is for income-yielding investments. This will not be the stock market, but the bond- and debt-based securities market. When you have established this, you will see how it compares to the real estate market. Remember that an equivalent percentage return on investment in the real estate field will have the added attraction of depreciation attached to it, and will, therefore, be a better annual yield.

The final decision will be what NIBDS (net income before debt service) to sell. If you have done your job correctly, your building will now have an ever-increasing cash flow due to the annual escalation of your NNN leases. The buyer will enjoy an instant or pending increase in NIBDS due to this fact. You can, if you have a strong market position, average the current year and the next projected year's NIBDS, or lower your cap rate a little. The resulting price should be at least 20 percent over competing gross-leased buildings.

Financing

To ensure that your building can sell for the price you are asking, it makes a great deal of sense to run the price by a lender. You might even go to the trouble to actually apply for financing on behalf of a buyer yet to be named. This will qualify the building, and the buyer can then qualify when he or she surfaces. The advantage of this is that it will save considerable time and forestall the financing contingency. If the building is pre-qualified, the buyer must only pass the credit check. This can be accomplished in a matter of days.

Once the building has qualified based upon the new leases, you will be faced with the possibility of funding the new financing. If you decide to do this, you must negotiate the buyer's right to assume the new financing upon payment of the 1 percent assumption fee. Of course, the ability to refinance at a greater dollar amount is going to demand that you consider keeping the building. We will discuss this in Chapter 31.

If we assume for the moment that you are going to sell, then you might want to prepurchase the commitment for the buyer. This might well facilitate the purchase if you have an individual buyer. If, however, you have done your job well, you might find that you will be selling to a REIT or another type of long-term holding company. It will want to arrange its own financing. In an effort to facilitate the sale, I would most likely stop short of actually purchasing the commitment. Having it available on short notice should be enough. Even to have a lender express interest at the figures you have produced, 75 percent of the proposed purchase price, will be a big boost to your sales program.

What to Do When You Sell

Once the decision to sell has been made, the checklist looks something like this:

- Spiff up the building.

- Fine-tune the leases.

- Enhance the cash flow.

- Set the price.

The final preparations for the sale do not need to be either elaborate or costly, especially if you have kept on top of the building since you purchased it.

> **CAUTION** **Better Believe It!**
>
> Don't stress over the leases at this stage of the game. You have what you have, and if you are about to sell, you are out of time. If you have followed the guidelines for fine-tuning your leases, they should be in better shape than most of the competition.

Spiff Up the Building

Taking the maintenance up a notch to present the building in the best possible light will cost a little more, and if the tenants object to the extra expense, you can pay for it below the line if necessary. It will help the sale if the building looks like you have maximized its potential.

Fine-Tune the Leases

At this point, you will not be able to do much more with your leases. You can, however, review them to see how they stack up to the NNN lease criteria spelled out in Chapters 19 and 21. You can document the leases' strengths by creating a spreadsheet outlining the critical assets in your standard lease. The buyer will, in the normal course of his or her due diligence, perform this chore.

Enhance the Cash Flow

Likewise, your cash flow should be maximized. Your expense recapture should be fine-tuned so that you are recapturing 100 percent of your monthly expenses for occupied spaces. This is an important aspect of your pro forma spreadsheet. Emphasize it and brag about it.

Set the Price

Most people agree that, in most things in life, timing is everything. You must select the time to sell when the market is good. In your case, you want a seller's market. When you purchased, hopefully, you bought the building in a buyer's market. The difference in dollars can be dramatic, so do not paint yourself into a corner where you are forced to sell when the market is against you. Obviously, these things can happen, but if you have a good project with consistent cash flow, and the market has turned sour, hang on to the building until it turns around. You should not consider sacrificing capital gain unless your back is to the wall.

The Sales Document

This document is as important to you as the purchase agreement was at the time of purchase. Your goal here is to allow the buyer a reasonable time for due diligence, but couch it in the framework of the documents you have prepared in advance.

Due Diligence

The buyer will want to have 30 days to review the preliminary title commitment, allowing you that time to assemble his or her list of documents needed. You need to tie the due diligence to 30 days from delivery of the documents to the buyer. If you have prepared these documents in advance, you can deliver them the day after the escrow opens.

The real lag time will entail the preparation and execution of the Estoppel certificates. You must, therefore, have them all prepared along with your due-diligence package. Send them out for execution the day after the escrow opens. Stay on top of them and make sure that they are all executed within the parameters spelled out in the lease.

Residual Guarantees

The real liability for you in any sale is the representations and the residual obligations associated with real estate sales. Any representations made by you will survive the close of escrow. Therefore, you must be very specific about what you represent, making sure that the buyer can easily verify the facts you have represented. If you have any verbal side agreements with the tenants or contractors, you must disclose them in writing and have them acknowledged by the other parties. While oral agreements are not enforceable in real estate transactions, there are agreements entered into between landlord and tenant that are routinely honored. Keep track of them on your to-do list and disclose them to the buyer.

The Least You Need to Know

- Make sure you want to sell versus trade or refinance. The grass is not always greener out there.

- Examine the market to see if it's the right time to be selling. There is never a single, best time.

- Check your competition; it could affect your decision to sell now or at all.

- Set up the sale for a win. Astute and systematic preparation will pay off handsomely at the bottom line.

Chapter 31

Pay Your Taxes or Reinvest

In This Chapter

- ◆ How much are the taxes?
- ◆ What are the alternatives?
- ◆ Only you can decide
- ◆ Building true wealth requires a strategy

I have alluded in previous chapters to the tax implications of real estate. When you sell, there will be two types of taxable income: capital gain and recapture of depreciation during your time of ownership. Capital gain is profit, and recapture is a paper adjustment intended for the government to "recapture" the tax benefit afforded to you during your period of ownership. All of these items will be examined in the light of your "basis" in the property. Since one of the reasons for becoming invested in real estate is the tax benefits, it is important that you understand them, and this chapter will help you do that. But note: *I am not a tax expert, and the following does not constitute tax advice. Consult your accountant for some clear direction before you take action.*

The Tax and You

The three most important parts of the tax code that will bear on the sale are basis, capital gain, and recapture.

Basis

Basis, on your original property, is defined as the purchase price of the property, plus any capital improvements that you have made since the purchase date, less any depreciation you have taken during your ownership of the property. All other expenditures are deemed to be operating or partnership expenses and are expensed during the current year for tax purposes. Your established basis will be used by your accountant, with the approval of the IRS, to determine the depreciation schedule during your tenure as the property owner.

Depreciation

If annual cash flow with a good return on invested capital was the sum total of the payment involved in a real estate investment experience, then it would be a great deal by anyone's standard. However, it gets even better! During the cash-flow period, the cash flow is tax sheltered, in part, by depreciation. In the past, the tax implications of building ownership could shape the fate of a project by overshadowing the feasibility. Tax options for accelerated depreciation resulted in projects that were built regardless of the return on investment.

The Tax Reform Act of 1986 put a stop to that consideration. Now all investment properties are depreciated on a straight-line basis over a period of approximately 27½ years for residential rentals and up to 39 years for commercial. Some people will say that this was the death of the development profession, but I think of it as having leveled the playing field. It helped eliminate the MBA development mills (large, well-heeled development companies employing hordes of unseasoned recent MBA graduates to play "boy wonder" developer) producing projects that had no real demand, simply because there was so much money available, and the "numbers" seemed to make sense. Today, a revamped lending market enables good developments to survive in an environment where only feasible projects are built.

Better Believe It!

This is an official disclaimer! Nothing in this book is intended to be legal or tax advice. You should consult both your attorney and your accountant for a fuller understanding of legal matters and the tax code as it applies to your situation.

The Effect of Depreciation

Depreciation is based on the assumption that each year the value of a real estate investment diminishes by a predetermined amount, currently based on a useful life of an arbitrary 30 years or more. This has been revised over the years, but concisely, if the building is theoretically wearing out over a 30-year period, then the government allows an annual tax break. The government allows owners to take a "depreciation allowance," calculated by taking the cost of the building and dividing it by the number of years allowed in the government's table of "useful life." In this way, the government provides a valuable incentive to developers and investors alike that is not available with other forms of investment.

Simplistically, a project purchased for $3,000,000, taken as having a 30-year useful life, will generate a paper loss of:

$3,000,000 \div 30$ years = $100,000 per year

This means that the first $100,000 of cash flow (NIBDS) each year is sheltered by the allowed, artificial "loss" of $100,000.

Recapture

The benefit of some "tax-free" income continues throughout your ownership of the project. When the project is sold, the straight-line depreciation you have taken during your ownership period is deducted from your basis (your original cost of acquisition), then the difference between your adjusted basis and the net sales price is used to determine your taxable income. This tax calculation does not necessarily take into account your actual profit made on the transaction. The calculated result will be taxed as capital gain if you have held the property for 12 months and a day or more.

Capital Gain

The balance of the profit over your adjusted basis is taxed at the federal rate of 15 percent, the maximum long-term (over one year) capital gain rate. The new owners are allowed to start all over, depreciating their new asset at their cost of acquisition.

What does this mean to you? You will have to consult your attorney and your accountant for this answer. You do, however, have some options when you sell. You do not necessarily have to pay the tax at that time.

Most people who pay the tax and move to other investments do so because they are not able to sustain the management requirements of real estate, or they need the cash for other obligations. Most investors with profits tend to seriously look at the exchange option.

The Exchange Option

If you wish to stay in real estate for the long term, you may "exchange" the property you are selling for another property or properties, of a "like kind" of equal or greater value than your sales price. There is some latitude in what the government allows as a like-kind exchange, so you should consult with attorneys and accountants who are experts in the field of 1031 exchanges. If you elect to "roll over" your original investment and the profit into a new investment, you are not avoiding the taxes, merely delaying the payment of them. The exchange option allows you to purchase new property and start the process all over again. In this scenario, your basis for depreciation purposes will be determined by taking your original basis in the property sold and adding in any new cost of the newly exchanged property. This new total is then used to determine your new basis and by extrapolation, your new depreciation schedule.

This process can be repeated ad infinitum. It is this sell-and-reinvest option that allows people to parley a profit into more ventures. It is a viable alternative to the refinance and reinvest scenario. Individual partners or LLC members may even part ways and exchange their percentage profits into individual new properties. Consult your tax attorney before attempting this maneuver, as it must pass IRS scrutiny.

Exchange Pros and Cons

Why don't all investors roll over their investment and profit when it is time to sell? The answer is not a simple one, as there are always outside factors that influence the individual's decision to sell or reinvest. The benefits of exchanging at the time of sale have been enumerated above, and the potential to build a real estate empire is not to be sneezed at.

Before you proceed, take a little time to examine the pitfalls in the exchange process. They are not necessarily daunting, but you need to take them into consideration before you act:

- ◆ To achieve a tax deferred exchange on all your sale proceeds, you must reinvest all your proceeds, including your original investment and your profit in the new property.

♦ You have a finite amount of time in which to find and arrange for the exchange of the new properties.

♦ Finally, there is the eternal difficulty of finding a good deal.

These considerations are the biggest reason for establishing sound, long-term relationships with your consultants. To pull off a good exchange, you will have to give your consultants plenty of notice when you decide to sell. You must start the search for new property immediately, so that all the required items will be available when they are needed to complete the transaction(s).

Your Exchange Consultants

At the very least, you will need a good broker to find you new properties, an attorney to handle the required exchange paperwork, and a good accountant to assemble the required financial analysis to make sense of the transaction.

Most tax-deferred 1031-qualified property exchanges are handled by a professional facilitator who deals with all the parties and expedites the process. You will also need the cooperation of the buyer of your property, because the buyer must "buy" your selected properties and exchange them with the property you are selling. This is facilitated by the middle man.

In addition to the above, I recommend that you also retain the services of a marketing consultant to oversee your activity with the broker on your new acquisitions. This will necessarily be a very busy time, as you will not only be selling but also buying. Both activities are time-consuming, and you might be prone to hurry and possibly overlook something in the process. Another pair of eyes and a third-party mind will be a big help.

The Attorney

The attorney will be necessary. The paperwork required during an exchange must be done correctly, or you might find yourself having to pay the taxes anyway. If the IRS does not approve the exchange, you will have to pay the tax after the fact as if you had sold and taken the cash.

Better Believe It!

Hire a good exchange attorney. You will find that it is money well spent. The results of improper legal representation can be disastrous.

The Big Decision

Which way will you jump? I believe it depends totally on your future plans and the results of the investment experience that you have during your first property acquisition and management. If you have followed the guidelines set down in this book, you should be in fairly good shape with your original investment. To go on, you will need to take it up a notch. If you review the contents of this book, you will realize that there are no earth-shattering revelations, no insider trade secrets, merely a collection of common-sense guidelines. This book merely puts them under one handy cover for you.

If you use the information in this book properly, you will use it as a guide to organize your thinking and occasionally refer to it for a double-check on your plans. Is it the definitive guide for profit-making in investment real estate? I doubt it. For you to prosper in the real estate investment game, you need to think, plan, exercise your common sense, and act in a timely manner, consistent with your well-defined goals. If I have done my job well, I will have been able to make you think about the implications of the real estate field and prompted you to be more organized in your approach.

To parlay a successful investment into an empire of any size will take some forward planning on your part. Good management is, as you have seen in this book, somewhat time-consuming. If you add the additional chores of multiple properties, then you are looking foursquare at expanding your operation to encompass the necessary management functions for more property. When this happens, someone must be delegated to manage the overall operation. When you form your first investment group, you need to be thinking along these lines. To hire and depend on a full-time, third-party manager is a decision that will definitely affect the bottom line. A manager without a stake in the profits is just an employee. Realistically, when partners or fellow members embark on an expansion plan, eventually one or more of the group will have to become a full-time manager for the enterprise. If it gets big enough, you will need an organization, replete with bookkeepers and the like.

Why Not Build Real Wealth While You're at It?

Since building a sizable portfolio is a distinct possibility for you, you need to examine the process from the start. I don't mean that you need to start creating a table of organization, but you should start organizing your thinking so that you are aware of the work involved. Look at it with an eye to evaluating the impact of multiple properties, in multiple locations on the management operation, as you proceed with your first investment. If you do this, you will be better prepared to make that sell-and-reinvest or refinance-and-hold decision when the time comes.

Refinancing can be very substantial once you have had property for a time. The following table is a typical example:

Assumptions	Effect	Financing	Cash yield
A 10-year-old office building, 20,000 SF	Rents started at $12 NNN and increased over time to $16 NNN	Original 75% of cost or at best 75% of value at completion @ a 9% cap rate = $1,999,999.00	GPI has increased from $240,000 to $320,000; NIBDS has increased to $340,000
	A 33% increase in rents	New potential loan at 9% cap rate, 75% of value	New value = $3,377,777.00; Loan = $2,533,333.00
The effect		New cash to invest	%553,333.00

Could you find a good use for this tax-free cash?

The Least You Need to Know

♦ While investing in income-producing real estate is a serious and challenging business, it can also be enjoyable and satisfying. It all depends on how you approach it. If you are a true entrepreneur, you will have an innate sense of adventure that will kick in when you start.

♦ You will meet a lot of people, and you will do things you have never done before. You will learn a lot.

♦ The process of investment and ownership will improve your life in all areas, because you will have to be organized, and an organized life can encompass many new experiences, not the least of which is a new way to make money.

♦ When you are organized, life gets better because you will have plenty of spare time for other things. In the end, that's what it's all about.

♦ Don't forget to spend some of your newly acquired largess on yourself and your family. Above all, enjoy life!

Glossary

absolute net   Income with no expense deductions, a.k.a. NNN.

absorption   The rate at which available space is leased.

acceleration   To call a note early and force a premature payoff.

acknowledgment   A document attesting to the fact that the tenant has taken possession, is occupying a premises, and is paying rent.

agency   The legal representation of another party; does not imply the ability to "bind" them to a transaction.

AIDT   All-inclusive deed of trust, a recorder lien wrapping an existing first deed of trust.

ALTA survey   A survey that includes the results of a physical inspection of the property.

ALTA title insurance   An insurance against any and all documented or undocumented flaws in the title to a property.

amortization   The prepayment of principal over time, creating level payments.

anchor tenant   A tenant with sufficient new worth to enable financing for a project.

arbitration   The binding settlement of disputes between parties, given by an agreed-upon third party.

assessment district   An area, usually contiguous involving two or more properties included in a special assessment district.

assessments   A special lien for a specific improvement benefiting two or more properties.

bankable   A loan commitment that can be borrowed against, easily financed.

bench appraisal   An estimate of value informally given by an appraiser.

beneficial title   As good as ownership rights to real property.

boundary survey   A map showing the boundaries, direction, and geographic orientation of a parcel of land.

bridge loan   A loan to tide one over until another can be funded.

broker   A licensed real estate agent who can employ other agents.

building department   A city function to evaluate and approve proposed building projects within a community.

build-to-suit   A project designed and built by a developer/contractor for one tenant or investor.

buy-sell agreement   A contract between the interim and permanent lenders and the borrower to pay off the interim loan.

call the loan   Accelerating a loan's due date.

CAM   *See* common area maintenance.

CAM charges   Costs of CAM passed on to the tenants.

campus   A collection of buildings in a parklike setting.

cap rate   *See* capitalization rate.

capitalization rate   The process of valuing an income stream by assessing a numerical factor to the probability of risk.

carry-back financing   Financing given by a seller to a buyer.

carry-back loan   A loan made by the seller to the buyer to finance part of the purchase price of real estate.

cash flow   Income less expenses.

cash on cash   Net income (NIBDS) divided by total project cost.

category   A use designation for a piece of real property; a zoning definition.

class A building   A high-rise of good quality construction; an "institutional" building.

co-housing   Housing sharing common features or amenities.

commercial   Nonresidential or residential on a large scale.

commercial real estate   (1) Real estate not single-family oriented. (2) The practice of development of investment property.

common area maintenance   Common expenses prorated to the tenants of a building; abbreviated as CAM.

compaction   The degree of compression of soil expressed in terms of its bearing capacity, or as a percentage of ideal requirements.

complex   Two or more buildings in one development.

contingency   An event that will preclude consummation of a contract.

continuing guarantee   A guarantee that survives a closing event.

contractor   One who is licensed to construct buildings and other improvements to the land.

convertible   A construction loan that may be converted to a permanent or semipermanent loan.

co-op   Residential units in a high-rise building, individually owned; does not include the land, which is held by co-op association.

core   The original center of a city.

corporation   A form of company ownership where the stockholders' liability is limited to the loss of their investment.

corridor   A linear description of land accessed by a specific traffic artery.

county board of supervisors   The elected governing body of a county.

coverage   The amount of building allowed on a given site area, generally defined as square feet per acre.

credit tenant   One with a "bankable" financial statement; in other words, an easily financed tenant.

critical path schedule   A sequence of events, the execution of which depends on the successful completion of a prior event.

cross-collateralization   Assets liened as a result of a loan on other assets.

debt coverage   The amount of NIBDS over the amount of a loan payment expressed as a percentage of total income; in other words, a 50 percent loan to value.

debt coverage ratio   The total net income before debt service (NIBDS) divided by the amount of the debt payment.

debt service   The mortgage payment.

deed of trust   A recorded lien on real property, generally a mortgage.

demised   The legal definition of a premises.

demographics   The statistical sampling of a population. Information pertaining to a specific population.

depreciation   The systematic accounting of building obsolescence through time.

depreciation allowance   The legal amount allowed for annual depreciation.

depreciation schedule   The unequal depreciation allowance over a period of time.

design-build   The construction contract wherein a contractor agrees to deliver a finished building within a certain price range, without the benefit of final plans and specs.

design review   The municipality's review of a project's proposed design.

developable   The ability to build on a piece of land.

developer   One who creates commercial real estate for a living, usually the principal or the owner.

developer's risk   The period of time during which the developer's cash is at risk.

development   The production of income-producing real estate.

disclosure   The process of revealing all the pro and con features involved in a project.

distressed   A property whose value has decreased due to loss of tenants, economic obsolescence, or both.

downsizing   The reduction of a workforce or leased premises.

draw   The tenant that attracts people to a shopping center.

due diligence   The process of discovery of all the pertinent facts about a piece of real property.

E&O   *See* errors and omissions insurance.

early call   An acceleration of a loan's due date, usually for cause.

earnest money   Money given as a deposit against the purchase price for real property.

easements   Portions of real property reserved for use by the public or third parties, generally restricted as to buildings thereon.

EIR   Environmental Impact Report. Also known as Environmental Impact Statement, or EIS.

EIS   Environmental Impact Statement. Also known as Environmental Impact Report, or EIR.

elevation   Height above sea level. Graphic depiction of a building's facade above ground.

encumbered property   Property with liens recorded against the title.

environmental   Dealing with the physical environment surrounding any given property. Pertaining to the physical world.

equity   The value evidenced by ownership.

errors and omissions insurance   A policy designed to protect architects' and engineers' clients from malpractice or error.

escrow   A third party real estate sales, purchasing, and financing facilitator.

escrow instructions   Executed instructions to the escrow agent from both buyer and seller in a real property transaction.

Estoppel certificate   A document stating that the tenant is in possession, paying rent, that the lease is in force, and that the landlord is not in default.

exchange   The process of trading one piece of real property for another to avoid immediate taxation of profits.

executed   A document that has been signed.

executory   A document ready for execution.

exhibits   Documents attached to a contract detailing specific issues.

feasibility study   The process of evaluating a deal.

fee   (1) The land, or (2) a payment for services rendered.

fee simple absolute   The unequivocal, unencumbered ownership of land.

fee title   Clean ownership rights to land.

fiduciary   An enforceable, legal obligation undertaken by an agent or partner to another person or entity.

first deed of trust   A recorded primary lien on real property, second only to the local taxes assessed.

flipping   The practice of reselling land before having purchased it.

floor plate   The layout of a building floor prior to tenant improvements.

force majeure   Acts of God or natural disasters.

free look   The time period in a real property contract during which the buyer's deposit is fully refundable.

free trade zone   A legal tax-free zone for import, export, and manufacturing of goods.

gap loan   The loan that covers the gap between equity and permanent financing; usually a land loan, or a seller carry-back loan.

general partner   A partner who is "jointly and severally" liable for all debts of a partnership.

general plan   A map showing the distribution of zoning categories in a designated area, i.e., township, city, or county.

general provisions   Boilerplate clauses in a legal document.

geotechnical   Pertaining to geology, seismology, and soil condition.

GLA   Gross Leasable Area.

going dark   A tenant's closing of a store, but continuing to pay rent.

GPI   *See* gross potential income.

gross lease   A lease which includes all costs of operation.

gross potential income (GPI)   The entire income before deductions or offsets.

hard costs   Construction costs.

hazardous materials   Materials defined by the government as hazardous to human beings and animals.

hazardous waste   Waste decreed by the U.S. government to be a hazard to human and animal health and well being.

health department   A government agency charged with protecting the health of the citizens.

high-rise building   A building containing over seven floors.

holding over   The month-to-month extension of a tenant's occupancy after a lease expires.

HVAC   Heating, ventilation, and air-conditioning.

improvement bonds   Bonds sold to the public to pay for improvements to real estate.

improvements   Construction; additions to land.

industrial building   Single- and multi-tenant manufacturing or warehouse buildings.

institution   A financial entity, usually a bank, a savings bank, a life insurance company, or a trust.

interim loan   Temporary or construction financing.

investment   Capital, money devoted to equity, or ownership of real property.

investment grade   A property worthy of investment for the long term.

joint and several   All parties are liable for the total amount of all unsecured obligations.

joint venture   A project undertaken by two or more entities.

land lease   A contract for the use of land without the transfer of ownership; it conveys a beneficial ownership.

leasable   Able to be leased (rented) for money.

lease   A written contract enabling the use of an item or premises for money.

leasehold interest   The legal right to occupy or possess real property. Not ownership rights, but enforceable and transferable.

legal notice   Notice recognized by the courts as having been duly received by the party being notified.

lessee   An occupant of a building, evidenced by written or oral agreement.

lessor   The owner or landlord.

leverage   The principle of increasing one's yield through borrowing money.

liability   A legal obligation.

lien   (1) A recorded legal obligation, a flaw in the title to a piece of property. (2) A legal notice of an obligation of the landowner.

limited liability company   A form of ownership with the limitation of liability of a corporation and the tax benefits of a partnership.

limited partner   A partner whose risk is limited to the loss of his or her investment.

limited partnership   A form of ownership where the general partner assumes the liabilities and the limited partners can lose only their investment.

lineal foot   A linear or lateral measurement.

liquidity   The relative speed of converting an asset to cash.

load factor   An added burden on the leasehold. A surcharge to pay for inefficiency in design or common areas.

loan package   A collection of documents that constitutes a complete loan application; the loan request, collateral description, and appraisal, financial statements and projections, and sample documentation.

location   The relative position of a parcel of land within a designated zone (city, town, and so on).

lot line   Property boundary.

main body   The business deal part of the lease.

majority in interest   Ownership totaling over 50 percent.

manufacturing plant   An industrial building where goods are produced.

market   The free, legal exchange of money, real property rights, and entitlements between parties.

master planned development   A planned development, usually a large residential community.

MBA shop   A company employing masters of business graduates in the 1980s, generally credited with causing the Great Recession of 1988 to 1991.

mediation   A process of negotiating a nonbinding settlement between opposing parties.

meets and bounds   A legal description of real property using geographical coordinates.

modified gross   A lease that includes only some of the operating expenses.

modified net   A lease that includes at least one expense of operation.

mortgage   A recorded loan on real property.

mortgage payment   Principal and interest payments calculated to amortize the principal over the term of the loan.

multifamily   A residential building housing more than one family.

multi-tenant building   Buildings designed for occupancy by more than one tenant.

multiuse complex   Projects mixing two or more of the following uses: office, retail, and industrial.

municipality   An aggregation of population acting as one political entity.

net income   The receipt of money over a designated period of time. Money left over after all bills are paid.

net lease   A lease that does not include operating expenses.

NI   Net income.

NIBDS   Net income before debt service is deducted.

NNN   Rent that excludes absolutely all operating expenses.

nonrecourse   A loan without personal guarantees.

note   A contract for repayment of a loan.

obsolescence   The process of rendering a building economically useless over time.

occupancy permit   A legal document entitling occupancy of a building.

office building   Single- and multi-tenant buildings housing office users only.

offset   The right to pay expenses and deduct the cost from rent or other monies due.

OPM   Other people's money, equity capital, or loans.

option   A right to purchase; a beneficial interest; generally transferable.

ordinance   A law passed by a community regulating land use.

over standard   Improvements other than those offered as standard.

parcel   A piece of land.

parcel number   A legal description of property within a county, generally assigned by the tax assessor (APN).

permanent loan   A loan for 10 or more years whose payments include principal and interest; examples are amortized or take-out loans.

personalty   Personal property.

planning commission   A government body charged with the oversight and approval of building projects, generally elected.

planning and zoning department   A governmental agency devoted to examination and evaluation of building projects.

point(s)   One percent of the principal. Money paid to secure a loan, either interim or permanent.

preleasing   Executing leases prior to the start of construction of a building.

preliminary lien notice   A legal notice that a supplier or contractor is starting work on a property that could result in a lien if unpaid.

premises   A specific location within a building, designed for and occupied by one tenant.

principal   (1) The owner. (2) The balance of a loan.

private placement   (1) The limited solicitation of equity capital. (2) The legal securing of investment capital from others without public solicitation.

pro forma   Projections of cost and income.

pro rata   A percentage share allotment.

project costs   Costs involved in the creation of a project.

property description   A legal definition of a piece of real property.

punch list   A list of unfinished or defective work.

purchase agreement   A contract to buy and sell real property.

quadrant   A one-quarter portion of any whole that is divided into four parts. Generally divided north to south and east to west.

rate of return   An annual or cumulative percent return on monies; abbreviated ROR.

real estate industry   Inclusive term denoting all individuals and entities, all property, skills, disciplines, and functions involved in the production of commercial real estate.

realty   Real property, generally defined as a house and land.

recourse   The ability to enforce repayment of a loan or obligation.

regional mall   A very large shopping center usually anchored by three or more department stores.

REIT   A real estate investment trust which owns multiple projects, usually publicly owned.

remedies   A negotiated or adjudicated compensation for a default.

rendering   A perspective graphic representation of a proposed project.

restrictions   A list of uses denied for a particular site.

retail building   Single- or multi-tenant buildings used for sale of merchandise to the public.

return on investment   Cash back from an investment; return of capital. Expressed as a percentage of the money invested. Abbreviated ROI.

right of offset   The ability to offset expenses against monies owed.

risk   An estimate of the likelihood of an event taking place; in other words, quantifying an investment's potential.

risk capital   Money invested in a nonguaranteed venture.

ROI   *See* return on investment.

roll over   The ability to convert an interim loan to a permanent loan.

ROR   *See* rate of return.

saleable   The marketability of an item.

salvage value   Value at forced sale.

schematic   A preliminary, rough graphic representation of a project.

section   (1) A graphic "slice" through a building. (2) 640 acres (a quarter of a mile square).

service the debt   Paying the mortgage or note.

setback   The distance from the property line in which nothing may be constructed.

shell   The outside of a building without tenant improvements.

signage   A coordinated group of signs designed to work closely together.

single-tenant building   A building designed for, built for, and leased to one tenant.

site   A location, including the land and the dirt.

site plan   A graphic depiction of site improvements and buildings on a parcel of land.

SMSA   A Standard Metropolitan Statistical Area, usually a core city and surrounding suburbs lumped together for statistical study.

soft costs   Costs of a project other than land and construction.

special assessments   Specific liens for specific benefits to real property.

specific density   The relative compaction of soil.

specifications   The specific description of an item as to use, dimension, construction, and quality.

speculation   The risking of capital for potentially inordinate gain due to possible increased demand for a commodity, such as land.

speculator   One who buys and resells unimproved land for a profit.

standard survey   A survey showing the physical boundary of a parcel of land with any recorded easements shown.

stipulations   A list of items to be done prior to improving or entitling a piece of real property.

strip commercial   A retail building, small and usually without an anchor tenant.

structure   (1) A building or constructed edifice. (2) The skeletal support for a building.

subcontractor   A contractor employed by another contractor or supplier rather than by the owner.

subdivision   The process of breaking up raw land into five or more separate and saleable parcels.

subject site (parcel)   A specific parcel of land.

subletting   The practice of executing a lease to a subtenant while the tenant remains on the original lease. Generally requires landlord's consent.

subordinated   Status of a lien, junior in position to another lien.

subordinated land lease   A land lease that is junior to financing in the event of default. The loan can foreclose out the land lease.

supply and demand   A prime determination of price; the greater the demand, the higher the price, and vice versa.

survey   The act of gathering data for the graphic legal description of a piece of land.

syndication   The raising of capital pools by public solicitation.

take-out loan   A permanent loan designed to pay off the interim or construction loan.

tenant broker   One who represents the interest of the tenant, rather than the interest of the landlord.

tenant improvement   Items constructed within a demised premises for the exclusive use of the tenant.

TI   Tenant improvements.

title   Ownership rights to real property or a document outlining the condition of a property's legal encumbrances.

title insurance   Insurance issued to protect the buyer or lender in the event of flaws to the ownership of real property.

title report   A written report regarding liens and claims recorded and not recorded on real property.

topographic map   A graphic description of the grades (contours and elevation) of a piece of land.

topography   The shape of land (hills and valleys, contours, and the like).

total costs   The all-inclusive number; nothing excluded. Includes land and hard and soft costs.

township   A map section used to locate land.

trade zone   A legally created tax-free zone used to promote international trade.

traffic count   The number of vehicles or people passing a specific point in an average 24-hour period.

traffic study   A report dealing with the extent and the effects of vehicular activity within a given area.

tri-party agreement   A contract, a buy-sell agreement, between the construction and permanent lenders and the borrower.

unsubordinated land lease   A land lease which has a higher lien priority than the loan.

urban renewal   A government-mandated land acquisition to promote the redevelopment of blighted areas of a city.

urban sprawl   The result of controlled low-rise development. New buildings spread out, rather than up.

useful life   The government's appraisal of the length of economic service of any given building.

use permit   A legal document, issued by a municipality or county that allows a specific activity on a particular site.

utility   Water, gas, electric, cable, sewer, telephone services.

visitor   Someone other than a tenant.

wrap loans   A loan that is in second position, but which assumed the responsibility to repay the first loan, under the existing terms.

0-lot line   The ability to build right up to the property boundary.

zoning   The process of categorizing uses for real property.

Sample Documents

Sample Purchase Agreement

THIS AGREEMENT, made this ___ day of_____, by and between [INSERT SELLER'S NAME], (hereinafter called "Seller") and [insert buyer's name] (hereinafter called "Buyer").

W I T N E S S E T H;

WHEREAS, Buyer has offered to purchase from Seller that certain real property, hereinafter more particularly described, which property is located in the County of _____, State of _____, (hereinafter referred to as the "Property"), for a purchase price equal to _____; for approximately _____ acres, subject to a complete and accurate survey to determine the precise number of acres contained in the property; and adjustment of the purchase price as provided in paragraph 3 hereof; and

WHEREAS, Seller is willing to sell the property on the terms and conditions contained herein; and

WHEREAS, the parties desire not only to enter into a formal detailed agreement of purchase and sale but also to establish an escrow through which the purchase and sale contemplated herein will be consummated.

NOW, THEREFORE, in consideration of the terms of this Agreement, the parties hereto agree as follows:

1. DESIGNATION OF ESCROW HOLDER. Buyer and Seller designate _____, the escrow holder (hereinafter referred to as the "escrow holder"). This Agreement shall constitute Escrow Instructions for the sale of the Property and a copy hereof shall be deposited with escrow holder for this purpose. Should escrow holder require the execution of its standard form printed Escrow Instructions, the parties agree to execute same; provided, however, that such instructions shall be construed as applying only to escrow holder's employment and that if there are conflicts between the terms of this Agreement and the terms of the printed Escrow Instructions, the terms of this Agreement shall control.

2. AGREEMENT TO SELL. Seller hereby agrees to sell, and Buyer hereby agrees to buy from Seller, the property located at _____ and described in Tax Assessor's Parcel #_____ which is attached hereto as Exhibit "A" and incorporated herein by reference which exhibit shall subsequently be replaced by a complete and accurate survey as soon as the same is available.

3. PURCHASE PRICE. Buyer agrees to purchase the property for the sum equal of the product of the number of square feet times $ _____, (which sum is hereinafter called the "purchase price"). The purchase price shall be payable in the following manner:

a) Cash in the amount of _____($ _____) shall be deposited with escrow holder in an account bearing a minimum of $5\frac{1}{4}\%$ interest to Buyer upon the execution of this Agreement and the designation by escrow holder of the "effective date." This payment shall constitute consideration for this contract. This payment shall be refundable except as noted hereinafter. This payment shall become nonrefundable and shall be released to Seller upon Buyer's completing to his satisfaction all items of work outlined in Paragraphs #4, #6, #7, #10. If the Buyer for any reason except as noted in Paragraphs #4 and #5 does not release the above payments, this Agreement becomes null and void with no further obligation or liability by either party. Escrow agent shall not release any funds to Seller until Seller has delivered the executed deed as outlined in Paragraph #8 herein.

b) The balance of the purchase price, approximately _____ ($ _____) shall be deposited in escrow on or before the date of closing and together with the original deposit of _____ $ _____) shall constitute 100% of the purchase price pursuant to Paragraph #3 herein.

4. TITLE OBLIGATIONS. Within fifteen (15) days from the effective date of this Agreement Seller shall cause to be delivered to the Buyer at Seller's sole cost and expense, a current title commitment for an ALTA owner's extended policy of title insur-

ance to be issued by escrow holder, showing the status of title of the Property and all exceptions, including leases, easements, restrictions, rights-of-way, covenants, reservations and other conditions, if any, affecting the Property, which would appear in an owner's extended policy of title insurance, if issued, and committing to issue such policy of title insurance to Buyer in the full amount of the purchase price for the Property. Accompanying such title commitment, Seller shall also cause to be furnished to Buyer legible copies of all documents, operating agreements, utility agreements, maintenance and management contracts, and any other existing agreements in effect, affecting the Property referred to in such title commitment. Provided Seller has timely provided Buyer with the preliminary title report (and copies of the exceptions) Buyer shall notify Seller of any objections which Buyer may have to the status of title within thirty (30) days from the date Buyer receives such title report. Buyer, at Buyer's sole option, may extend the subsequent dates in this agreement by the amount of time seller is late delivering this title commitment and accompanying documents to Buyer. If Buyer fails to give such notice of dissatisfactions as to any exception or other matter within such thirty (30) day period, such exception(s) shall be deemed approved by Buyer. If Buyer disapproves of condition of title, the earnest money deposit shall be returned to Buyer, the Agreement shall terminate, and neither party shall have any liability or obligation to the other. Time is of the essence in this agreement. Should Seller not deliver title commitment within the time frame specified then all dates in this agreement are automatically extended by the amount of the delay of Seller's submittal.

Seller shall convey marketable title to the property to Buyer by grant deed in fee simple absolute, subject to no exceptions other than those specifically set forth in this Agreement and those approved in writing by Buyer. Any exceptions to title approved in writing by Buyer in the aggregate are referred to herein as "permitted exceptions," and they shall not constitute a breach of Seller's duty to convey marketable title or of Seller's implied covenants of title arising from said deed. Buyer shall be provided, at Seller's cost, at close of escrow a policy of title insurance written by escrow holder on American Land Title Association (ALTA) Title Insurance Policy Standard Form with liability in the amount of the purchase price (hereinafter referred to as "title policy"). Such title policy shall show no exceptions other than the permitted exceptions; the usual printed exceptions and/or conditions and stipulations of the ALTA Standard Form policy.

5. RIGHT OF CANCELLATION.

a) Anything to the contrary notwithstanding in this Agreement, including but not limited to Paragraphs #3(1) and #4 hereof, Buyer may, for any reason, cancel this Agreement and the escrow provided for herein, at any time within the first thirty (30) days following receipt by Buyer of the preliminary title report to be furnished by Seller. Such cancellation shall be effected by Buyer providing Seller and the escrow holder with written notice of election to terminate prior to the expiration of such thirty (30) day period, in which even escrow holder shall pay to Buyer the initial _____ ($ _____) earnest money deposit, at which time this Agreement shall terminate and be of no further force and effect and neither party shall have any further obligation or liability to the other. If Buyer does not cancel this Agreement within such thirty (30) day period as provided for herein, the initial _____ ($ _____) earnest money deposit shall be released to Seller, upon completion and approval by Buyer of items covered in Paragraphs #4, #6, #7, #10. Such cancellation shall be effected by Buyer providing Seller and the escrow holder with written notice of election to terminate prior to the expiration of such _____ day period.

6. RIGHT OF INSPECTION. Buyer shall have _____ days from the effective date of this Agreement at Buyer's sole cost to effect an inspection of the subject property. Buyer and Buyer's Engineers, employees and representatives have the right to enter upon the Property for the purpose of making the necessary investigations, including but not limited to, building inspection, surveying, soils tests, location of utilities, storm drainage and any other tests Buyer deems necessary. If Buyer shall enter the subject property during the term of this Agreement for any reason whatsoever, Buyer hereby agrees to indemnify and hold Seller harmless from and against any and all claims, liabilities, causes of action and damages which Seller may have filed against it or may suffer or incur, arising out of or attributable to the entry upon the subject property and the acts thereon of Buyer, its agents, employees and representatives. Such indemnification shall extend to the costs of litigation incurred by Seller, if any, and to the reasonable attorney's fees which may be expended by Seller in connection therewith.

7. SURVEY. During the first thirty (30) days after the effective date of this Agreement, Seller shall furnish an ALTA As Built Survey acceptable to escrow holder and Buyer. The contents of the survey and map shall be deemed approved by Buyer unless disapproved by Buyer in writing conveyed to Seller within ten (10) days of the receipt of the survey.

8. PLACING DEED IN ESCROW. On the _____ day after the effective date of this Agreement or Buyer's approval of the Title commitment and prior to escrow holder releasing to Seller, Seller shall execute and deliver to escrow holder the duly executed and acknowledged deed conveying the property to Buyer. Buyer then, subject to having approved all items in paragraphs 3,4,5, & 7 within _____ days of the

effective date of this Agreement, shall instruct escrow holder to release to Seller the _____ ($ _____) earnest money deposit. Said deposit shall be nonrefundable and deemed earned by Seller subject to Paragraphs #3, #4, #5, #7, and #23 herein.

9. PLACING PURCHASE PRICE IN ESCROW. Prior to the close of escrow, Buyer shall deliver or cause to be delivered to escrow holder, as set forth in Paragraph #3 (b) above, cash and all other documents in the amount of the balance of the purchase price inclusive of all deposits plus those closing costs to be paid by Buyer.

10. CONDITIONS PRECEDENT. The following conditions are conditions precedent to Buyer's obligation to consummate its purchase of the property:

a) Seller shall have performed each and every, all and singular, its obligations, and promises contained in this Agreement.

b) Bonds and assessments. Buyer understands that there are not outstanding assessments against the property. Seller shall deliver title to Buyer free of all liens and encumbrances at the close of escrow.

c) Buyer shall give written notice to Seller, through escrow agent, thirty (30) days prior to closing of escrow to vacate the property.

If any of the above conditions precedent shall fail to occur, Buyer's obligation under this Agreement shall terminate by Buyer's giving written notice thereof to Seller and the escrow holder. Thereupon, Seller shall instruct the escrow holder to return all payments to Buyer, unless forfeited as provided for hereinabove, and both Buyer and Seller agree to execute such documents, releases, and/or instructions as may be necessary to reflect fully the termination of Buyer's obligations hereunder.

The Conditions of Closing are exclusively for the benefit of Buyer, and Buyer may, in writing (at his option), at any time waive any such condition. In the event Buyer shall fail to notify Seller in writing prior to the end of such investigation period that all such Conditions of Closing have occurred or been waived, then this Agreement shall immediately terminate and neither party shall have any further obligation or liability hereunder, and Buyer's deposit of _____ shall be immediately returned to Buyer.

11. CLOSING OF ESCROW. Escrow holder shall not close escrow until it holds the following items in its file:

a) The moneys, documents and instruments specified in Paragraphs #3, #4, #7, #8, and #9 hereof.

b) The title policy insuring that Buyer holds title to the property as of the time of closing escrow and showing the following additional matters:

1) The permitted exceptions; and

2) The usual printed exceptions and/or conditions and stipulations of the title policy.

c) A duplicate original of this Agreement executed by Seller and Buyer.

This escrow shall close within fifteen (15) days of receipt of building permits for Buyer's contemplated project.

d) Notwithstanding anything to the contrary above, Buyer has the right at Buyer's discretion to extend the escrow two times for a period of _____ (___) days each upon payment by Buyer to Seller to escrow of _____ (_____) for each _____ (___) day extension. Said funds shall be paid into escrow and released to Seller at Buyer's option, and shall be subject to Paragraph #23 as additional earnest moneys.

12. CLOSING COSTS AND PRORATION OF EXPENSES. Escrow holder shall pay immediately upon closing the required documentary transfer tax and recording fees on the conveyance charging the same to Buyer. Seller shall pay the title insurance premium for the title policy as set forth in Paragraph #4 above. Property taxes shall be prorated as of the date of closing on the basis of the latest available information. The amount of any bond(s) or assessment(s) which is a lien against the property shall be paid in full by Seller as of the date of closing. Seller and Buyer shall share equally in paying the escrow fees of escrow holder. Other charges shall be allocated in the manner customary in _____ County.

13. EXISTING INFORMATION. Seller shall provide Buyer with all existing information in Sellers possession, but not limited to, Engineering, Civil and Geology, Land Plans, Architecture, Appraisals, Market Studies, and potential leases within 48 hours from opening of escrow. If Buyer fails to complete this purchase, all items delivered hereunder shall be immediately returned to Seller.

14. REPRESENTATIONS. All of Seller's representations stated in this Agreement and in any addendum attached hereto shall be true and correct as of the date of execution of this Agreement, and Seller shall notify Buyer immediately in writing if at any time prior to Close of Escrow, Seller believes that it would not be able to make any one or more of the representations provided herein. All of Seller's representations shall be true and correct as of the date of Close of Escrow and shall survive Close of Escrow. Seller hereby represents as follows:

a) Seller is the owner of and has full right, power and authority to sell, convey and transfer the Property to Buyer as provided in this Agreement and to carry out Seller's obligations under this Agreement and shall convey to Buyer at Close of Escrow marketable fee title to the Property, free and clear of all liens, assessments, covenants, conditions, restrictions, easements, encroachments, leases, rights of third parties, encumbrances, exceptions and other title defects.

b) Until Close of Escrow, Seller shall maintain the Property in its present condition, and shall not enter into any lease of the Property or any contracts or agreements pertaining to the Property without first obtaining the prior written consent of Buyer.

c) Seller has not received any notice and has no knowledge of:

(1) Any requirement by any governmental authority requiring that expenditures be made in connection with the Property:

(2) The widening of the streets adjacent to the Property;

(3) Any proceeding to change the zoning applicable to assessments upon all or any part of the Property. To the best of Seller's knowledge, the Property is in full compliance with all applicable building codes, environmental zoning, subdivision, and land use laws and any other applicable local, state, and federal laws and regulations.

d) To the best of Seller's knowledge, the Property does not contain and no activity upon the Property has produced any hazardous or toxic waste, deposit, or contamination which violates any federal, state, local or other governmental law, regulation or order or requires reporting to any governmental authority. See Paragraph #15.

e) To the best of Seller's knowledge, there exists no management, maintenance, operating, service or any other contract of similar nature, commitments, agreements or obligations of any kind, written or oral, affecting the Property which would be binding upon Buyer after close of escrow except those enumerated in the title report and approved by buyer as permitted exceptions.

f) To the best of Seller's knowledge, there are no existing actions, suits, or proceedings pending or threatened against or involving the Property.

g) To the best of Seller's knowledge, Seller has not filed or been the subject of any filing of a petition under the Federal Bankruptcy Code or any insolvency laws, or any laws for composition of indebtedness or the reorganization of debtors.

h) To the best of Seller's knowledge, Seller has obtained all licenses, permits, easements, and right of way requested for the normal use and operation of the Property and to insure vehicular and pedestrian ingress and egress from the Property.

i) To the best of Seller's knowledge, all documents submitted to Buyer for Buyer's review shall be true, correct, complete, and not misleading, and Buyer shall be immediately notified if any documents are altered, amended, modified, terminated or canceled.

j) At the Close of Escrow, there are no sums due, owing or unpaid for labor or materials furnished to the Property at the request of Seller which might give rise to a mechanics', material men's or other liens attaching to the Property.

k) There exists no breach, nor any state of facts which with the passage of time, the giving of notice or both, would constitute a default under any contract which relates to the Property and will be assumed by Buyer at the Close of Escrow.

15. DOCUMENTATION. Prior to Close of Escrow, Seller shall furnish Buyer any and all documentation required by Internal Revenue Code 1445 ("1445") including without limitation, a Certificate of Non-Foreign Status. Seller further agrees that in the event that Seller does not furnish Buyer a Certificate of Non-Foreign Status, Buyer is authorized to withhold and deduct from the Purchase Price any and all amounts required by 1445 and transfer said sum within ten (10) days to the Internal Revenue Service.

16. HAZARDOUS WASTE. Seller warrants that, to the best of Seller's knowledge, no toxic materials have been stored on or under the soil, used or disposed of on the property; nor have toxic materials migrated on or into the subject property, including but not limited to asbestos, heavy metal, petroleum products, solvents, pesticides or herbicides, unless otherwise disclosed in writing to the Buyer. Seller agrees to indemnify, defend and hold the Buyer harmless from and against any claims, costs, liabilities, causes or action, and fees, including attorney's fees arising from the storage use or disposal of existence of any toxic materials on the Property which result in contamination or deterioration of ground water or soil at a level of contamination greater than established by any governmental agency having appropriate jurisdiction.

In the event that the soil, subsoil, ground water or other constituent parts of the Property are determined contaminated as provided above, Buyer shall have the option to either (a) require Seller to clean up and otherwise restore the soil, subsoil, ground water or other constituent parts of the Property to a condition which would comply with the requirements of any governmental agency or body having any jurisdiction over the property, or (b) terminate this agreement without further liabilities on the part of either party. In the event of such termination, the Deposit shall be returned to the Buyer. Buyer and Seller acknowledge that neither Broker nor their sales people have made any representations regarding the absence of toxic materials on the property, and further warrant that neither Broker nor their salespeople are qualified to detect the presence of toxic materials on the property.

17. COOPERATION. Seller agrees to fully cooperate with Buyer and to use its best efforts in obtaining all Governmental approvals, to execute all necessary applications and related documents in such form as may be required by such Governmental authorities, all without cost to Seller.

18. LIQUIDATED DAMAGES. **IF BUYER FAILS TO COMPLETE SAID PURCHASE AS HEREIN PROVIDED BY REASON OF ANY DEFAULT OF BUYER, SELLER SHALL BE RELEASED FROM HIS OBLIGATIONS TO SELL THE SUBJECT PROPERTY TO BUYER AND MAY PROCEED AGAINST BUYER UPON ANY CLAIMS OR REMEDY WHICH HE MAY HAVE IN LAW OR EQUITY, PROVIDED, HOWEVER, THAT BY PLACING THEIR INITIALS HERE BUYER(S) (____) (____) SELLER(S): (____) (____) AGREE THAT IT WOULD BE IMPRACTICAL OR EXTREMELY DIFFICULT TO FIX ACTUAL DAMAGES IN CASE OF BUYER'S FAILURE TO COMPLETE THE PURCHASE DUE TO BUYER'S DEFAULT, THAT THE DEPOSIT(S) ACTUALLY PAID AS LIQUIDATED DAMAGES AND AS AND FOR HIS SOLE AND COMPLETE REMEDY.**

19. SIGNS. Buyer shall be allowed to place marketing signs upon the property.

20. DISTRIBUTION OF TITLE POLICY. Escrow holder shall distribute to Buyer as immediately as possible after close of escrow the Buyer's policy of title insurance mentioned above.

21. POSSESSION. Possession of the property shall be delivered to Buyer at closing. Notwithstanding the foregoing, at any time or times prior to closing, Buyer, its agents and contractors, shall have the right to enter upon and inspect the property, testing the physical properties thereof and evaluating the feasibility of development activity thereon as set forth in Paragraph #6 above.

22. AMENDED ESCROW INSTRUCTIONS. Amended or additional instructions may be received into escrow at any time until escrow is ready to close. To be effective, such amended or additional instructions must be in writing and signed by both Buyer and Seller. Buyer and Seller agree to execute such other documents and papers consistent with the provisions of this Agreement as may be required by escrow holder to complete escrow.

23. ENTIRE AGREEMENT. The terms of this Agreement contain the entire agreement between the parties and supersede any and all previous agreements. No

representation, covenant, agreement, or conditions not included herein has been or is relied upon by either of the parties.

24. WAIVER. Any condition contained herein for the benefit of either one of the parties may be waived only by the party to be benefited.

25. REAL ESTATE COMMISSIONS. Commission shall be the sole obligation of the Seller. Buyer and Seller agree that they are as follows and shall be paid from proceeds of escrow:

Commission Amount: _____

Paid as follows: _____

26. MULTIPLE ORIGINALS. This Agreement may be executed in one or more counterparts, each of which shall be deemed an original.

27. TIME IS OF THE ESSENCE. Time is of the essence in the performance of this Agreement.

28. BINDING EFFECT. This Agreement is binding upon the parties hereto and upon their successors and assigns.

29. NOTICES. Any notice or written direction required or designed to be given pursuant to this Agreement may be given personally or by United States mail, certified mail, return receipt requested, with postage thereon fully prepaid, addressed to Buyer at:

[INSERT BUYER'S NAME]_____

ADDRESS_____

PHONE #S_____   _____

Fax:_____

E-mail_____

To Seller at:

[INSERT SELLER'S NAME]_____

ADDRESS_____

PHONE #S_____   _____

Fax:_____

E-mail_____

To Escrow Holder at:

[INSERT ESCROW HOLDER'S NAME]_____

ADDRESS_____

PHONE #S_____ _____

Fax:_____

E-mail_____

or to such other address as either party may designate from time to time by written notice to the other. The date of service of such notices, certificates, documents, statements, or requests required by this Agreement shall be the date such notices are received as evidenced by the return receipt or the date such notices are refused if such be the case.

30. ATTORNEY'S FEES. If either party to this Agreement resorts to legal action to enforce any of the terms or provisions hereof or to recover damages for the breach hereof, the prevailing party shall be entitled to recover reasonable attorneys' fees, court costs and other expenses incurred from the unsuccessful party.

31. ASSIGNMENT. Seller agrees that Buyer may assign its rights under this Agreement to other persons or entities and it will deliver title to such nominee upon written notice prior to the close of escrow of the identity of the nominee taking title. Seller agrees that this Agreement shall be binding on its heirs, assigns, and successors.

32. RECORDATION. If Buyer records this Agreement, Buyer shall simultaneously deliver an executed quitclaim deed to the escrow holder to be recorded by the escrow holder upon termination of this Agreement or default by Buyer.

33. COVENANT TO SIGN DOCUMENTS. Within five (5) days of presentation thereof, Buyer and Seller agree to execute such other documents as may be required.

34. EXPIRATION. This Agreement expires if Seller's written acceptance or response is not received by Buyer on or before _____ at 5:00 P.M.

35. EXTENDED CLOSING. Buyer may, at buyer's sole option, extend the closing date of this agreement by 90 days. To exercise this option, buyer must notify escrow holder and seller in writing no later that 30 days prior to the scheduled closing, and, pay into escrow an additional Fifty Thousand and no/00 Dollars ($50,000.00) earnest money. This additional earnest money deposit shall immediately be released by escrow holder to seller as additional liquidated damages pursuant to article 18 herein. This additional deposit shall/(shall not) accrue to the purchase price at the close of escrow.

Signatures

BUYER: [INSERT BUYER'S NAME]

by _____   Date: _____

SELLER: [INSERT SELLER'S NAME]

by _____   Date: _____

"Effective Date": This Agreement, fully executed by Seller and Buyer, together with the cash deposit, has been received by escrow holder on the date specified below. Such items, together with the deposits to be received within five (5) days of the effective date will be held in escrow, and handled by escrow holder pursuant to this Agreement by the under-signed escrow agent. Escrow agent accepts this Agreement as its escrow instructions without the necessity of executing its standard printed form of escrow instructions.

Effective Date: _____

Agreed and Accepted by: [INSERT TITLE COMPANY] _____

_____

Escrow Officer

[ATTACH NOTARY PAGE]

[ATTACH EXHIBITS: A—PROPERTY DESCRIPTION, AND B—LIST OF LEASES]

Sample Commercial Lease Main Body

For and in consideration of the rental and of the covenants and agreements here-inafter set forth to be kept and performed by the Lessee, Landlord hereby leases to Lessee and Lessee hereby leases from Landlord the Premises herein described for the term, at the rental, and subject to and upon all of the terms, covenants and agreements hereinafter set forth.

ARTICLE 1—SUMMARY OF CERTAIN LEASE PROVISIONS

DATE OF EXECUTION: XXXXXXXXXXXX

LANDLORD / LESSOR: [Insert Landlord's Name]

TENANT / LESSEE: XXXXXXXXXXXXXXXXXXXXX

Guarantor (s): XXXXXXXXXXXXXXXXXXXXX

TENANT'S TRADE NAME: XXXXXXXXXXXXXX

LEASE TERM: **Five [5]** years. Provided Lessee has not defaulted under any terms and conditions of the lease, the Landlord will extend for **[2] five [5]** year options. If and in the event Lessee wishes to exercise an option to renew the lease, Lessee shall give written notice to Landlord one-hundred twenty (120) days before the expiration of the then current term. Tenant's failure to provide timely notice to Landlord shall be interpreted by Landlord as Tenant's rejection of any and all remaining options and Landlord shall be free to seek other tenants or make other arrangements for the Premises without any liability or further obligation to Lessee. (USE FOR LEASES WITH OPTIONS ONLY!)

MINIMUM RENT: Minimum monthly rent on a triple net basis.

Years 1-5	$ XX.00 / SF / Year $ X.XX /SF / Month
Years 6-10	$ XX.XX / SF / Year $ X.XX / SF /Month
Years 11-15	$ XX.XX / SF / Year $ X.XX / SF / Month

As additional rent, Lessee shall pay its pro rata share of real property taxes, insurance, and common area expenses on a pro rata basis per *Article 6* herein, subject to the CPI adjustment in *Exhibit C*.

PERCENTAGE RENT: None

SECURITY DEPOSIT: First month's rent **$ XXXXXXXXX** plus a security deposit of **$ XXXXXXXXX**

APPROXIMATE SIZE OF PREMISES: Tenant's premises shall contain approximately **[XXXX]** square feet. The final square footage and layout will be determined by a mutually approved space plan.

USE OF PREMISES: The primary business shall be a
XXXXXXXXXXXXXXXXXXXXXXXXXXXXXXXXXX

ADDRESSES FOR NOTICES: To Landlord: [INSERT LANDLORD"S NAME] [Insert address and phone Nos.]

To Lessee (s):

XXXXXXXXXXXXXXXXXXXXXXXXXXXXXXXXXXXXXXXXXXXXXXXXX

EXHIBITS:

A	Site Plan	B	Construction
C	CPI Adjustment & Acknowledgment of Commencement	D	Signs
E	Lessee Offset and Estoppel Certificate	F	Guarantor's Obligations
G	Special Conditions		

Exhibits "A" through "G" are incorporated herein by this reference as if set forth at length.

The foregoing is a summary only and reference should always be made to the full Lease provisions. References have been provided for convenience and designate some, but not necessarily all, of the other Articles and/or Sections where references to the particular Summary of Certain Lease Provisions appear. Each reference in this Lease to any of the summarized lease provisions contained in this *Article 1* shall be construed to incorporate all of the terms provided under each summarized lease provision and in case of any conflict with the balance of the Lease, the latter shall control.

ARTICLE 2—PREMISES

a. Landlord hereby leases to Lessee and Lessee hereby leases from Landlord that certain space (the "Premises") indicated on *Exhibit "A"* hereto, the Premises being agreed, for the purpose of this Lease, to have an area of approximately **XXXXX square feet** and being situated in that Building (as hereinafter defined) known as XXXXXXXXXXXXXXXXXXXX located on the property described on *Exhibit "A"* hereto and depicted on the project site plan attached as *Exhibit "A"* hereto.

b. This Lease is subject to the terms, covenants and conditions herein set forth and Lessee covenants as a material part of the consideration for this Lease to keep and perform each and all of said terms, covenants, and conditions by it to be kept and performed and that this Lease is made upon the condition of said performance.

c. **The Premises shall be used solely for _____**

ARTICLE 3—TERM

The term of this Lease shall be for **Three years**, commencing (except as provided in *Exhibit "C"* hereto) **on XXXXXXXXXX** (the date of commencement of the Lease term sometimes herein called the ("Commencement Date") and, unless sooner terminated in accordance with the terms hereof, **ending on XXXXXXXXXX,** or if, under *Exhibit "C"* hereto, the Commencement Date is other than the date specified above, ending **on the XXXXXX** anniversary of the Commencement Date of this Lease as determined under *Exhibit "C"* hereto.

ARTICLE 4—POSSESSION

a. If Landlord, for any reason whatsoever, cannot deliver possession of the Premises to Lessee on the Commencement Date of the term hereof, this Lease shall not be void or voidable, nor shall Landlord be liable to Lessee for any loss or damage resulting therefrom, and the expiration date of the above term shall be extended for an equal period so the term of the Lease shall be as indicated in *Article "3"*, above, but in that event, all rent shall be abated during the period between the Commencement Date of said term and the time when Landlord delivers possession. If within twenty-four (24) months from the date of execution hereof Landlord has not delivered the premises to Lessee this Lease shall be automatically terminated with no liability to Landlord or Lessee.

b. In the event Landlord shall permit Lessee to occupy the Premises prior to the Commencement Date of the term, such occupancy shall be subject to all the provisions of this Lease and the term of the Lease shall expire, unless sooner terminated in accordance with the terms hereof, on the **XXXXX anniversary** of the date of occupancy by Lessee.

ARTICLE 5—RENT AND RENT ADJUSTMENT

a. Lessee agrees to pay Landlord at such place as Landlord may designate without deduction, offset, prior notice or demand and Landlord agrees to accept as rent for the Premises the total **sum of XXXXXXXXXXXXXXXXX in** lawful money of the United Stated in monthly installments **of $XXXXXXX** payable in advance on the first day of each month during the term of this Lease, except that the rent installment for the first full calendar month shall be paid upon execution of this Lease. The rent for any portion of any calendar month of the term preceding, the first full calendar month shall be paid on the first day of the first full calendar month. The rent payable for any portion of a calendar month included in the term of the Lease shall be a pro rate portion of the rent payable for a full calendar month. The date for commencement of Lease rent shall be the Commencement Date except as provided to the contrary in *Article 4* hereof.

b. Lessee shall also pay Landlord a sum equal to the aggregate of any municipal, city, county, state or federal excise, sales, use, gross receipts or transaction privilege taxes now or hereafter levied or imposed, directly or indirectly, against or on account of the amounts payable hereunder or the receipt thereof by Landlord, which sum shall be paid with each installment of rent as hereinabove provided.

c. Lessee has deposited with Landlord the sum of **$XXXXXX** as security for the full and faithful performance of each and every provision of this Lease. If at any time Lessee shall be in default with respect to any term, covenant, condition or provision of this Lease, including without limitation any payment of rent or payment of any other sums due Landlord as and for any other purpose whatsoever, Landlord may, but shall no obligation to use, apply or retain all or part of the security deposit for payment of rent or any other sum in default, or for payment of any other amount which Landlord may spend or become obligated to spend because of Tenant's default, including without limitation the repair of damage, or to compensate Landlord for any other loss or damage which Landlord may suffer because of Tenant's default. In such event Lessee shall on demand pay to Landlord as additional security an amount sufficient to restore the security deposit to its original amount, and Tenant's failure to do so shall be a material breach of this Lease. If Lessee is not in default at the termination of this Lease, Landlord shall return the deposit to Lessee, except any portion used as a cleaning fee as hereafter provided. Landlord shall not be required to keep this security deposit separate from its general funds, and Lessee shall not be entitled to interest on such deposit. Landlord may use a reasonable portion of this deposit as a non-refundable cleaning fee [not to exceed $100.00] to clean the Premises upon any termination (by expiration of term, default or otherwise) of this Lease.

d. Lessee shall be entitled to reasonable parking in common with other tenants of the Building. Lessee agrees not to overburden the parking facilities and agrees to cooperate with Landlord and other tenants in the use of parking facilities. Landlord reserves the right in its absolute discretion to determine whether parking facilities are becoming overcrowded and in such event to allocate parking spaces among Lessee and other tenants. Landlord may also require Lessee and its employees to obtain parking off the site of the Building and adjacent parking areas in the event Tenant's customers, clients, or invitees appear to be using for their own purposes the number of parking spaces that would otherwise be attributable to a reasonable number of spaces for Tenant's use. There will be no assigned parking.

e. If the term of this Lease is greater than one year, then the rent payable under subparagraph a. of this *Article 4* and *Exhibit "C"* shall be subject to adjustment as hereinafter provided for in *Exhibit "C"* herein.

ARTICLE 6—ADDITIONAL RENT: DIRECT OPERATING EXPENSE

a. Commencing with the first month of the term of this Lease, Lessee shall pay to landlord monthly within three (3) days of demand as additional rent its pro rata share of any Direct Expenses (as hereinafter defined) for the operation and maintenance of the Building as such Direct Expenses are estimated by Landlord. Tenant's pro rata share of any such estimated expenses shall equal a sum obtained by multiplying the Direct Expenses as estimated by Landlord for the month for which the demand is made times a percentage obtained by dividing the total square footage contained in the Building into the total square footage contained in the Premises leased to Lessee herein.

b. The term "Direct Expenses" as used herein includes: All direct costs of operation and maintenance of the buildings, real property and improvements of which the Premises are a part, as determined by standard accounting practices, including without limitation the following costs by way of illustration: real property taxes and assessments; water and sewer charges; insurance premiums; utilities; security; window washing; trash removal ; costs incurred in the management of the Building and property, if any, including administrative overhead or property management fees not exceeding 10% of gross expenses; reserves for replacement of machinery and equipment; supplies; materials; equipment; and tools; costs of maintenance and upkeep and replacement when required of all landscaping, parking and common areas. ("Direct Expenses" shall not include depreciation on the Building or equipment therein, loan payments, executive salaries, or real estate brokers' commissions).

Following the end of each calendar quarter, Landlord shall submit to lessee a statement of the actual Direct Expenses for the preceding calendar quarter. If the payments made by Lessee, as provided hereinabove, for said preceding calendar quarter based upon Landlord's estimate of Direct Expenses were less than Tenant's share (based upon the formula provided hereinabove) of the actual Direct Expenses, Lessee shall pay the difference by the date the next regular monthly rent payment is due. If said payments made by Lessee were more than Tenant's share of the actual Direct Expenses, the overpayment by Lessee shall, so long as Lessee is not then in default and Landlord has no claim against Lessee for any prior default, be credited against the next monthly rent falling due. The estimates of Direct Expenses by Landlord as well as the quarterly statements of actual Direct Expenses may each contain, in the case of items such as, but not limited to, property taxes and insurance premiums which may be paid less frequently than monthly, an allocation for each month based on the actual (or if the actual amounts are not know, Landlord's estimate thereof) cost of such items. If an estimated amount for any such item is used in a quarterly statement of actual Direct Expenses, then, at such time as the actual amount is know, it shall be set forth in the next quarterly statement of actual Direct Expenses prepared by Landlord and shall be reflected in the adjustment described above. If the Lease commences on other than the first day of a calendar month or expires on other than the last day of a calendar month, any amount due under this *Article* shall be prorated based upon the number of days during the month which were included in the term of the Lease.

c. Lessee hereby acknowledges that late payment by Lessee to Landlord of Rent and other sums due hereunder will cause Landlord to incur costs not contemplated by this Lease, the exact amount of which are unknown and will be extremely difficult to ascertain other than such charges and late charges which may be imposed on Landlord by the terms of any mortgage or trust deed covering the Premises. Accordingly, if any installment of Rent or any other sums due from Lessee shall not be received by Landlord or Landlord's designee within ten (10) days after such amount shall be due, Lessee shall pay to Landlord in addition to the late charges incurred by Landlord under any mortgage or deed of trust covering the Premises, a late charge equal to ten percent (10%) of the amount (s) past due and additionally all such installments of Rent or other sums due shall bear interest at the rate provided for on Past Due Obligations as provided in *Article 11* from the date the same became due and payable. The parties hereby agree that such late charge represents fair and reasonable estimate of the costs Landlord will incur by reason of late payment by Lessee. Acceptance of such late charge by Landlord shall in no event constitute a waiver of Tenant's default with respect to such overdue amount, nor prevent Landlord from exercising any of the rights and remedies granted hereunder.

d. Accordingly, if any installment of Rent or any other sums due from Lessee shall not be received by Landlord or Landlord's designee within ten (10) days after such amount shall be due, Landlord shall give Lessee written notice of Lessee's non payment of rent. Lessee shall have three working days from the date of Landlord's written notice to cure the late payment. Upon failure of Lessee to cure, Landlord may declare Lessee to be in default under this lease pursuant to *Article 11* hereto.

ARTICLE 7—ASSIGNMENT AND SUBLETTING

Lessee shall not, either voluntarily or by operation of law, assign, transfer, mortgage, pledge, hypothecate or encumber this Lease or any interest therein, and shall not sublet the Premises or any part thereof, or any right or privilege appurtenant thereto, or suffer any other person (the officers, employees, agents, servants, invitees and guests of Lessee excepted) to occupy or use the Premises, or any portion thereof, without the written consent of Landlord first had and obtained, which consent shall not be unreasonably withheld. Any such assignment or subletting without such consent shall be void, and shall, at the option of the Landlord, constitute a default under this Lease. Regardless of Landlord's consent, no subletting or assignment shall release Lessee or Tenant's obligation to pay the rent and to perform all other obligations to be performed by Lessee hereunder for the term of this Lease. The acceptance of rent by Landlord from any other person shall not be deemed to be a waiver of any provision hereof. Without regard to whether Landlord consents to an assignment or a subletting, if Lessee or any assignee or sublessee assigns this Lease or sublets the Premises or any portion thereof for a rental rate greater than that paid to the Landlord, such excess shall be paid to the Landlord.

ARTICLE 8—INSURANCE

(a) Lessee shall, at Tenant's expense, obtain and keep in force during the term of this Lease a policy of comprehensive general public liability insurance insuring Landlord and Lessee (naming Landlord as an additional named insured) against any liability arising out of the use, occupancy, maintenance, repair or improvement of the Premises and all areas appurtenant thereto including without limitation coverage against "occurrences". Such insurance shall provide single limit liability coverage of not less than $1,000,000 per occurrence for bodily injury or death and property damage. The limits of said insurance shall not, however, limit the liability of the Lessee hereunder, and Lessee is responsible for ensuring that the amount of liability insurance carried by Lessee is sufficient for Tenant's purposes. Lessee may carry said insurance under a blanket policy, providing, however, said insurance by Lessee shall have a Landlord's protective liability endorsement attached thereto in form and substance satisfactory to Landlord. If Lessee shall fail to procure and maintain said insurance, Landlord may, but shall not be required to, procure and maintain same but at the expense of Lessee. Insurance required hereunder shall be in companies rated A+, AAA or better in "Best's Insurance Guide". Lessee shall deliver to Landlord prior to occupancy of the Premises copies of policies of liability insurance required herein or certificates evidencing the existence and amounts of such insurance with evidence satisfactory to Landlord of payment of premiums and thereafter within thirty (30) days after any demand therefore by Landlord. No policy shall be cancelable or subject to reduction of coverage except after thirty (30) days prior written notice to Landlord and Landlord's lender. Lessee acknowledges and agrees that insurance coverage carried by Landlord will not cover Tenant's property within the Premises or the Building and that Lessee shall be responsible, at Tenant's sole cost or expense, for providing insurance coverage for Tenant's movable equipment, furnishings, trade fixtures and other personal property in or upon the Premises or the Building, and for any alterations, additions or improvements to or of the Premises or any part thereof made by Lessee, in the event of damage or loss thereto from any cause whatsoever. Lessee shall furnish Landlord with renewals or "binders" of any such policy at least ten (10) days prior to the expiration thereof.

(b) RENT LOSS ENDORSEMENT. Landlord may at its option require that the above described policies of insurance shall be written with rent loss endorsements in favor of Landlord in amounts sufficient to pay Tenant's obligations hereunder including, without limitation, the Minimum Rent, Promotional Costs, insurance premiums, taxes, Common Area expenses and utility costs excluding only Tenant's and/or Landlord's avoided costs.

ARTICLE 9—SERVICES AND UTILITIES

Provided that Lessee is not in default hereunder, Landlord agrees to furnish to the Premises during reasonable hours of generally recognized business days, to be determined by Landlord in its sole discretion, and subject to the rules and regulations of the Building, the parking areas, common entries in the Building. Landlord shall not be liable for, and Lessee shall not be entitled to, any reduction or abatement of rental by reason of Landlord's failure to furnish any of the foregoing when such failure is caused by casualty, Act of God, accident, breakage, repairs, strikes, lockouts or other labor disturbances or labor disputes of any character, or by any other cause, similar or dissimilar, beyond the reasonable control of Landlord. Landlord shall not be liable under any circumstances for injury to or death of or loss or damage to persons or property or damage to Tenant's business, however occurring, through or in connection with or incidental to failure to furnish any of the foregoing.

ARTICLE 10—HOLDING OVER

If Lessee remains in possession of the Premises or any part thereof after the expiration of the term hereof, with the express written consent of Landlord, such occupancy shall be a tenancy from month-to-month at a rental, payable monthly in advance, in double the amount of the last monthly rental, plus all other charges payable hereunder and upon all the terms hereof applicable to a month-to-month tenancy. In such case, either party may thereafter terminate this Lease at any time upon giving not less than thirty (30) days' written notice to the other party.

ARTICLE 11—DEFAULT

The occurrence of any one or more of the following events ("Events of Default") shall constitute a material default and breach of this Lease by Lessee.

(a) The vacating or abandonment of the Premises by Lessee.

(b) The failure by Lessee to make any payment of rent or any other payment required to be made by Lessee hereunder, as and when due, where such failure shall continue for a period of three (3) days after written notice thereof by Landlord to Lessee.

(c) The failure by Lessee to observe or perform any of the covenants, conditions or provisions of this Lease to be observed or performed by Lessee, other than as described in *paragraphs a., b., or d. of this **Article 11***, where such failure shall continue for a period of thirty (30) days are reasonably required for its cure, then Lessee shall not be deemed to be in default if Lessee commences such cure within said thirty (30) day period and thereafter diligently prosecutes such cure to completion, and if Lessee provides Landlord with such security as Landlord may require to fully compensate Landlord for any loss or liability to which Landlord might be exposed.

(d) The making by Lessee of any general assignment or general arrangement for the benefit of creditors; or the filing by or against Lessee of a petition to have Lessee adjudged a bankrupt, or a petition for reorganization or arrangement under any law, now existing or hereafter amended or enacted, relating to bankruptcy or insolvency (unless, in the case of a petition filed against Lessee, Lessee has not consented to, or admitted the material allegation of said petition and said petition is dismissed within sixty (60) days); or the appointment of a trustee or a receiver (other than in a bankruptcy or insolvency proceeding) to take possession of substantially all of Tenant's assets located at the Premises or of Tenant's interest in this Lease, where possession is not restored to Lessee within thirty (30) days; or the attachment, execution or other judicial seizure of substantially all of Tenant's assets located at the Premises or of Tenant's interest in this Lease, where such seizure is not discharged in thirty (30) days; or if Lessee becomes insolvent within the meaning of the federal bankruptcy code.

ARTICLE 12—REMEDIES UPON DEFAULT

(a) In the event of any such Event of Default then, and in any such event (regardless of the pendency of any proceeding which has or might have the effect of preventing Lessee from curing such Default), Landlord, at any time thereafter, may invoke, simultaneously or successively, any one or more of the powers, rights and remedies set forth in this Lease and/or which Landlord may now or hereafter have at law or in equity or by statute or otherwise. "Default" as used in this Lease shall mean any condition or event which constitutes or which, after notice or lapse of time, or both, as provided in *Article 11* would constitute an Event of Default.

(b) If an Event of Default shall have occurred, Landlord may, at any time thereafter, either:

(1) Terminate this Lease by written notice to Lessee, or

(2) Re-enter the Premises by summary proceedings or otherwise, with or without terminating this Lease, remove all persons and property from the Premises without liability to any person for damages sustained by reason of such removal and

re-let, in the name of Landlord or Lessee or otherwise, the Premises at such rental and upon such other terms and conditions (which may include, without limitation, concessions or free rent) as Landlord in its sole discretion may deem advisable. In such event, Lessee shall remain liable for all rent, additional rent and all other obligations hereunder plus the reasonable cost of obtaining possession of and reletting the Premises and of any repairs and alterations, including without limitation replacement of or changes in Lessee improvements, necessary to prepare them for reletting, less the rents received from such reletting, if any. Any and all monthly deficiencies so payable by Lessee shall be paid monthly on the date herein provided for the payment of rent. Notwithstanding any such reletting without termination, Landlord may at any time thereafter elect to terminate this Lease for such previous breach.

(c) Should Landlord at any time terminate this Lease for any breach, in addition to any other remedies it may have, it may recover from Lessee all damages it may incur by reason of such breach, including, without limitation, the cost of recovering the Premises (including without limitation reasonable attorneys' fees) the portion of the leasing commission paid by Landlord in connection with this Lease and applicable to the unexpired term of this Lease, and including the worth at the time of such termination of the excess, if any, of the amount of rent and charges equivalent to rent reserved in this Lease for the remainder of the term over the reasonable rental value of the Premises for the remainder of the term, all of which amounts shall be immediately due and payable from Lessee to Landlord. No re-entry of taking possession of the Premises by Landlord shall be construed as an election of its part to terminate this Lease unless a written notice of such intention be given to Lessee.

All amounts due Landlord under this *Article* shall bear interest at the rate of twelve percent (12%) per annum from the date due until paid. In addition to the foregoing remedies and so long as this Lease is not terminated, Landlord shall have the right but not the obligation to remedy any default of Lessee and to add to the rent payable hereunder all of Landlord's reasonable costs in so doing, with interest thereon until the same is repaid at the rate of the lower of twelve percent (12%) per annum or the maximum rate then allowed by law.

All remedies herein conferred upon Landlord shall be cumulative and not exclusive of any other remedy conferred herein or at law or in equity. If Lessee is in default, Landlord may prevent removal of property from the Premises by any lawful means it deems necessary to protect its interests.

ARTICLE 13—COVENANTS TO OPERATE

13.1 Lessee covenants and agrees that, continuously and uninterruptedly from and after the commencement of the term of this Lease it will operate and conduct within the Premises the business which it is permitted to operate and conduct under the provisions hereof, except while the Premises are untenantable by reason of fire or other casualty, and that it will at all times keep and maintain within and upon the Premises an adequate stock of merchandise and trade fixtures to service and supply the usual and ordinary demands and requirements of its customers and to maximize sales volume upon the Premises and that it will keep its Premises in a neat, clean and orderly condition.

13.2 Lessee shall refrain from dumping, disposal, reduction, incineration or other burning of trash, papers, refuse or garbage of any kind in or about the Premises. Lessee shall store all trash and garbage within the Premises or at a location designated by Landlord in covered metal containers so located as not to be visible to customers or business invitees in the Shopping Center. Lessee shall also arrange for and bear the expense of the prompt and regular removal of such trash and garbage from the Premises. Landlord may provide central trash removal facilities for Lessee and Lessee shall pay costs upon demand for such removal on a pro rata basis providing such costs to Lessee are not more than if Lessee made its own arrangements for trash removal with a reputable firm. Landlord may include such costs and expenses thereof in the Common Area costs.

13.3 Lessee shall complete, or cause to be completed, all deliveries, loading, unloading and services to the Premises, during times designated by Landlord, and in a manner that will not interfere with Landlord, other tenants, or employees or customers of Landlord or other tenants, nor shall Lessee permit delivery vehicles to park in front of the customer entrances to any shops, between the hours of 10:00 A.M. and 6:00 P.M. of each day. The Landlord reserves the right to further regulate the activities of the Lessee in regard to deliveries and servicing of the Premises, and Lessee further agrees to abide by such further nondiscriminatory regulations of Landlord.

13.4 Commencing with the opening for business by Lessee in the Premises and for the remainder of the term of this Lease, Lessee shall conduct its business in the leased Premises and will keep the leased Premises open for business not less than the following hours: 10:00 A.M. to 6:00 P.M. Monday through Saturday, except for Thanksgiving, Christmas, and January 1. In no event shall Lessee remain open for business longer hours than any anchor store without Landlord's written permission.

13.5 Lessee agrees that it will not, during the term of this Lease, directly or indirectly, operate or own any similar type of business within a radius of two (2) miles from the location of the Premises. The preceding sentence shall not apply to any such similar business which Lessee owns or operates on the execution date of this Lease, the existence of which was previously disclosed to Landlord. Without limiting Landlord's remedies in the event Lessee should violate this covenant, Landlord may, at its option, include the "net sales" of such other business in the "net sales" transacted from the Premises for the purpose of computing the Percentage Rent due hereunder.

ARTICLE 14—AMERICANS WITH DISABILITIES ACT

Lessee shall, at all times during the term of this Lease, and at Tenant's sole cost and expense, maintain and keep the Property in full compliance with the Americans With Disability Act of 1990, Public Law No. 101-336, 42 USC 12101 et. eq.(the "ADA"), for its intended use by Lessee as approved herein. Lessee shall indemnify, defend, and hold Landlord harmless from and against any and all claims arising from noncompliance or alleged noncompliance with the provisions of ADA in effect during the term hereof, including any extensions and renewals, and from and against all costs, attorneys fees, expenses and liabilities incurred in or from any such claim. Lessee, upon notice from Landlord, shall defend the same at Tenant's expense by counsel reasonably satisfactory to Landlord. Lessee, as a material part of the consideration to Landlord, hereby waives all claims in respect thereof against Landlord.

ARTICLE 15—BROKERS

Lessee warrants that it has had no dealings with any real estate broker or agents in connection with the negotiations of this Lease excepting only Rider Land & Development LLC and that it knows of no other real estate broker or agent who is entitled to a commission in connection with this Lease. Lessee agrees to indemnify and hold Landlord harmless from and against any and all claims, demands, losses, liabilities, lawsuits, judgments, and costs and expenses (including without limitation reasonable attorneys' fees) with respect to any alleged leasing commission or equivalent compensation alleged to be owing on account of Tenant's dealings with any real estate broker or agent other than the aforesaid broker.

The parties hereto have executed this Lease on the dates specified immediately adjacent to their respective signatures.

15.1 ENTIRE AGREEMENT. THIS LEASE IS THE RESULT OF NEGOTIATIONS THAT OCCURRED OVER THE COURSE OF SEVERAL MONTHS, WHICH NEGOTIATIONS INVOLVED WRITTEN AND ORAL COMMUNICATIONS BY AND BETWEEN THE PARTIES, THEIR ACCOUNTANTS, AND ATTORNEYS. THE NEGOTIATIONS THAT PRECEDED THIS LEASE AT TIMES CONSIDERED ARRANGEMENTS THAT WERE AT VARIANCE WITH THE PROVISIONS OF THIS LEASE. ALL THE PRECEDING AND CONTEMPORANEOUS ORAL AND WRITTEN

STATEMENTS, UNDERSTANDINGS, REPRESENTATIONS, WAR-
RANTIES, AND PROMISES, WHETHER CONSISTENT OR INCONSIS-
TENT HEREWITH, ARE AGREED TO BE OF NO FORCE OR EFFECT
FOR ANY PURPOSE WHATSOEVER UNLESS EXPRESSLY OR EXPLIC-
ITLY STATED IN THIS LEASE. THIS LEASE, TOGETHER WITH ALL
ATTACHMENTS, SCHEDULES, AND SPECIFIC REFERENCES REPRE-
SENTS THE COMPLETE AND FINAL AGREEMENT OF THE PARTIES
AND IS INTENDED AS THE COMPLETE AND EXCLUSIVE STATE-
MENT OF THEIR INTENT, AND IT SUPERSEDES ALL PRIOR AND
CONTEMPORANEOUS CONSISTENT AND INCONSISTENT STATE-
MENTS, REPRESENTATIONS, WARRANTIES, UNDERSTANDINGS,
NEGOTIATIONS, AND AGREEMENTS, AND IT MAY NOT BE SUPPLE-
MENTED, MODIFIED OR AMENDED BY EVIDENCE, EITHER ORAL
OR WRITTEN, OF ANY SUCH MATTERS OR BY COURSE OF DEAL-
ING, BUT ONLY UPON THE WRITTEN AGREEMENT OF THE PAR-
TIES. THE PARTIES HEREBY STIPULATE THAT EACH AND EVERY
PROVISION CONTAINED IN THIS LEASE WAS BARGAINED FOR AND
THE PLAIN MEANING OF SAID PROVISIONS MEMORIALIZES THE
INTENT OF THE PARTIES HERETO.

15.2 SCRUTINY. THIS LEASE HAS BEEN SUBMITTED TO THE
SCRUTINY OF ALL PARTIES AND THEIR RESPECTIVE LEGAL COUN-
SEL AND SHALL BE GIVEN A FAIR AND REASONABLE INTERPRETA-
TION IN ACCORDANCE WITH THE WORDS HEREOF WITHOUT
CONSIDERATION OR WEIGHT BEING GIVEN TO ITS BEING
DRAFTED BY OR FOR ONE OF THE PARTIES. IF IN FACT ONE OF
THE PARTIES HAS NOT SUBMITTED THIS LEASE TO THE
SCRUTINY OF THEIR LEGAL COUNSEL, SUCH PARTY STIPULATES
THAT, DESPITE HAVING HAD THE OPPORTUNITY TO DO SO, THEY
WAIVED THE SAME AND ELECTED TO PROCEED WITHOUT THE
BENEFIT OF SUCH LEGAL REVIEW.

Initials   _____ _____

Executed this Sunday, July 31, 2005, at YYYY,YYY

Landlord: _____   [INSERT LANDLORD'S NAME]

         _____   [Insert Address]

By:_____   [Insert Name of Signatory]

[ATTACH NOTARY PAGE (OPTIONAL)]

Sample Commercial Lease General Provisions

ARTICLE G-1—USE

Lessee shall use the Premises for the purposes permitted in **paragraph c. of *Article* 2** hereof and shall not use or permit the Premises to be used for any other purpose without the prior written consent of Landlord.

Lessee shall not do or permit anything to be done in or about the Premises nor bring or keep anything therein which will in any way increase the existing rate of or affect any fire or other insurance upon the Building or any of its contents, or cause cancellation of any insurance policy covering the Building, or any part thereof, or any of its contents. Lessee shall not do, or permit anything to be done, in or about the Premises which will in any way obstruct or interfere with the rights of other tenants or occupants of the Building, or injure or annoy them, or use or allow the Premises to be used for any improper, immoral, unlawful or objectionable purpose, nor shall Lessee cause, maintain or permit any nuisance in, on or about the Premises. Lessee shall not commit or suffer to be committed any waste in or upon the Premises.

Lessee shall not do nor permit anything to be done in or about the Premises in violation of the covenants and restrictions governing the property. By signing this Lease Lessee assumes responsibility for making himself/herself aware of all covenants and restrictions governing the property.

EXCLUSIVES. It is herewith agreed that this Lease contains no restrictive covenants, and Lessee shall have an *exclusive right be the* _____ within the boundaries of the property described in *Exhibit* "A".

ARTICLE G-2—COMPLIANCE WITH LAW

Lessee shall not use the Premises or permit anything to be done in or about the Premises which will in any way conflict with any law, statute, ordinance or governmental rule or regulation now in force or which may hereafter be enacted or promulgated. Lessee shall, at its sole cost and expense, promptly comply with all laws, statutes, ordinances and governmental rules, regulations or requirements now in force or which may hereafter be in force, and with the requirements of any board of fire insurance underwriters or other similar bodies now or hereafter constituted, relating to, or affecting the condition, use or occupancy of the Premises. The judgment of any court of competent jurisdiction or the admission of Lessee in any action against Lessee, whether Landlord be a party thereto or not, that Lessee has violated any law, statute, ordinance or governmental rule, regulation or requirement, shall be conclusive of that fact as between Landlord and Lessee.

ARTICLE G-3—ALTERATIONS AND ADDITIONS, SURRENDER OF POSSESSION

Lessee shall not make or suffer to be made any alterations, additions or improvements to or of the Premises or any part thereof without the written consent of Landlord first had and obtained and any alterations, additions or improvements to or of the Premises, including, but not limited to, wall covering, paneling and built-in cabinet work, but excepting movable furniture and trade fixtures, shall on the expiration of the term become a part of the realty and belong to Landlord and shall be surrendered with the Premises. In the event Landlord consents to the making of any alterations, additions, or improvements to the Premises by Lessee, the same shall be made by Lessee at Tenant's sole cost and expense, and any contractor or person selected by Lessee to make the same must first be approved of in writing by Landlord, which approval shall not be unreasonably withheld. Any such alterations, additions or improvements made by Lessee shall be performed in accordance with all applicable laws, ordinances and codes, and in a first class workmanlike manner, and shall not weaken or impair the structural strength, or lessen the value, of the Building. Prior to commencement of any alterations or additions, Lessee shall cause its contractors to provide Landlord with certificates of insurance from the insurer certifying that each contractor has in full force and effect insurance meeting all the requirements of *Article 8* hereof. In making any such alterations, additions, or improvements, Lessee shall, at Tenant's sole cost and expense:

(1) File for and secure any necessary permits or approvals from all governmental departments or authorities having jurisdiction, and any utility company having an interest therein; and

(2) Notify Landlord in writing at least fifteen (15) days prior to the commencement of work on any alteration, addition or improvement so that Landlord can post and record appropriate notices of non-responsibility.

Upon the expiration or sooner termination of the term hereof, Lessee shall, upon written demand by Landlord given at least thirty (30) days prior to the end of the term, at Tenant's sole cost and expense, forthwith and with all due diligence remove any alterations, additions, or improvements made by Lessee, designated by Landlord to be removed; provided that Lessee shall, forthwith and with all due diligence at its sole cost and expense, repair any damage to the Premises caused by such removal. Lessee may also, upon the expiration or sooner termination of the term hereof, and provided that Lessee is not then in default hereunder, remove Tenant's movable equipment, furnishings, trade fixtures and other personal property (excluding any alterations, additions or improvements made by Lessee not specifically designated by Landlord to be removed), provided that Lessee shall, forthwith and with all due diligence at its sole cost and expense, repair any damages to the Premises caused by such removal. Upon the expiration or sooner termination of this Lease or upon the termination of Tenant's right of possession, Lessee shall immediately surrender possession of the Premises to Landlord and remove all of its property therefrom as permitted or required herein, and if such possession is not immediately surrendered, Landlord may reenter the Premises and remove all persons and property therefrom. If Lessee fails or refuses to remove any such property from the Premises, Lessee shall be conclusively presumed to have abandoned the same, and title thereto shall thereupon pass to Landlord without cost, setoff, credit allowance or otherwise, and Landlord may accept title to such property, or, at Tenant's expense, remove the same or any part thereof in any manner that Landlord shall choose and store the same without incurring liability to Lessee or any other person.

ARTICLE G-4—REPAIRS

a. By taking possession of the Premises, Lessee shall be deemed to have accepted the Premises as being in good, satisfactory, and sanitary order, condition and repair. Lessee shall, at Tenant's sole cost and expense, keep the Premises and every part thereof in good condition and repair, damage thereto from causes beyond the control of Lessee (and not caused by any act or omission of Tenant's agents, officers, employees, contractors, servants, invitees, licensees or guests) and ordinary wear and tear excepted. If Lessee does not make such repairs, Landlord may make such repairs and replacements, and Lessee shall pay Landlord the cost thereof upon receipt of a statement therefore unless Landlord deducts the same from the security deposit pursuant to *Article 5 c.* hereof and is entitled to reimbursement pursuant thereto. Lessee shall, upon the expiration or sooner termination of this Lease, surrender the Premises to Landlord in good condition, ordinary wear and tear and damage from causes beyond the control of Lessee (and not caused by any act or omission of Tenant's agents, officers, employees, contractors, servants, licensees, invitees or guests) excepted. Except as specifically provided in an addendum, if any, to this Lease, Landlord shall have no obligation whatsoever to alter, remodel, improve, repair, decorate or paint the Premises or any part thereof and the parties hereto affirm that Landlord has made no representations to Lessee respecting the condition of the Premises or the Building except as specifically herein set forth.

b. Notwithstanding the provisions of *Article* G-4 a., above, Landlord shall repair and maintain the structural portions of the Building, including the basic plumbing, air conditioning, heating and electrical systems installed or furnished by Landlord, unless such maintenance or repairs are caused in part or in whole by the act, neglect, fault or omission of any duty by the Lessee, its agents, officers, employees, contractors, servants, licensees, invitees or guests, in which case Lessee shall pay to Landlord the reasonable cost of such maintenance or repairs. Landlord shall not be liable for any failure to make any such repairs or to perform any maintenance for which Landlord is responsible as provided above unless such failure shall persist for an unreasonable time after the written notice of the need of such repairs or maintenance is given to Landlord by Lessee and is due solely to causes within Landlord's reasonable control. Except as provided in *Article G-11* hereof, there shall be no abatement of rent, and in any event there shall be no liability of landlord by reason of any injury to or interference with Tenant's business arising from the making of any repairs, alterations or improvements in or to any portion of the Building or the Premises or in or to fixtures, appurtenances and equipment therein. Lessee, to the extent permitted by law, waives the right to make repairs at Landlord's expense under any law, statute, or ordinance now or hereafter in affect. Landlord may enter the Premises at all reasonable times to make any repairs Landlord deems necessary or desirable, or as Landlord may be required to do by a government authority.

ARTICLE G-5—LIENS

Lessee shall keep the Premises, the Building and the property in which the Premises are situated free from any and all mechanics', material men's, and other liens, and claims thereof, arising out of any work performed, materials furnished or obligations incurred by or for Lessee. Landlord may require, at Landlord's sole option, that Lessee shall provide to Landlord at Tenant's sole cost and expense a lien and completion bond, or its equivalent, in an amount equal to one and one-half times any and all estimated costs of any improvements, additions or alterations of or to the Premises, to insure Landlord against any liability for mechanics' and material men's liens and to insure completion of the work and Landlord's cost of defending against any such claims and liens.

ARTICLE G-6—HOLD HARMLESS

Lessee shall indemnify and hold Landlord harmless from and against any and all claims arising out of (i) Tenant's use of the Premises or any part thereof or the conduct of its business, or (ii) any activity, work or other thing done, permitted or suffered by Lessee in or about the Building or the Premises, or any part thereof, or (iii) any breach or default in the performance of any obligation on Tenant's part to be performed under the terms of this Lease, or (iv) any act or negligence of the Lessee, or any officer, agent, employee, contractor, servant, licensee, invitee or guest of Lessee, and in each case from and against any and all damages, losses, liabilities, lawsuits, judgments, and costs and expenses (including without limitation expert witness fees and reasonable attorneys' fees) arising in connection with any such claim or claims as described in clauses (i) through (iv), above, or any action or proceeding brought thereon. If any such action or proceeding be brought against Landlord, Lessee upon notice from Landlord shall defend the same at Tenant's sole expense by counsel reasonably satisfactory to Landlord. Lessee as a material part of the consideration to Landlord hereby assumes all risk of damage or loss to property or injury or death to persons, in, upon, or about the Premises, from any cause other than Landlord's sole negligence, and Lessee hereby waives all claims in respect thereof against Landlord.

Landlord or its agents shall not be liable for any damage or loss to property entrusted to employees of the Building, nor for loss or damage to any property by theft, or otherwise, nor for any injury to or death of or damage or loss to persons or property resulting from any accident, casualty or condition occurring in or about the Building or the Premises, or any part thereof, or any equipment, appliances or fixtures therein, or from any other cause whatsoever, unless caused solely by the negligence of Landlord, its agents, servants or employees. Landlord or its agents shall not be liable for interference with the light or other incorporeal hereditaments or any loss of business by Lessee, nor shall Landlord be liable for any latent defect in the Premises or in the Building. Lessee shall give prompt written notice to Landlord in case of fire or accidents in the Premises or in the Building or of defects therein or in the fixtures or equipment.

ARTICLE G-7—SUBROGATION

As long as both of their respective insurers so permit, Landlord and Lessee hereby mutually waive their respective rights of recovery against each other for any damages and losses to the extent such damage or loss is reimbursed by insurance under fire, extended coverage and other property insurance policies existing for the benefit of the respective parties. Each party shall obtain only special endorsements, if required by its insurer, to evidence compliance with the aforementioned waiver.

ARTICLE G-8—PROPERTY TAXES

Lessee shall pay, or cause to be paid, before delinquency, any and all taxes levied or assessed and which become payable during the term hereof upon all Tenant's leasehold improvements, equipment, furniture, fixtures and personal property located in the Premises; except only that which has been paid for by Landlord and is the standard of the Building. In the event any or all of the Tenant's leasehold improvements, equipment, furniture, fixtures or personal property shall be assessed and taxed with the Building, Lessee shall pay to Landlord its share of such taxes within ten (10) days after delivery to Lessee by Landlord of a statement in writing setting forth the amount of such taxes applicable to Tenant's property. If Tenant's leasehold improvements, equipment, furniture, fixtures, and personal property are not separately assessed on the tax statement or bill, Landlord's good faith determination of the amount of such taxes applicable to Tenant's property shall be a conclusive determination of Tenant's obligation to pay such amount as so determined by Landlord.

ARTICLE G9-9—RULES AND REGULATIONS

Lessee shall faithfully observe and comply with the rules and regulations attached to this Lease as *Exhibit* **"E"** and such other reasonable rules and regulations as Landlord may from time to time promulgate. Landlord reserves the right from time to time to make all reasonable modifications to said rules. The additions and modifications to those rules shall be binding upon Lessee upon delivery of a copy of them to Lessee. Landlord shall not be liable to Lessee for the non-performance of any said rules and regulations by any other tenants or occupants of the Building.

ARTICLE G-10—HAZARDOUS SUBSTANCES

(a) **Compliance with Environmental Laws**. Lessee shall conduct all operations or activities upon the Premises, or any portion thereof, in compliance with all Environmental Laws, as hereinafter defined. Lessee shall not engage in or permit any dumping, discharge, disposal, spillage or leakage (whether legal or illegal, accidental or intentional) of such Hazardous Substances, as hereafter defined, at, on, in or about the Premises, or any portion thereof.

(1) For purposes of this Lease, "Hazardous Substance Law" means any federal, state or local statute, regulation, rule, ordinance or common law principle concerning the presence, possession, handling, storage, treatment, transportation, disposal or cleanup of, or liability for, a Hazardous Substance, as currently in effect and as hereafter enacted or modified, including but not limited to the Comprehensive Environmental Response, Compensation and Liability Act as amended by the Superfund Amendments and Reauthorization Act (42 U.S.C. § 9601 et seq.), the Safe Water Drinking Act (42 U.S.C. § 300F et seq.), the Toxic Substances Control Act (15 U.S.C. § 2601 et seq.), the Resource Conservation and Recovery Act (42 U.S.C. § 6901 et seq.), the Federal Water Pollution Control Act (33 U.S.C. § 1251 et seq.), the Hazardous Waste Management Act of 1983, and other applicable statutes passed and enacted by the Washington Legislature, and common law principles of tort and strict liability.

(2) For purposes of this Lease, "Hazardous Substance" means any chemical, compound or material which is deemed a hazardous substance, hazardous waste, hazardous material, infectious waste or toxic substance, or any combination or formulation of substances defined, listed or classified by reasons of deleterious properties

such as ignitability, corrosivity, reactivity, carcinogenicity, toxicity, reproductive carcinogenicity, extraction procedure toxicity, toxicity characteristic, leaching procedure toxicity,
petroleum, including crude oil and any fractions thereof; "hazardous waste," "restricted
hazardous waste," and "waste" with the above stated properties, as defined in Washington code; and any other chemical material or substance that because of its quantity,
concentration, physical or chemical characteristics exposure to which is limited or regulated for health, safety, and environmental reasons by any governmental authority with
jurisdiction, or which poses significant present or potential hazard to human health and
safety or to the environment if released to the work place or environment.

(b) **Indemnification.** Lessee agrees to indemnify, protect, defend (with counsel
reasonably approved by Lessor) and hold Lessor, any assignee of Lessor, the directors, officers, shareholders, employees and agents of such entities and their respective
heirs, executors, administrators, legal representatives, successors and assigns, harmless
from and against: any claims (including, without limitation, third party claims for personal injury or real or personal property), actions, administrative or other proceedings
(including informal proceedings), demands, liabilities, liens, judgments, damages
(including punitive damages and all foreseeable and unforeseeable consequential damages), penalties, fines, suits, defenses, offsets, obligations, duties, costs (including all
remedial, removal, responsive, abatement, cleanup, compliance, legal investigative,
preventive, planning and monitoring costs and other related costs, expenses and disbursements, such as attorneys', paralegals', consultants' and experts' costs and
expenses, and also including, without limitation, any such fees and expenses incurred
in enforcing the Lease or collecting any sums due hereunder), charges, expenses,
interest or losses (including, without limitation, diminution in the value of the
Premises), together with all other costs and expenses of any kind or nature (collectively, "Costs"), which arise out of, are connected with or are attributable to, directly
or indirectly, the presence, suspected presence, release or suspected release of any
Hazardous Substance in or into the air, soil, surface water, groundwater or soil vapor
at, on, about, under or within the Premises, or any portion thereof. If Lessor shall
suffer or incur any such Costs, Lessee shall pay Lessor the total of all such Costs suffered or incurred by landlord upon demand therefore by lessor. Without limiting the
generality of the foregoing, the indemnification provided by this *Article* **G-10** shall
specifically cover Costs, including capital, operating and maintenance costs, incurred
in connection with any investigation or monitoring of site conditions, any cleanup,
containment, remedial, removal or restoration work required or performed by any
federal, state or local government agency or political subdivision, or performed by

any nongovernmental entity or person because of the presence, suspected presence, release or suspected release of any Hazardous Substance in or into the air, soil, groundwater, surface water or solid vapor at, on, about, under or within the Premises (or any damage due to such Hazardous Substance).

ARTICLE G-11—ENTRY BY LANDLORD

Landlord reserves and shall at any and all times have the right to enter the Premises, inspect the same, supply janitorial service and any other service to be provided by Landlord to Lessee hereunder, submit the Premises to prospective purchasers, mortgagees or tenants, post notices of non-responsibility, and alter, improve or repair the Premises and any portion of the Building that Landlord may deem necessary or desirable, without any abatement of rent, and may for such purpose erect scaffolding and other necessary structures where reasonably required by the character of the work to be performed, always providing that the entrance to the Premises shall not be blocked thereby, and further providing that the business of the Lessee shall not be interfered with unreasonably. Lessee hereby waives any claim for damages or for any injury or inconvenience to or interference with Tenant's business, any loss of occupancy or quiet enjoyment of the Premises, and any other damage or loss occasioned thereby. For each of the aforesaid purposes, Landlord shall at all times have and retain a key with which to unlock all of the doors in, upon and about the Premises, excluding Tenant's vaults, safes and files, and Landlord shall have the right to use any and all means which Landlord may deem proper to open said doors in an emergency in order to obtain entry to the Premises without liability to Lessee except for any failure to exercise due care for Tenant's property under the circumstances of each entry. Any entry to the Premises obtained by Landlord by any of said means or otherwise shall not under any circumstances be construed or deemed to be a forcible or unlawful entry into, or a detainer of, the Premises, or an eviction of Lessee from the Premises or any portion thereof.

ARTICLE G-12—RECONSTRUCTION

In the event the Premises or the Building are damaged by fire or other perils covered by the extended coverage insurance carried by Landlord for the Building, Landlord agrees to repair the same with reasonable promptness and this Lease shall remain in full force and effect, except that Lessee shall be entitled to a proportionate reduction of the rent while such repairs are being made, such proportionate reduction to be based upon the extent to which the making of such repairs shall materially interfere with the business carried on by the Lessee in the Premises. If the damage is due to the fault or neglect of Lessee, or its agents, officers, employees, contractors, servants, invitees, licensees or guests, there shall be no reduction or abatement of rent.

In the event the Premises or the Building are damaged as a result of any cause other than the perils covered by the fire and extended coverage insurance carried by Landlord on the Building, then this Lease shall remain in full force without rent reduction and Landlord shall forthwith repair the same, provided the extent of the destruction be less than ten percent (10%) of the then full replacement cost of the Premises or the Building, as applicable. In the event the destruction of the Premises or the Building is in to an extent greater than ten percent (10%) of the full replacement cost thereof, then Landlord shall have the option (i) to repair or restore such damage, this Lease continuing in full force and effect, but the rent to be proportionately reduced as hereinabove provided in this *Article* unless the damage is due to the fault or neglect of Lessee, or its agents, officers, employees, contractors, servants, invitees, licensees or guests, or (ii) to give notice to Lessee at any time within sixty (60) days after such damage terminating this Lease as of the date specified in such notice, which date shall be no less than thirty (30) and not more than sixty (60) days after the giving of such notice. In the event of giving such notice, this Lease shall expire and all interest of the Lessee in the Premises shall terminate on the date so specified in such notice and the rent, reduced (if Lessee is entitled to a reduction under this *Article*) by a proportionate amount based upon the extent, if any, to which such damage has materially interfered with the business carried on by Lessee in the Premises, shall be paid up to the date of such termination.

Notwithstanding anything to the contrary in this *Article* or Articles 10 b. or 16, Landlord shall not have any obligation whatsoever to repair, reconstruct or restore the Premises when any damage thereto or to the Building occurs during the last twelve (12) months of the term of this Lease or any extension thereof (however, this sentence does not relieve Landlord of the obligation to perform such routine maintenance as it is obligated to provide under this Lease).

Landlord shall not be required to repair any injury or damage by fire or other cause, or to make any repairs or replacements, of any panels, decoration, office fixtures, furniture, or any other portable property installed in the Premises by Lessee.

Lessee shall not be entitled to any compensation or damages from Landlord for loss of the use of the whole or any part of the Premises, for damage to or loss of any of Tenant's fixtures or personal property, or for any damage to Tenant's business, or any inconvenience or annoyance occasioned by such damage, or by any repair, reconstruction or restoration by Landlord, or by any failure of Landlord to make any repairs, reconstruction or restoration under this *Article* or any other provision of this Lease.

ARTICLE G-13—EMINENT DOMAIN

If more than twenty-five percent (25%) of the area of the Premises shall be taken or appropriated for any public or quasi-public use under the power of eminent domain, or conveyed in lieu thereof, either party hereto shall have the right, at its option, to terminate this Lease by written notice to the other party given within ten (10) days of the date of such taking, appropriation or conveyance, and Landlord shall be entitled to any and all income, rent, award, or any interest therein whatsoever which may be paid or made in connection with such public or quasi-public use or purpose, and Lessee shall have no claim against Landlord for the value of any unexpired term of this Lease. If any part of the Building other than the Premises may be so taken, appropriated or conveyed, Landlord shall have the right at its option to terminate this Lease, and in any such event Landlord shall be entitled to the entire award as above provided whether or not this Lease is terminated. If less than twenty-five percent (25%) of the Premises is so taken, appropriated or conveyed, or more than twenty-five percent (25%) thereof is so taken, appropriated or conveyed and neither party elects to terminate as herein provided, the rental thereafter to be paid hereunder for the Premises shall be reduced in the same ratio that the percentage of the area of the Premises so taken, appropriated or conveyed bears to the total area of the Premises immediately prior to the taking, appropriation or conveyance, and in any such event Landlord shall be entitled to the entire award as above provided.

ARTICLE G-14—ESTOPPEL CERTIFICATE

Within ten (10) days of written request by Landlord at any time, or from time to time, Lessee shall execute, acknowledge and deliver to Landlord a statement in writing, (a) certifying that this Lease is unmodified and in full force and effect (or, if modified, stating the nature of such modification and certifying that this Lease as so modified is in full force and effect), and the date to which the rental and other charges are paid in advance, if any, and (b) acknowledging that there are not, to Tenant's knowledge, any uncured defaults on the part of the Landlord hereunder, or specifying such defaults if any are claimed. Any such statement may be relied upon by any prospective purchaser or encumbrancer of all or any portion of the real property of which the Premises are a part or any interest therein. Tenant's failure to deliver such a statement within such time shall be conclusive against Lessee that (i) this Lease is in full force and effect, without modification except as may be represented by Landlord, (ii) there are no uncured defaults in Landlord's performance, and (iii) not more than one month's rent has been paid in advance.

ARTICLE G-15—GENERAL PROVISIONS

a. **Plats, Riders and Exhibits.** Clauses, plats and riders, if any, signed by Landlord and Lessee and endorsed on or affixed to this Lease are a part hereof. The Exhibits (including without limitation **Exhibits "A" through "G"**) hereto, including without limitation any agreements therein, constitute part of this Lease. Lessee acknowledges and agrees that the site plan shown on *Exhibit* **"A"** hereto is subject to such reasonable modifications as Landlord may desire to make prior to completion of construction of the Building.

b. **Waiver.** No waiver shall be binding unless executed in writing by the party making the waiver. The waiver by Landlord of any term, covenant, or condition herein contained shall not be deemed to be a waiver of such term, covenant or condition on any subsequent breach of the same or any other term, covenant or condition herein contained. The subsequent acceptance of rent hereunder by Landlord shall not be deemed to be a waiver of any preceding breach by Lessee of any term, covenant or condition of this Lease, other than the failure of the Lessee to pay the particular rental so accepted, regardless of Landlord's knowledge of such preceding breach at the time of the acceptance of such rent.

c. **Notices.** All notices or demands of any kind required or desired to be given by or to Landlord, Lessee, or Guarantor (s) hereunder shall be in writing. All notice between the parties shall be deemed received when personally delivered or when deposited in the United States mail postage prepaid, registered or certified, with return receipt requested, or sent by facsimile transmission or telegram or mail-o-gram or by recognized courier delivery (e.g. Federal Express, Airborne, Burlington, etc.) addressed to the parties, as the case may be, at the address set forth in *Article* **1** of this Lease or at such other addresses as the parties may subsequently designate by written notice given in the manner provided in this section.

Notice personally delivered will be effective upon delivery to an authorized representative of the party at the designated address. Notice sent by mail or courier in accordance with the above will be effective upon receipt or upon the date the party refuses to accept receipt, or the date upon which such notice is returned to sender as undeliverable. Notices sent by facsimile transmission or telegram or mail-o-gram will be effective upon transmission.

d. **Joint Obligations.** If there be more than one Lessee the obligations hereunder imposed upon Tenants shall be joint and several.

e. **Marginal Headings.** The captions of paragraphs and *Article* titles of the

Articles of this Lease are not a part of this Lease and shall have no effect upon the construction or interpretation of any part hereof.

f. **Time.** Time is of the essence of this Lease and each and all of its provisions in which performance is a factor.

g. **Successors and Assigns.** The covenants and conditions herein contained, subject to the provisions as to assignment, apply to and bind the heirs, successors, executors, administrators, legal representatives and assigns of the parties hereto.

h. **Recordation.** Neither Landlord nor Lessee shall record this Lease or a short form or memorandum hereof without the prior written consent of the other party.

i. **Quiet Possession.** Upon Lessee paying the rent reserved hereunder and observing and performing all of the covenants, conditions and provisions on Tenant's part to be observed and performed hereunder, Lessee shall have quiet possession of the Premises for the entire term hereof, subject to all the provisions of this Lease.

j. **Late Charges.** Lessee hereby acknowledges that late payment by Lessee to Landlord of rent or other sums due hereunder will cause Landlord to incur costs not contemplated by this Lease, the exact amount of which are impracticable or extremely difficult to ascertain. Such costs include, but are not limited to, processing and accounting charges and late charges which may be imposed upon Landlord by terms of any mortgage or trust deed covering the Premises or any part of the real property of which the Premises are a part. Accordingly, if any installment of rent or any other sum due from Lessee shall not be received by Landlord or Landlord's designee within three (3) days after written notice that said amount is past due, then Lessee shall pay to Landlord, in each case, a late charge equal to ten percent (10%) of such overdue amount. The parties hereby agree that such late charge represents a fair and reasonable estimate of the cost that Landlord will incur by reason of late payment by Lessee. Acceptance of any late charges by Landlord shall in no event constitute a waiver of Tenant's default with respect to such overdue amount, nor prevent Landlord from exercising any of its other rights and remedies hereunder.

k. **Prior Agreements.** This Lease contains all of the agreements of the parties hereto with respect to any matter covered or mentioned in this Lease, and no prior agreements or understanding pertaining to any such matters shall be effective for any purpose. No provision of this Lease may be amended or added to except by an agreement in writing signed by the parties hereto or their respective successors in interest. This Lease shall not be effective or binding on any party until fully executed by both parties hereto.

l. **Inability to Perform.** This Lease and the obligations of the Lessee hereunder shall not be affected or impaired because the Landlord is unable to fulfill any of its obligations hereunder or is delayed in doing so, if such inability or delay is caused by reason of strike, labor troubles, Acts of God, or any other cause, similar or dissimilar, beyond the reasonable control of the Landlord.

m. **Attorneys' Fees.** In the event of any action or proceeding brought by either party against the other under this Lease the prevailing party shall be entitled to recover all its costs and expenses, including without limitation expert witness fees and the fees of its attorneys in such action or proceeding in such amount as the court may adjudge reasonable as attorneys' fees.

n. **Sale of Premises by Landlord.** In the event of any sale of the Building, Landlord shall be and is hereby entirely freed and relieved of all liability under any and all of its covenants and obligations contained in or derived from this Lease arising out of any act, occurrence or omission occurring after the consummation of such sale; and the parties or their successors in interest, or between the parties and any such purchaser, to have assumed and agreed to carry out each and every of the covenants and obligations of the Landlord under this Lease, and Lessee will look solely to Landlord's successor in interest in and to this Lease. Landlord, upon notice to Lessee of any such sale, may transfer any security deposit to its successor in interest and Landlord will thereupon be discharged from further liability in reference thereto.

o. **Subordination, Attornment.** Landlord reserves the right to place liens and encumbrances on and against the Premises, the Building and the property of which the Premises are part, superior in lien and effect to this Lease and the estate created hereby, and Lessee will execute and deliver, upon Landlord's demand, any instrument or instruments necessary to subordinate this Lease to such liens or encumbrances; provided, however, that any such subordination is conditioned upon the holders of any such lien or encumbrance agreeing not to disturb Tenant's possession of the Premises so long as Lessee remains in full and complete compliance with the terms hereof, notwithstanding any foreclosure of such lien or encumbrance. This Lease is and shall be subordinate to the lien of any deed of trust or mortgage placed upon the Premises, Building, and property of which the Premises are a part or any part thereof.

p. **Name.** Lessee shall not use the name of the Building or of the development in which the Building is situated for any purpose other than as an address of the business to be conducted by the Lessee in the Premises.

q. **Severability.** Any provision of this Lease which shall prove to be invalid, void or illegal shall in no way affect, impair or invalidate any other provision hereof and all such other provisions shall remain in full force and effect.

r. **Cumulative Remedies.** No remedy or election hereunder shall be deemed exclusive but shall, wherever possible, be cumulative with all other remedies at law or in equity.

s. **Choice of Law.** This Lease shall be governed by the laws of the State of Arizona.

t. **Signs and Auctions.** Lessee shall not place any sign in or upon the Premises, windows or Building or conduct any auction thereon without Landlord's prior written consent.

u. **Gender and Number.** Wherever the context so requires herein, each gender shall include any other gender and the singular number shall include the plural and vice-versa.

v. **Consents.** Whenever the consent of Landlord is required herein, the giving or withholding of such consent in any one or any number of instances shall not limit or waive the need for such consent in any other or future instances.

ARTICLE G-16—BUILDING PLANNING & EMPLOYEE PARKING

(a) In the event Landlord requires the premises to be used in conjunction with another suite or for other reasons related to the building planning program, upon notifying Lessee in writing, Landlord shall have the right to move Lessee to other space in the premises of which the premises forms a part, at Landlord's sole cost and expense. The terms and conditions of the original Lease shall remain in full force and effect, save and excepting that a revised *Exhibit* "A" shall become a part of this Lease and shall reflect the location of the new space in *Article* 2 of this Lease shall be amended to include and state all correct data as to the new space. However, if the new space does not meet the Tenant's approval, Lessee shall have the right to cancel said Lease upon giving Landlord thirty (30) days notice within ten (10) days of receipt of Landlord's notification.

(b) It is understood that the Lessee and employees of Lessee shall not be permitted to park their automobiles in the automobile parking areas which may from time to time be designated for patrons of the Shopping Center. Lessee and its employees shall park their cars only in those portions of the parking areas, if any, designated for that purpose by Landlord. Lessee shall furnish Landlord with its and its employees' license numbers within fifteen (15) days after taking possession of the Premises and Lessee shall thereafter notify Landlord of any changes within five (5) days after such change occurs. If Lessee or its employees fail to park their cars in designated parking areas, then Landlord may give notice of such violation. If Lessee does not cease such violation, or cause such violation by its employees to be ceased as the case may be within two (2) days after Landlord's said notice is given, Lessee shall pay to Landlord an amount equal to twenty-five dollars ($25.00) per day per violating vehicle calculated from and including the day on which Landlord's notice was given to and including the day when all violations by Lessee and its employees cease. If, from time to time, after such cessation, Lessee or any of its employees again violate this *Article*, Landlord need not give Lessee any further notice of violation and the said twenty-five dollar ($25.00) per day per violating vehicle charge shall commence against Lessee for each violating vehicle immediately upon such further violation and run until such violation ceases. All amounts due under the provisions of this *Article* shall be payable by Lessee, as additional rent within ten (10) days after demand therefore. Lessee shall notify each of its employees of the provisions prior to their commencing any employment connected with the demised Premises and shall also inform them that their cars are subject to being towed away at such employees' expense in case of any violation.

ARTICLE G-17—DISCRIMINATION

The Lessee herein covenants by and for the Lessee and Tenant's heirs, personal representatives and assigns and all persons claiming under the Lessee or through the Lessee that this Lease is made subject to the condition that there shall be no discrimination against or segregation of any person or of a group of persons on account of race, color, religion, creed, sex, sexual orientation, or national origin in the leasing, subleasing, transferring, use, occupancy, tenure or enjoyment of the land herein leased, nor shall the Lessee or any person claiming under or through the Lessee establish or permit any such practice or practices of discrimination or segregation with reference to the selection, location, number, use or occupancy of tenant's, lessees, sub lessees, subtenants, or vendees in the land herein leased.

ARTICLE G-18—AUTHORITY OF PARTIES

a. **Corporate Authority.** If Lessee is a corporation, each individual executing this Lease on behalf of the corporation represents and warrants that he/she is duly authorized to execute and deliver this Lease on behalf of the corporation, in accordance with a duly adopted resolution of the board of directors of the corporation or in accordance with the bylaws of the corporation, and that this Lease is binding upon the corporation in accordance with its terms.

b. **Limited Liability Company.** Landlord is an XXXXXX Limited Liability Company, it is understood and agreed that any claim by Lessee on Landlord shall be limited to the assets of the Limited Liability Company, and, furthermore, Lessee expressly waives any and all rights to proceed against the individual Members, except to the extent of their interest in the Limited Liability Company.

_____

[Insert Authorized Signatory]   Date : Sunday, July 31, 2005

[Insert Landlord]

_____ and _____

Lessee: **XXXXXXXXXXXXXXX**   Lessee: **XXXXXXXXXXXXX**

Index